JAMES HERRIOT
The Life of a Country Vet

Graham Lord's first biography was of the legendary British journalist, drinker and womaniser Jeffrey Bernard, *Just the One: The Wives and Times of Jeffrey Bernard*, which was revised and reissued by Headline in 1997 following Bernard's death. He has also published an autobiographical book about his childhood in Mozambique and Zimbabwe, *Ghosts of King Solomon's Mines*, and several novels, most recently *A Party to Die For* in 1997. He was for many years Literary Editor and weekly books columnist of the *Sunday Express*, during which time he interviewed almost every major novelist and bestseller, from P.G. Wodehouse and Graham Greene to Ruth Rendell – and James Herriot.

ALSO BY GRAHAM LORD

NOVELS

Marshmallow Pie

A Roof Under Your Feet

The Spider and the Fly

God and All His Angels

The Nostradamus Horoscope

Time Out of Mind

A Party to Die For

AUTOBIOGRAPHY

Ghosts of King Solomon's Mines

BIOGRAPHY

Just the One:
The Wives and Times of Jeffrey Bernard 1932–1997*

Available in paperback from Headline

GRAHAM LORD

JAMES HERRIOT

The Life of a Country Vet

HEADLINE

First published in 1997
by HEADLINE BOOK PUBLISHING

First published in paperback in 1998
by HEADLINE BOOK PUBLISHING

10 9 8 7 6 5 4 3

ISBN 0 7472 5720 5

Typeset by
Letterpart Limited, Reigate, Surrey

Printed and bound in Great Britain by
Mackays of Chatham PLC, Chatham, Kent

HEADLINE BOOK PUBLISHING
A division of Hodder Headline PLC
338 Euston Road
London NW1 3BH

For my brother

Rod,

another perfect gentleman

Contents

Acknowledgements   ix

Introduction   1

One   *Ink and Showbiz*   9

Two   *A Glasgow Tenement*   19

Three   *Lah We and Whe Ho*   41

Four   *Beaumont, the Belt and Barbirolli*   51

Five   *Beer and Stardust*   79

Six   *A Yorkshire Vet At Last*   107

Seven   *The Phoney War*   133

Eight   *Perfect Peace*   147

Nine   *The Ex-Hairdresser From Pinner*   165

Ten   *The Interior Decorator From New York*   199

Eleven   *The Reluctant Millionaire*   229

Twelve   *Timothy, Tim and the TV Series*   273

Thirteen   *The Mellow Years*   303

Fourteen   *The Rich Man in His Castle*   319

Postscript   345

Index   355

Acknowledgements

First and above all I am especially grateful to the late Alf Wight himself for all the kindness and generosity he showed me over more than twenty years. He was a rare example of a genuinely good man and — even rarer — a gentleman. It is good to know that his warmth and decency were able to touch the hearts of millions.

I would also like to thank the following for their help, tolerance and patience in giving me interviews, anecdotes and guidance, lending me photographs, introducing me to other witnesses and checking facts:

John Alderton, Professor Sir James Armour, Derry Brabbs, Alan Brooke, Dorothy Campbell, Heulwen Campbell, Maisie Cessford, Nell Clark, William Crawford, Ken Cunningham, Doreen Dalrymple, Peter Day, Dick Douglas-Boyd, Carol Drinkwater, Pam Dunning, Mervyn Gould, Janet Grey, Rupert Grey, Robert Hardy, Susan Hill, Sir Anthony Hopkins, Jim Kinlay, Harry Locke, Ian McColl, Neil McColl, Sandra McCormack, Tom McCormack, Diana Mackay, Eddie McSween, Cal Morgan, John Morrison, Kathleen Morrison, Victor Morrison, Chris Page, Bruce Peter, Dominic Prince, May Ritchie, Freda Roberts, Mary Roger, John Rush, Alan Samson, Jean Schreiber, Bette Steele, Jimmy Steele, Eddie

Straiton, Penny Straiton, Harold Summers, Raleigh Trevelyan, Simon Ward, Richard Whiteley, Professor Norman Wright, Andy Young and Philip Ziegler.

I would also like to thank for their invaluable help the staffs of the superb Mitchell Library and City Archives Library in Glasgow, especially Anne Escott, Jan McLaughlin and Rob Urquhart; Michael Moss and his staff in the Glasgow University Archives; the Glasgow University Library, and especially Elizabeth Watson in the Special Collections Department; the James Herriot Library at Glasgow Veterinary School; Janet McBain, the Curator of the Scottish Film Council; the British Film Institute; the Sunderland Library; Elizabeth Rees of the Tyne and Wear Archives Service at Newcastle Library; the Press Association and British Museum Newspaper libraries in London; the Thirsk Museum; the Royal Air Force Personnel Management Centre Headquarters at RAF Innsworth, Gloucester; and the London libraries of the *Veterinary Record* and the Royal College of Veterinary Surgeons.

I am grateful too for being able to quote from many newspapers and magazines, most notably the *Daily Mail*, *Mail on Sunday*, *Daily Telegraph*, *Sunday Telegraph*, *Times*, *Sunday Times Magazine*, *Sunday Express*, *Sun*, *Today* and the *Veterinary Record*.

I must also acknowledge the huge amount of information I have been able to glean from the following authors' books, pamphlets and unpublished manuscripts:

Anderson, Albert, *A Century of Sunderland Cinemas 1896–1996*, Black Cat Publications, 1995
Bolitho, William, *Cancer of Empire*, Putnam & Co., 1924

Callan, Michael Feeney, *Anthony Hopkins: In Darkness and Light*, Sidgwick and Jackson, 1993

Campbell, Alastair D., *Hillhead High School, 1885–1961*, Hillhead High School Pavilions Improvements Fund Committee, 1962

Campbell, Marilyn, *The Development of the Theatre in Sunderland*, unpublished typescript

Dingwall, Patricia and Hillery, Caroline, *Herriot Country*, Discovery Publishing

Falk, Quentin, *Anthony Hopkins: Too Good to Waste*, Columbus Books, 1989

Fisher, Joe, *The Glasgow Encyclopaedia*, Mainstream, 1994

The Glasgow Veterinary College (Incorporated): Records of 80 Years' Progress, 1941

Glasgow Veterinary School, 1862–1962, Glasgow University Archives

Gould, Mervyn, *Sunderland's Golden Age of Entertainment*, unpublished typescript, 1975

Hillhead High School Magazine, 1927–33

Junor, John, *Listening For a Midnight Tram*, Chapmans, 1990

Kinematograph Weekly, *Playing to Pictures*, 1914

McArthur, Tom, and Waddell, Peter, *The Secret Life of John Logie Baird*, Hutchinson, 1986

McKinlay, Alan, *Making Ships Making Men*, Lomond Print, 1991

Michael Joseph Ltd, *At the Sign of the Mermaid: Fifty Years of Michael Joseph*, Michael Joseph, 1986

Morton, Henry Brougham, *A Hillhead Album*, Maclehose, 1973

Peter, Bruce, *100 Years of Glasgow's Amazing Cinemas*, Polygon, 1996

Pryde, George S., *Scotland from 1603 to the Present Day*, Thomas Nelson, 1962

Reid, J.M., *Glasgow*, B.T. Batsford, 1956

Service, Robert, *Ploughman of the Moon*, Ernest Benn, 1946

Sinclair, Maureen, *Murder, Murder, Polis!: Glasgow Street Songs and Games Rhymes*, Ramsay Head Press, 1986

Smith, J.W. and Holden, T.S., *Where Ships Are Born: a History of Shipbuilding on the River Wear*, Thomas Reed & Co, 1953

Sternlicht, Sanford, *All Things Herriot: James Herriot and his Peaceable Kingdom*, Syracuse University Press, 1995

Straiton, Eddie, *Animals Are My Life*, J.A. Allen, 1979

Straiton, Eddie, *A Vet on the Set*, Arrow, 1985

Webster, Jack, *Alistair MacLean: A Life*, Chapmans, 1991

Yoker Secondary School Pupils, *Both Sides of the Burn: The Story of Yoker*, Bell, Aird and Coghill, 1966

Young, Jimmy, *Jimmy Young*, Michael Joseph, 1982

Introduction

ALF WIGHT, the quiet, modest Scottish vet who wrote hugely bestselling books under the pseudonym James Herriot, always insisted that he owed his success to me. I told him often that this could not possibly be true but he said time and again that he was convinced that it was my big review of his second book, in the *Sunday Express* in 1972, that orbited him to international stardom.

He always claimed that the critics had ignored his first book, *If Only They Could Talk*, a homely, humorous fictionalised account of one year in the life of a country vet. It was set in the 1930s, before the discovery of antibiotics, when a vet had to rely on grisly old equipment and deal with rough country farmers who would treat a sick cow by dosing it with Jeyes' Fluid and beer, or by chopping a piece off the end of its tail 'to let the bad out'. One farmer told Alf that he could not understand why his horse was still so shaky even though he had already tried the old Yorkshire remedy of ramming raw onions up its rectum.

On the face of it, that first book seemed so unlikely to be a success that the first British publisher to see the manuscript left it lying around for eighteen months before rejecting it. His American publisher took three months to read it and eventually, in 1970, the British publisher Michael Joseph brought it out in a respectable but small edition of just 3,000 copies that did not sell in any vast numbers at first.

Undeterred, Alf wrote a sequel, *It Shouldn't Happen to a Vet*, which was published in London in 1972 in the quiet month of January when few books were published and literary editors had more time to look at those that were not obvious bestsellers. I was at that time literary editor of the London *Sunday Express* and, in search of something a little different that quiet week, I picked up the second Herriot book and found it so engaging that I led my column with a long review. In it I predicted: 'James Herriot is on to a winner . . . a delightful new collection of medical stories that would make a marvellous basis for a TV series.'

Alf insisted that it was this one review – and the subsequent serialisation of the book in the *Sunday Express* – that gave him a crucial boost at the start of his career as a writer. The day after the review appeared he wrote me the most astonishingly self-effacing letter I have ever received from any author. I mention it here not to bask in reflected glory but to show what a thoroughly *nice* and humble man Alf Wight was and how astonished he was by his success. He said that since he was only a beginner he did not know whether it was the done thing for an author to thank a reviewer but that he had long been an admirer of my weekly column so that for me to review his book was for him a dream come true. He was, he said, not so stupid as to think that money was the most satisfactory target, and no matter how much money he might make in future out of his writing nothing would ever give him a bigger thrill than that moment when he had sat in his car on the cobbles of Thirsk marketplace, opened the *Sunday Express* and read my review.

When he died in 1995 his daughter Rosie told the *Sunday Express*: 'Dad was always very aware that it was the *Sunday Express* literary editor Graham Lord who gave him the first big break with a crucial review in 1972', and in 1996 Alf's son Jimmy confirmed his sister's recollection, telling me: 'My father always said how much he owed you for what you had done for him.'

Alf never forgot what he saw as his debt to me, even though he became impossibly famous. Coachloads of tourists from all over the world turned up at his surgery in Thirsk (which he called Darrowby in the books) in pursuit of his autograph – so many that eventually he could hardly clench his right hand. Queues of fans formed outside the surgery. Letters arrived by the sackful. He was harassed by so many requests for interviews and public appearances that he often had to decline invitations. But he never refused me.

In the year after my review appeared his success was certainly phenomenally sudden. By the time his third book was published in 1973 he was already a massive bestseller on both sides of the Atlantic and had been translated into twelve languages, including Japanese. He was utterly bewildered by it all. 'I mean, can you imagine it?' he said to me then. 'Yorkshire dialect in Japanese?' The first two books were published together in America under the title *All Creatures Great and Small*, becoming a huge bestseller, and before long Christopher Timothy, Carol

Drinkwater and Robert Hardy were starring in the long-running British TV series of the same name.

None of this success and adulation seemed to change Alf Wight at all. Despite his wealth he and his wife Joan lived in a cosy, unassuming two-bedroom bungalow and he continued to practise as a vet. Indeed, except for his Scots childhood – he was educated at Glasgow's Hillhead High School and then at Glasgow Veterinary College – and his service in the RAF during the Second World War, he spent all his life in Thirsk, where he worked as a vet for more than fifty years.

Even the choice of his pseudonym was amazingly casual. 'I was writing in front of the TV,' he told me once, 'watching a football match, and there was the Scottish international Jim Herriot playing in goal for Birmingham City. He had such a good game that I borrowed his name.'

Like many people, Alf Wight had been convinced for years that he had a book in him, but he did not quite get it right until he was over fifty, when, after years of practice, he managed at last to sell *If Only They Could Talk*.

He wrote under a pseudonym because he felt it was wrong for a professional man to advertise. 'I'm just a working vet whose hobby happens to be writing, and I only write in my spare time,' he told me. 'It's very satisfying and it'd be silly to change my whole life pattern now. The only thing the success has done is to give me security. I don't do anything now that I didn't do before and I haven't bought anything I wouldn't have done. I can't see the point. I like doing my work, taking the dogs for a walk, drinking a pint of beer with friends. I don't like high living or high society or expensive things.'

In 1988, nearly twenty years after my review of his second book, I went up to Thirsk to interview Alf again and met his seventy-seven-year-old partner Donald Sinclair, the real 'Siegfried Farnon' of the books. After lunch at the Golden Fleece hotel, Alf took me across the road to show me the newsagent's shop in the marketplace where he had bought the paper containing that first review. 'Oh, what a lift that was,' he said. 'A whole page. It was better than selling a million copies. I read it that Sunday morning right *there*, on the cobbles outside the news-agent, and couldn't believe it. I'll never forget it.'

Nor did he, right to the end. When I became editor of a new short-story magazine, *Raconteur*, in 1994, I wrote to every author I knew to solicit unpublished stories with which to launch the magazine. The first to respond was Alf, who sent me, just a few weeks before he died, a rare collector's-item story that he had written many years previously. The story, 'La Vie en Rose', is not about animals at all but about a happily married man's sudden temptation when he notices a beautiful woman eyeing him in a restaurant. He had written it, he told me in his last letter to me, about thirty years earlier, when he had still been 'practising' writing and trying to find his way into print. That was the sort of man he was: he had taken the trouble to help me even though his shaky signature betrayed his obvious frailty.

Some people have been surprised that I should embark on a biography of 'James Herriot', suggesting that Alf must surely have covered his life fully in his own books. In fact his famous books are heavily fictionalised – they are novels, not autobiography – and he left out an enormous amount, saying virtually nothing about his parents or his poverty-stricken Glasgow childhood and adolescence, and sometimes glossing over the truth in such a way that many myths have grown up around him.

It was not until I was well into the research for this book that I discovered that he owed his vast success almost entirely to an ex-hairdresser from Pinner, an interior decorator from New York and an unknown book reviewer from Chicago. Most of the Herriot myths have been fully absorbed and recycled by almost everyone who has written about him. The official Yorkshire Dales guide *Herriot Country*, for instance, claims quite incorrectly that Alf's wife Joan was a farmer's daughter, that they married before he went into the RAF, that he was in the RAF in Scarborough when his son was born, and that he never wrote anything until he was over fifty – all inaccurate allegations that have been taken from the Herriot books without a second thought.

The most hilarious example of this unquestioning recycling of the Herriot novels is an American book called *All Things Herriot: James Herriot and his Peaceable Kingdom*, which was written by Sanford Sternlicht, a 'part-time professor of English at Syracuse University'. Not only does Sternlicht repeat many of the untrue stories, but the book is frequently inaccurate, sometimes carelessly so. Sternlicht claims, for instance, that Alf's parents took him when he was three weeks old to live in 'Hillhead, near Glasgow': Hillhead is, in fact, in the heart of Glasgow, but in any case the family never lived there. He states that the principal of Glasgow Veterinary College when Alf was there was a Dr Waterhouse: in fact he was Dr Whitehouse. Sternlicht says on one page that Alf graduated from the college in 1937 and on another that it was 1938, when the correct date is 1939. He claims quite incorrectly that Alf started working at the famous veterinary practice in Thirsk in 1938 (it was 1940); that he served in the RAF from 1943 to 1945 (1941 to 1943); that Alf's son was born in 1944 (1943) and was called Nicholas James (James Alexander); that Alf's daughter Rosemary was born in 1949 (1947); that Alf took his pseudonym from the name of a Bristol City footballer (Birmingham City). And so it goes on, an extraordinary catalogue of errors that one can hardly believe can have come from a 'professor of English' – even a 'part-time' one – and been published by a reputable university.

Sternlicht's book is also such a wonderfully earnest, pompous, 'politically correct' treatise that Alf would have roared with laughter had he read it. As Alf himself told *Maclean's* magazine in 1978: 'It's only the Americans who seem to get very intense about my writing. They read into it all kinds of weighty, humanitarian, sociological meanings. It astonishes me, something I can't see. Not many of the villagers around here can see any of this in my books either. A local farmer once told me, "Your books are about *nowt*".'

Sternlicht even manages to accuse James and Siegfried of being 'remarkably sexist' and suggests that the young James Herriot is not only an alcoholic but also possibly a closet homosexual. As Dorothy Parker once remarked of a book she was reviewing: 'This is not a novel to be tossed aside lightly. It should be thrown with great force.'

As I started the research for *this* book – interviewing Alf's old friends and acquaintances, dating from his earliest primary-school days in Glasgow through his years at veterinary college and as a vet in Yorkshire – I was amazed to discover some remarkable revelations about his life. I have seen his humble birthplace, researched his parents' background and his desperately poor childhood, dug up pictures of him as a boy at school and veterinary college, found what may be his very earliest teenage writings, obtained copies of his school and college reports, discovered who his first girlfriend was and the *real* reason he was invalided out of the RAF. I have also uncovered the truth behind the widely accepted myth of how he first came to write his books, and the truth behind both the books themselves and the TV series.

Yet none of these revelations detracts at all from our image of James Herriot as one of the gentlest, kindest authors ever to put typewriter to paper. Alf Wight was among the nicest men I have ever met.

CHAPTER ONE

Ink and Showbiz

THE BABY BOY who was destined to become James Herriot was born in his maternal grandparents' tiny two-up-two-down terraced house in the working-class Roker area of Sunderland, just five minutes' walk from the shipyards on the northern bank of the great shipbuilding river Wear.

He was born on 3 October 1916, in the middle of the First World War, to the sound of clattering steel and clanging rivets as the Sunderland shipyard workers – his father among them – raced to build more and more ships to defeat the German enemy.

His grandparents' house, 111 Brandling Street, was just five hundred yards away from the spot where six months earlier a German Zeppelin bomb had fallen, killing twenty-two people, injuring nearly a hundred and destroying the new Star Cinema. It was Sunderland's worst Zeppelin raid of the war. Two minutes' walk from the house was Roker Park, the home since 1898 of his beloved Sunderland Football Club, which he was to support all his life and which was to make him its life president in 1992.

He was named James Alfred Wight but was never called James or Jimmy. Instead he was always known as Alfie, to distinguish him from his father, Jim – James Henry

Wight, a gentle-looking, open-faced twenty-six-year-old journeyman ship plater, himself the son of yet another James Wight, who was also a ship plater.

Alfie's mother, Hannah ('Nan', *née* Bell), was a striking twenty-four-year-old who had herself been born only three streets away, in Church Street. Her parents, Robert and Jane Bell, had gone no further than four hundred yards in twenty-four years, but although her fifty-one-year-old father had not moved far sideways in the world he had at least moved upwards. He owned the little house in Brandling Street – he had bought it several years earlier – and although he had started out in life as a tripe dresser, like *his* father, he was now a senior printer. So there were words and ink and literature in the future James Herriot's veins right from the start, as well as the rich red blood of the Wearside Victorian working class.

There was also in Alf Wight's genes a talent for entertaining others that was eventually to make him a multimillionaire. His mother was a singer, perhaps in the music hall, and his father was an accomplished pianist, something that was much more common in Victorian and Edwardian times, even in working-class families, than it is today. At some period of his life Jim Wight began to boost his meagre shipyard wages by playing in the early cinemas, where pianists or even entire orchestras were hired to accompany the silent movies while extras behind the screen provided sound effects as necessary. He may already have started earning a little extra as a cinema pianist by the time his son was born because by 1916 the cinema had become the working classes' favourite recreation in every large town in Britain. On the day that Alfie was born, you could pay tuppence to watch D.W. Griffiths' legendary 1915 film about the American Civil War, *The Birth of a Nation*, 'the greatest picture ever made', from the gallery at the Sunderland Empire. For 4d you could sit on the balcony, for 6d in the pit, for 1/6d in the grand circle, for two shillings in the orchestra stalls and for 7/6d you could take a sumptuous box. Or you could see *The Butterfly on the Wheel* at the King's Theatre or *The Sins of the Rich* at the Theatre Royal. In Sunderland the theatres and variety music halls often doubled as cinemas, and there were plenty of them: the Royal; the King's, with its 2,500 seats; the vast People's Palace that held 3,000; the Empire; the Wear Music Hall; the Villiers; the Avenue Theatre and Opera House in Gillbridge Avenue (now part of the Vaux Brewery), where Sir Henry Irving had made his farewell appearance on 28 October 1904 and where the last of the great music-hall stars, the comedian Wee Georgie Wood, started his career in 1906.

Few of Sunderland's wartime theatrical records have survived and none of the many indexed playbills and posters at Sunderland Museum refers to either Jim or Hannah Wight – or to Hannah under her maiden name, Bell – but just a year before Alfie was born the Roker Variety Theatre opened nearby in Roker Avenue, which ran across Brandling Street. The theatre employed a ten-piece orchestra to brighten up the silent 'flickers', and it is possible that Jim Wight was the orchestra's pianist or organist. In those early days of the cinema a film's distributors would send the cinemas advance lists of suggested tunes to match each scene. The musical suggestions for the film *Marked Money*, for instance, listed the suggested music, and the style in which it should be played, for the following scenes:

6 AT CROOK TELEPHONING . . . AGITATO MISTERIOSO . . . MISTERIOSO

7 AS MAN SNATCHES BAG . . . STORM AT SEA AND DANGER . . . AGITATO HEAVY

8 AS COOK IS SEEN COMING DOWNSTAIRS . . . HEAVE HO . . . NAUTICAL ALLEGRO

9 AS CAPTAIN READS LETTER . . . FAREWELL . . . ANDANTE ROMANTIC

18 SEGUE . . . JEALOUSY . . . APPASSIONATO

As the film reached its climax – 'attack on girl . . . crooks in car . . . smash with milk cart . . . attack on crook' – the musical suggestions throbbed and pounded with increasingly urgent suggestions of *Agitato*.

'They used to send a synopsis of the film and a music score but we always had a run-through with the orchestra to ensure that they played the right music at the right time,' said Arthur Ratcliffe, who started his cinema career as a 'lime boy' – working the spotlight, carrying films, etc – in the year that Alf Wight was born, and went on to become the Roker Variety Theatre's chief projectionist until it closed in 1961.

Had Jim Wight been playing full-time in the cinema he could have earned about £3 a week, a very respectable sum in those days, but since there was plenty of work to be had in the shipyards during the war he was more likely to have been an occasional part-timer filling in for the regular pianist, perhaps one of those cheap-rate semi-amateurs castigated in the professional cinema musicians' handbook, *Playing to Pictures*, which was published by *The Kinematograph Weekly* in 1914. 'It is lamentable,' said the paper, 'that so few proprietors engage good musicians; cheapness seems to be the one thing they aim at. To give a few glaring instances: men are now playing nine hours daily for 20s. and 30s. a week, and ladies are playing four hours daily for 15s. a week. This is not a dustman's wage, let alone a living wage.'

It was certainly not easy work playing in the cinema. The pianist – 'the backbone of the band', according to *The Kinematograph Weekly* – was expected not only to be technically competent but also to bone up in advance on the new films he was to accompany by reading the trade papers' summaries; to buy and plan music appropriate for each scene and in keeping with the mood of the film as a whole; to rehearse before performing; and then to play constantly for as long as three hours at each showing and to do so in very poor light. 'In some halls,' reported *The Kinematograph Weekly*, 'the bad light makes one think they are looking for a black cat in a coal cellar.'

If the projectionist should put on the wrong reel at the wrong time, as he often did, the pianist was expected to cope with the crisis. If there should be a short circuit or a blown fuse, or if the film caught fire, he was expected to calm the multitude with a merry, reassuring melody. There is even a section in *Playing to Pictures* entitled 'Music Preventing a Panic'.

The Wights left Hannah's parents' house just three weeks after Alfie's birth and moved with the baby to Glasgow. It is not difficult to understand why they moved out, for number 111 Brandling Street was much too small for them all now that they had a squalling baby as well. But why did they go all the way to Glasgow, 120 miles away to the north-west? Their motives seem baffling. A few years earlier, during the terrible shipyard depression of 1907 to 1909, some of the Sunderland yards had come to a complete standstill and their workers had been forced to move all over Britain in search of work. But by 1916 the shipyards were booming again because of the vast worldwide demand for ships. In 1914 no fewer than seventy-four ships were built on the river Wear, and throughout the war the British navy suffered such huge losses of warships because of the attacks by German U-boats that by 1918 two new yards were opened in Sunderland and even women were being employed for the first time in the shipyard offices.

Yet the Wights chose this very moment to uproot themselves and give up Jim's steady job to go to Glasgow. Could it perhaps have been because of the Zeppelin that had fallen just five hundred yards away, when Hannah was three months pregnant with Alfie? Had she been terrified by the explosion and the twenty-two sudden deaths? Did she fear for her baby's future and think that perhaps Glasgow would be a safer place to live – further from the Zeppelin raids? Hannah was certainly by all accounts a strong-willed, forceful young woman who would have been perfectly capable of persuading her gentle, retiring young husband to abandon his home town, job and family to go north.

Or did they leave Sunderland perhaps because Jim had been supplementing his shipyard income by playing the piano in the Star Cinema, which had now been destroyed by the Zeppelin raid? Had he maybe found it difficult to find another cinema job? Or had he suddenly been offered another job as a pianist in Glasgow? It seems particularly unlikely that he would have abandoned his job as a ship plater to become a full-time musician just at the moment that he had another mouth to feed, because in those days a cinema pianist was paid appreciably less than a skilled shipyard worker, who could earn around £5 a week during the war – nearly double what a pianist could expect. Four days after the Zeppelin raid on Sunderland, for instance, the Lyceum at Dumfries in Scotland was advertising in *The Era* showbiz magazine for a violin soloist to work at £2-5s-0d a week – the same rate of pay that the Grand Hotel in Folkestone was offering in *The Era* on 12 April 1916 for a pianist to play seven evenings a week from 4.30 to 6, 7.30 to 8.30 and 9 to 10 (and until midnight on Saturdays). On 18 October 1916, under 'Musicians Wanted', this advertisement appeared in *The Era*:

Wanted, Wanted, Wanted, Wanted.

———

To open immediately
for
THE PICTURE HOUSE,
DUMBARTON,
REPETITEUR VIOLINIST, ALSO
'CELLIST.

———

For
THE PICTURE PALACE,
GREENOCK.

**PIANIST, REPETITEUR VIOLIN and
'CELLIST.
Experience in High-Class Programmes
essential. Ladies or Gents.**

———

A.M.U. Terms.

———

Full particulars to

———

**MR. CON. WILLIAM,
The Grand Central Picture House,
Glasgow.**

Could Jim or Hannah Wight have suddenly spotted this opportunity for a new life north of the border? And did they perhaps giggle over another advertisement, inserted by the late King Edward VII's infamous ex-mistress in the same issue?

**The Versatile Comedienne
MISS LILLIE LANGTRY.**

———

**This week
LONDON**

———

G. Barclay, or direct.

King Edward had been dead for six years but his beloved Jersey Lily – who had in her prime earned $6,000 a week as an actress in America – was still making ends meet by treading the boards of Britain's provincial theatres at the age of sixty-three.

Or maybe there was a much simpler, more human reason for the move to Glasgow. Until now Britain had relied on volunteers to fight the First World War but in 1916 conscription was introduced for the first time. Perhaps the Wights feared that if Jim stayed much longer in Sunderland he would – like so many of his fellow shipyard workers – be conscripted into the army and felt that there might be less chance of being called up if he left home and submerged himself in a different, huge, anonymous city.

Alf Wight himself always claimed later that his father went to Glasgow to play in a cinema. In 1992 he told Stephen Pile of the *Daily Telegraph* that Jim 'had found a new career as a cinema pianist in Glasgow', and Lynda Lee-Potter of the *Daily Mail* that his father started playing the piano 'as leader of an orchestra which provided background music for silent films at the Picturedrome' as soon as they arrived in Glasgow. 'He could play anything,' he told Miss Lee-Potter. 'Once there was a religious film on and it came to the bit where Christ was walking on the water. Somebody said to the pianist, "For goodness' sake do something appropriate" and he played "Life on the Ocean Wave".' Alf also told Tony Hardisty of the *Sunday Express* that his father's 'work as an orchestra leader and pianist took him to Glasgow'. And yet there is a huge question mark over all these claims. For the next twenty years, whenever Jim Wight had to fill in an official form, he always said that he was a ship plater or a joiner – or even, in the 1930s, a fishmonger. It was not until 1937 that he first described himself officially as a musician.

Why? If he had been a musician right from the start, why would he have claimed to have several other much more humble jobs? It is the first of many mysteries about Alf's life, and maybe the first example of how he began to massage the facts into fiction.

Whatever the reason, the Wights and their baby left Sunderland at the end of October 1916 just as *The Millionaire and the Woman* was on at the Theatre Royal (tickets from Boots the Chemists, 62 Fawcett-street). The family moved into a cramped little apartment on the first floor of a grim tenement building in the working-class Yoker district of Glasgow, right outside the gates of the shipyards on the northern bank of the Clyde. From Roker to Yoker – 120 miles, but they had exchanged one life of grinding hardship for another. Only the venue had changed. They were to live there in precarious poverty for more than twenty years.

In 1997 there was still no blue commemorative plaque on the wall of the simple red-brick house at 111 Brandling Street. Behind their net curtains the house's present occupants have no idea that they are living in the birthplace of one of the most popular storytellers of the twentieth century. Their outside wall is adorned with nothing more than a black television satellite dish. Yet maybe a TV aerial is more appropriate than any plaque or memorial, for in the end it was television that was to make the James Herriot books such a huge success, beaming their stories to millions around the entire globe.

CHAPTER TWO

A Glasgow Tenement

JIM, HANNAH AND ALFIE WIGHT arrived in Glasgow at the end of October 1916. Even then it was the biggest city in Scotland and the heart of its industrial and commercial muscle, with a population of more than 800,000 people. It was an elegant city of solid, stylish Victorian buildings, monuments and spacious parks, with a notable university, museum and art galleries; it was also known for its Clyde-bank shipbuilding yards, engineering and other heavy industries, and was notorious for the turbulent slums and tenements of the Gorbals, where thousands of people existed in terrible poverty and often in drunken despair. Two out of every three Glaswegians lived in those days in just one or two rooms, their conditions vividly described by William Bolitho in a 1924 pamphlet, *Cancer of Empire*:

'We enter the Close. On each landing opens the water-closet, which the municipality installed thirty years ago. This is clean – the municipal inspectors are vigilant; but on an average twenty-five persons share its use. In some houses this number is nearer fifty. On the other side of the tiny landing opens a long, impenetrably black gulf; the central corridor of five homes. We feel our way, knock at a door and enter, calling out "Sanitary". A small room, one side of which is taken up by the Scots' fireplace, like an enclosed iron altar, with two hobs on which the teapot is kept everlastingly on the boil. The floor is worn wood, there are irregular square inches of frayed oilcloth. An enormous drabbled woman, who is dressed in dish clothes which do not show the dirt so plainly, however, as her face, explains the arrangements ... She has five children, and the gas is kept burning all day at the glimmer. The elements are simple and human. There is the bed, set into a niche, deep, evil-smelling, strewed with heaps of the same material as her dress ... Bed, hearth and chair; humanity's minimum, as simple as the Parables.'

Even more graphic is the picture painted in *Animals Are My Life*, the autobiography of Eddie Straiton. Straiton, a contemporary of Alf Wight, was also raised on Clydebank, pulled himself out of poverty by sheer hard work and went to Glasgow Veterinary College. He became a close friend of Alf and famous in his own right as 'The TV Vet' of the 1970s and 80s. While Alf Wight was an only child, Eddie Straiton was one of three, and consequently his family was poorer than Alf's, but otherwise their lives as children in the deprived western end of 1920s Glasgow would have been similar.

'Life in Scotland's industrial towns in those days was grim and hard,' wrote Straiton. 'Bare feet from the end of February to nearly Christmas. Porridge and broth for breakfast, dinner, tea and supper; meat seen only once a week. Occasionally a mother would scream from an upstairs tenement window: "Come up for the top of yer feyther's egg!" A rare delicacy indeed.'

His memories were nightmarish: 'The Saturday shopping

for a ha'pennyworth of turnip, carrot, leek, parsley and lentils. The evening scramble at the butcher's back door for the scrap beef bones. The ever-simmering pot of broth beside the open fireplace; the broth getting thinner and thinner as each weekend approached. It was ladled out before each meal of porridge with the reassuring words that will live in my mind for ever: "This'll stick tae yer ribs." ' On Sundays there would be a special treat: a blob of margarine on a pile of potatoes and a slice of sausage.

And then there was the fighting: 'The fighting! Everyone always seemed to be fighting. I remember when I was very small my father telling me: "Always get the first yin in and if he's bigger than you, kick him on his shins afore ye hit 'im".' A street brawler's favourite weapon was the notorious 'Glesga Kiss', in which the attacker's head was crunched into the bridge of his opponent's nose. 'The sight of blood usually finished the argument,' said Straiton. 'We learned at an early age how to use that devastating weapon the "heid" and we never hesitated to aim our kicks at the tender areas when the battle wasn't going well.'

Eddie's father was a self-employed (but not always employed) builder and plumber, and the family survived on £1 a week. Other families somehow managed to keep going on as little as twelve shillings a week unemployment pay, often spending hours day after day raking around in dustbins to try to find empty jam jars – 'jeelie jars' – that they could sell back to the local grocer for a farthing or a halfpenny. Times were so tough that on the day after he turned eight, little Eddie was forced to take his first job, rising at four each chilly morning to help the milkman on his delivery rounds and earning threepence a week for his pains. Although he was tiny, undernourished and had had no breakfast, he had to carry half-gallon cans of milk up three flights of stairs in each 'close' of the tenement buildings, pouring the milk into the jugs and cups outside each door and taking the money that had been left out to pay for it. 'I found my heart aching for the pathetic poverty of the people,' wrote Straiton in his autobiography. 'On every floor there was one jug or cup with a note saying "Pay ye on Saturday." '

Eddie, like Alf, was sufficiently clever and hard-working to pass the entrance examination to one of the Glasgow high schools and so escape the tenements and become a professional man, but 'most of my boyhood companions finished up as wine drinkers,' he wrote. 'If they didn't have at least average intelligence, they simply had no chance. There was absolutely no future. With parents on the dole, their only prospects when they left school were endless days of lounging around street corners and billiard rooms until they were old enough to sign on at the "burroo" – the unemployment exchange. Inevitably many, like their parents, turned to drink.'

In the week that the Wights arrived in this urban maelstrom there was opera on at the city's Theatre Royal – *Rigoletto* and *Carmen* ('All tickets from Boots the Chemists, 101–5 Sauchiehall-street') – plays at the Coliseum, King's, Metropole and Princess's, and variety shows at the Alhambra, Empire, Olympia and Pavilion. But Jim and Hannah did not as yet have time for their showbiz careers, much as they might have wanted to.

They took rented lodgings four miles west of the city centre and just outside the city limits, moving into a tiny two-room apartment in Balmoral Terrace in Yoker Road. Here in the heart of the shipbuilding area the streets and houses were still lit with gas, the rich smell of the sea drifted rank across the streets, and crowded electric trams clanged and rattled in and out of the city.

'There were few motor cars anywhere in those days,' wrote Sir John Junor, the former editor of the *Sunday Express*, describing his own 1920s Glasgow childhood in his memoirs *Listening For a Midnight Tram*. 'Often the only sound as I lay in the stillness of the night was a tramcar clattering along the rails.'

The 'close' in which the Wights lived at 750 Yoker Road – now renamed Dumbarton Road – was owned by a Mrs Isabell Jones of 316 Golfhill Drive, Dennistoun, Glasgow. It was extremely crowded by modern standards, with two small apartments on the ground floor and three tiny two-room 'but and bens' on each of the first and second floors. Into these eight minute apartments were crammed no fewer than eighteen *voting* adults – let alone all their wives, who were not yet enfranchised and were thus not listed in the voters' register. Including the children of all these families there could well have been as many as fifty people jammed into the three-storey close – with just one outdoor lavatory at the end of the shabby little back yard to accommodate them all. The queues for the privy each morning must have stretched the length of the yard.

It is also difficult to imagine how dark houses were in those days. For a small child there must have been shadows and nightmares on every landing. 'There was still no electricity in the streets or school, just gas,' I was told by William Crawford, an eighty-one-year-old lifelong

resident of Yoker who went to primary school with Alfie
Wight. 'I remember when I was about nine [in 1924] and
we got electricity and we were up and down switching it
on and off.'

'Yoker Road would have been *pretty* slummy, though it
was a better tenement than some,' I was told by Eddie
Straiton. Certainly it was not a desperate slum area like
the teeming cesspit of the Gorbals on the other side of the
river, where the children wore rags and the poverty and
overcrowding were truly terrible. In the Gorbals one of
the children's favourite songs went like this:

> Murder murder polis!
> Three stairs up.
> The wummin in the middle door
> Hit me wi' a cup.
> Ma head's a' blood
> An' ma face is a' cut.
> Murder murder polis!
> Three stairs up.
> Send fur the doctor.
> The doctor widnae come.
> Send fur the ambulance.
> Run run run!

Another began:

> My mother and your mother
> Were hanging out some clothes.
> My mother gave your mother
> A punch on the nose . . .

Yoker may have been a working-class area but it was *respectable* working class. John Logie Baird, the twenty-eight-year-old future inventor of television, was working as an electrical engineer at Yoker Power Station and living in a terraced house at 17 Coldingham Avenue, where he was possibly already messing about with the tea chest, biscuit tin, bits of cardboard, fourpenny lenses, darning needles, string, sealing wax, wire, glue and second-hand electric motor that would allow him ten years later to transmit the first television picture.

Later Baird described his life in Glasgow, with its 'sordid and mean lodgings, in soul-destroying surroundings, under grey skies'. Or as Tom McArthur and Peter Waddell put it in their biography *The Secret Life of John Logie Baird*: 'He trudged to work in the cold dawn through cobbled streets flanked by tenements where families lived on the breadline. Smoke from giant chimneystacks fouled the air, making the glimpses of the green slopes of the Campsie Fells on the skyline even more tantalising. He was frequently coughing, choking with a cold, or just recovering from one. He wrote: "What a wave of resentment and anger comes over me, even now, when I think of the awful conditions of work in those Glasgow factories – the sodden gloom, the bitter, bleak, cold rain, the slave-driven workers cooped in a vile atmosphere with the incessant roar and clatter of machinery from six in the morning to six at night, and then home to lodgings surrounded by sordid squalor, too worn out to move from my miserable bedroom."' It is little wonder that Baird became a lifelong socialist, like so many others who were raised and worked on what eventually became notorious as 'Red Clydeside'.

The Wights' neighbours in the building at 750 Yoker Road were respectable enough to include an engineer surveyor, Gavin Brand; an engineer, Alex Turnbull, and his wife Jane; and an engineering draughtsman William Carruthers, and his wife Eliza; as well as a boilermaker, a smith, a sailor and their wives. Unlikely though it sounds, one witness says she was told in later years by Hannah that the Wights soon installed a grand piano in their tiny new home. Some of Hannah's stories, however, need to be treated with care, for she was always renowned for her vivid imagination.

Respectable or not, Yoker was still a tough, hard-drinking, hard-talking district, like every Scottish working-class area. John Junor, the future *Sunday Express* editor who was to give Alf Wight's writing career a vital boost more than fifty years later when he decided to serialise the second James Herriot book, was two years younger than Alf, and was born two miles away from Yoker in Shannon Street, in a similar two-room red-stone tenement flat. Junor, whose father was a steelworker, wrote in his memoirs: 'My father was a good man, an honest man, a hard-working man. But . . . Every Friday night, after he had handed over the weekly housekeeping allowance to my mother, he would use the few shillings left in his pocket to go to the pub and get drunk, as did many working-class Scotsmen of the time. I hated Friday nights. I hated the shouting, the rowing, the cursing monster my father became.'

Another favourite children's rhyme of the time asked:

Does yer maw drink wine?
Does she drink it a' the time?
Does she ever get the feelin'
That she's gonni hit the ceilin'?
Does yer maw drink wine?
Does yer maw drink gin?
Does she drink it oot a tin?
Does she ever get the feelin'
That she's gonni hit the ceilin'?
Does yer maw drink gin?

There is no suggestion that either Jim or Hannah Wight was a drunk but many of their neighbours were and they lived in a desperately alcoholic society. The stresses, strains and anxieties of a working-class life in those days must have been immense and it is highly understandable that so many workers and their wives 'drowned their sorrows' in drink whenever they had a penny or two to spare. Yoker was certainly no exception: *Both Sides of the Burn*, a history of the area compiled by fifteen-year-old pupils at the secondary school in 1966, reports that on Saturday nights the police had to be reinforced to deal with drunks.

The best aspect of the move to Glasgow must have been that Jim Wight probably had little trouble finding work as a ship plater. The gates of one of the yards, Yarrow, were right opposite his new home, John Brown's, employing 9,700 men, was just down the road, and the Glasgow shipyards, like those of Sunderland, were booming in those middle years of the First World War. Although Jim, as a plater, would have had to seek work as one of the 'black squad' – the casual pieceworkers who were hired only when needed to do a particular job – platers were skilled men and wages in the boom years at the end of the war rose as high as £4-18s-0d for a forty-seven-hour week.

Even so, an unemployed plater might well have to look for work by standing each day outside the shipyard gates in a milling throng of dozens of other unemployed men – platers, riveters, caulkers, boilermakers – in the hope of catching the eye of a foreman who was looking for casual workers to hire. 'In Brown's there used to be a daily market,' one old shipyard worker told Alan McKinlay for his pamphlet about the Glasgow yards during those years, *Making Ships Making Men*. 'If you were a riveter or whatever you used to go down in the morning and wait outside the foreman's office and he would say "you, you and you" and give you a start. Sometimes the foreman would walk up and down the lines of men waiting for work without saying a word, not even a grunt – which most of them were capable of. That meant there was no work for you that day. They were just reminding you that they had all the power and you had none.' Said another contemporary witness: 'It was like a slave market – talk about the Deep South.'

The foremen ('the bastards in bowlers') had such wide-ranging powers in the shipyards – hiring and firing on a whim, handing out the best and worst jobs – that casual workers like Jim Wight were forced to grovel to them if they were to stay in work and feed their families. Some foremen had to be bribed with drinks in the pub by men desperate for work; others were deeply stained by the bitter Catholic-versus-Protestant hatreds of the area and refused to hire workers who were of a different religious denomination from themselves. John Junor tells how at the age of four he was taken to hospital suffering from diphtheria and scarlet fever. As he recovered consciousness he heard the boy in the next bed asking him: 'Are you a cup or a plate?'

'I did not know what he meant,' says Junor, 'but replied "a plate" – an answer which met with his approval. It was quite some time before I discovered, and he could not have been much older than myself, that he had been asking whether I was Catholic or Protestant. Religious feelings ran high and early in working-class Glasgow.'

Prejudiced or not, fair or brutal, in the shipyards the foremen all wore bowler hats. 'That was their badge of office,' Alan McKinlay was told. 'But the bowler was also his protection. If he was an unpopular man and walking near where a ship was being built and they were riveting up the bows, many a time a hot rivet came down on top of his skull or a spanner just missed him.'

Being a ship plater was a hard, dirty, noisy and dangerous job. A plater took the vast, flat plates of cold steel that would go to make a ship's hull, used huge hydraulic machines to cut, roll, smooth and shape them into the exact size and curve required, drilled lines of rivet holes into them by hammering them with pointed steel rods, and then hung them in their exact positions on the ship's frame ready for the riveters. Platers often had to work in dangerous positions – on wooden stages, for instance, suspended high above the ground and the echoing depths of the ship's skeleton. The noise of banging, clattering and hammering was deafening and 'operating these huge machines,' says McKinlay, 'not only required skill but great physical strength as well. The plates and the tools were extremely heavy and the slightest slip could result in a serious accident. And while the plates were prepared inside sheds these provided little protection against the elements.' One shipyard worker told him: 'The sheds were only a roof over your head and dirt floors with the wind and rain blowing in on you. I've seen us wi' a heavy job working the punch wi' the sweat blinding ye and the icicles hanging to the machines. It was that bitter cold that there were icicles but you were sweating you were working that hard!' The enormous plates, says McKinlay, had to be shifted by hand ('shouldered') between different machines 'and manually moved from the shed to the ship. To protect themselves against the razor-sharp edges of the steel plates the platers wore "bratties", aprons made of the heavy canvas bags used to hold washers.'

'There was very little transport,' an old plater told McKinlay. 'You had to push or carry most of your work in bogeys or barrows. Nowadays they have trailers and conveyors for carrying plates about the yard. In those days you'd to bogey it if you couldnae carry it. Many a time I went hame wi' ma shoulders raw wi' carrying heavy angles all about the shed on ma shoulders.'

If Jim Wight was lucky enough to find plenty of work right away that icy winter of 1916, his baby son would have seen him leaving home each day long before dawn – dressed in his warmest clothes because most of his work was done outside, whatever the weather – and returning home, raw and exhausted, long after the wintry winds were gusting down the dark evening streets. Each morning, if he had found work, Jim would have joined the thousands of other tradesmen who surged in through the shipyard gates at 6 a.m. to toil away until 5.30 p.m. in a raucous turmoil of clattering, crashing and hammering, with only brief breaks for breakfast and lunch. 'You could tell when the men went into the yard what they were working at,' one old shipyard worker told Alan McKinlay. 'You'd see the electricians and the engineers going in in boilersuits, nice clean overalls. And you'd see the black squad coming in and they'd have any sort of old clothes – old patched trousers with a dirty cardigan, an old jacket with the elbows out, a muffler round the neck and maybe an old bonnet.'

If Jim Wight had arrived at the shipyard gates even a minute after 6 a.m. he would have found them locked and would have lost half a day's pay. If he was working at John Brown's he would have had to put in a fifty-four-hour week for his first two years in Glasgow, until 1919, when the shipyard workers staged a Forty Hours Strike that managed to reduce their working week to forty-seven hours, meaning that they did not need to report for work until 7.30 a.m. The strike also won them a half-day off on Saturdays so that now at last they could follow the fortunes of their local football clubs.

Jim Wight was an obsessive football fan, taking with him to Glasgow a lifelong passion for Sunderland Football Club – which was widely known as The Team of All the Talents and had been Football League champions five times in the late 1890s and early 1900s. Jim's burning passion was inherited by his son, despite the fact that Alfie had lived in the town for no more than three weeks. By the time he was three his father was already teaching him to recite the names of the Sunderland team. 'I swear I never learned nursery rhymes,' Alf told Tony Hardisty of the *Sunday Express* many years later. 'I merely recited the names of the great players he had watched at Roker Park. As a very young child I knew of Buchan, Mordue, Holley, Cuggy and all the others my father idolised. To my father anyone who played for Sunderland was a god in red and white. The early part of Saturday evenings was filled with suspense as we waited for our *Glasgow Evening Times* and the football results. Tea was never enjoyed when Sunderland had lost. It was a banquet when they won.' It was the beginning of a lifelong love affair with Sunderland soccer that was to reach a fantastic climax seventy-two years later when Alf Wight was elected life president of the club.

At first, of course, Alfie was far too young to notice his father's daily exhaustion. By the time he was old enough to understand, Jim Wight was probably out of work more often than he was in it, for a brief boom in the shipyards after the end of the First World War was followed by a slump that brought hardship and anxiety to almost every family on Clydeside. From 1920 onwards the British shipyards sank into a deep depression that meant unemployment for thousands of workers and hunger for their families. The huge production of the wartime years had led to a gross overcapacity. This was worsened by a general slump in world trade, as well as the 1921 Washington Naval Treaty, which placed restrictions on naval shipbuilding. Not one British naval vessel was launched in the 1920s, and the number of workers employed in Scottish shipbuilding declined by 37 per cent between 1921 and 1931, from 124,000 to 78,000. Even John Brown's yard faced closure at the end of 1930 and was saved only when it landed the contract to build the biggest ship in the world, the legendary Cunard transatlantic liner *Queen Mary*. But despite having that plum job on its books, John Brown's was employing no more than 3,556 men in 1931 – as opposed to 9,700 during the First World War – and the economic crisis of the depression meant that work even on the *Queen Mary* soon had to be put in mothballs for more than two years, with the launch of the great liner delayed until September 1934. In the early 1930s the shipyards of Britain were using just 5 per cent of their potential capacity. Clydeside production fell from 153,000 tons of shipping in 1931 to 67,000 in 1932 and 56,000 in 1933. The average income of a Scots worker dropped from £1-12s-0d a week in 1925 to £1-6s-0d a week in 1932, and by the end of 1933 30 per cent of Scots were unemployed. The situation did not improve until new warships were once again needed in the mid-1930s to counter the growing threat from Nazi Germany.

What was Jim Wight to do during these terrible years? There was no point in moving back to Sunderland, for the slump was just as bad there. After the war hundreds of redundant old ships were being sold off for less than they cost to build, new orders were suspended or cancelled and Wearside faced its worst depression ever, worse even than the slump of 1907–9. In 1920 the joiners went on strike when the shipyard owners tried to reduce their wages, and by 1923, when the boilermakers were locked out of the yards, there were 14,000 men unemployed in Sunderland. By the end of the 1920s the world was moving towards the worst depression it had ever known.

Platers like Jim Wight were particularly vulnerable because they were laid off as soon as they had completed the work they had been hired to do. For the boilermakers and platers 'it was always feast or famine', as one old worker told Alan McKinlay, 'either too much work or none at all'. Jim Wight spent almost his entire shipyard life in Glasgow under the shadow of unemployment, never knowing whether he would be able to feed his wife and son. In desperation he kept changing his job, describing himself in the official city valuation rolls as a ship plater (1916–26), a joiner (1927–31) and even a fishmonger (1932–6). It was probably this constant uncertainty, anxiety and maybe even desperation that forced him to look for regular work playing the piano in a cinema.

By 1920 the cinemas in Glasgow had been booming for years as the excitements of the flickering screen began to replace the allure of the old music halls in the affections of working-class Glaswegians. There was plenty of work for musicians and every week the theatrical magazine *The Era* was packed with small classified advertisements seeking musicians to play in cinemas all over the country for wages ranging from £2 to £4 a week, depending on hours and venue. Whatever the rate of pay, it was better than standing hopelessly at the shipyard gates each morning.

Playing the piano in a cinema was also a great deal more fun than staggering about in the bitter wind and rain carrying heavy plates of steel. Describing the early days of the silent films, George Singleton, the son of a Glasgow cinema owner, told Bruce Peter, the author of *100 Years of Glasgow's Amazing Cinemas*: 'As the film started we'd all be plunged into darkness – there were no dimmers in those days – and my father, who loved music, would be thumping away on the piano at the side. Babies would cry, conversations would continue and those who could read would repeat the captions in loud voices for the benefit of the illiterate and short-sighted around them. When a spool broke, everyone would hiss and stamp their feet.'

Until 1910 Glasgow's 'kinematograph' cinemas were in fact theatres or musical halls that sandwiched the screening of films in between other shows and variety performances – places like the Panopticon, once the Britannia Music Hall, where the young Stan Laurel first appeared on the variety stage, and where Cary Grant made his début under his real name, Archie Leach, and wowed the girls in the audience by dancing on stilts. Glasgow's first proper 'picture palace' cinema, the Charing Cross Electric Theatre, opened in Sauchiehall Street in 1910, and after that new cinemas sprouted everywhere and competition was brisk. Leading the new fad were the Greens, a circus family from Wigan who moved north, branched out into the cinema business and eventually employed Jim Wight as a pianist at their brand-new, purpose-built, 1,100-seat Picturedrome cinema in the Gorbals at numbers 21/23 Govan Street, opposite the Govan Street synagogue.

'The Picturedromes, typically, had twin towered, pavilion-like façades and plain rectangular interiors ornamented with simple plaster scrollwork incorporating Art Nouveau motifs,' says Bruce Peter in *100 Years of Glasgow's Amazing Cinemas*. When the Summerstoun

Road Picturedrome was opened in 1912 its arrival was heralded by this advertisement:

GREEN'S GOVAN PICTUREDROME OPENS TOMORROW
COMPLETE PICTURE PROGRAMME
THE PICK OF THE WORLD'S PRODUCTIONS
People's Prices – Pit 2d – Stalls 4d – Balcony (plush tip-ups) 6d
In Order To Place This Entertainment Within The Reach Of All
There Will Be A Few Seats At One Penny
Twice Nightly 7 and 9

The slum-dwellers of the Gorbals loved the cinema, which had become their main form of entertainment, offering them a world of fantasy and glamour to take their minds off their own wretched lives. Children collected empty jam jars and sold them back to the grocers in exchange for a few pence to buy a cinema ticket for the afternoon matinée. And they sang about it when they played their street games:

> *Skinny malinky long legs*
> *Big banana feet*
> *Went tae the pictures*
> *An' couldnae find a seat.*
> *When the picture started*
> *Skinny malinky farted,*
> *Skinny malinky long legs*
> *Big banana feet.*

To play in the Picturedrome, Jim Wight would have travelled three miles each way each day – across the river by ferry and then into the Gorbals by tram – maybe taking Hannah with him to sing between screenings, if she could find someone to look after the baby. The cinemas were still partly music halls and staged singing and variety acts in between the silent films. 'The Govan Street Picturedrome had a small five- or six-piece orchestra,' Bruce Peter told me. 'The Picturedromes were very basic and only the Playhouse had a real big orchestra with fifteen or sixteen musicians. As a rule the cinemas had only a pianist playing during the day and the orchestra would not come on until five or six o'clock. And since many cinemas were also still music halls it is quite probable that James and Hannah Wight performed together at the same venues. The shipyards and the cinemas were certainly closely linked. The cinema was a working-class entertainment tradition and a remarkable number of shipyard people went into the cinema or showbiz, like Billy Connolly.'

Few of these old cinemas still exist. Most of them – and the tenements in which their customers lived – were demolished during the huge redevelopment of the central slum areas of Glasgow in the 1960s and 70s. The cinema where Jim Wight played was closed in 1958 and demolished in about 1966. Today the bleak site where Green's Picturedrome stood in Govan Street – now Ballater Street – is occupied by the huge, red-brick Central Glasgow Mosque and Islamic Centre. Every building around it has been demolished.

*

It was in this rough, tough but honest society that Alfie Wight was raised until he was twenty. As he grew through his childhood and teens he must have been deeply affected by the poverty, unemployment and anxiety all around him. In his Herriot books he never wrote about the fears and hardship of his youth, but they must surely have shaped his character as he saw his father exhausted or worried night after night, his mother tense or brave. The raw nature of his childhood environment could easily have turned him into a bitter, angry or violent young man, into a raging communist or anarchist, or into a hopeless alcoholic. Instead he emerged from this social cauldron not only as a staunch Conservative (who in later years greatly admired Margaret Thatcher), but also as one of the kindest, gentlest, most straightforward men you could hope to meet. There must have been milk and honey in his veins as well as printer's ink. Perhaps it helped that his father too was kind and gentle; that Alfie was an only child; that his good-looking, strong-willed mother worshipped him and drove him on. 'Alf's father was a very nice person,' Eddie Straiton told me, 'and would *never* upset anyone. He was just the same as Alf, always ruled by the mother. Alf had a happy home as a child but his mother ruled them all. She was a very, very strong personality.'

You can see in Alf Wight's earliest photograph (picture section I), showing him at the age of nine among his classmates at Yoker Primary School, the eager, open face of a child who is deeply loved and excited by the world and all it has to offer. It is the face of a boy of whom things are expected, not least by himself. It helped too, of course, that this was a boy of real intelligence and ability. He was always going to go far. He had not only brains but determination and character.

Alfie Wight was admitted to Yoker Primary School on 30 August 1921, five weeks before his fifth birthday. By then John Logie Baird, now thirty-four, was living in London, but it is tempting to imagine that he may have returned to Yoker at some time and perhaps have passed Alf in the street as he trotted along Yoker Road to the school half a mile away; that perhaps the inventor and the bright-eyed little boy stared unknowingly at each other, Baird pale, sickly and bronchitic as always after a long night wrestling with the mysteries of his extraordinary invention that would one day make the little boy famous all around the world.

It is tempting to imagine that Baird and Alfie Wight looked at each other on Yoker Road and smiled.

CHAPTER THREE

Lah We and Whe Ho

FOR SEVEN YEARS, from August 1921 until June 1928, from just before his fifth birthday until he was nearly twelve, Alfie Wight left his poky little tenement home at 8.45 a.m. every day during term-time and walked to the local primary school half a mile away, past the little park with the stark memorial to the fallen dead of the First World War, past more rows of grim, dull-red tenements, past the Auld Hoose Pub (now The Anchorage) on the corner of Kelso Street, past the old ferry building. At 12.15 he would walk back home for a bite of lunch, returning to school at 1.15 and going home again at 4 o'clock. Saturdays and Sundays were free.

Yoker Road is now Dumbarton Road and the primary school has been turned into a community centre. The area has about it an air of neglect, with shops empty, boarded up and for sale, but in 1921 it would have been buzzing with crowded street life and noisy with the cries of children. The headmaster of Yoker Primary throughout Alfie Wight's time there was William Malcolm, MA, and as the shipyards slid into recession his pupils were increasingly the sons and daughters of the workers in the local factories, distillery or brick kilns.

One of Alf Wight's classmates, William Crawford, also

the son of a shipyard worker, was still living in 1996, at the age of eighty-one, in a second-floor flat just a hundred yards away from the school, his kitchen window overlooking what used to be the playground. He was born in 1915 'round the corner' and spent all his life in the area – working for thirty years as a boilermaker – except for two years in a munitions factory in England. Mr Crawford's life was what Alf Wight's might have been had he not done well enough to win a place at the academically distinguished Hillhead High School. If things had been different, Alf might well have gone on instead to Yoker Secondary and, like Wullie Crawford, left school at fourteen to become a grocer's messenger boy. When Alf was going to veterinary college, Mr Crawford was joining Yarrow's shipyard as a rivet heater, later working as a shipyard machineman and then as a boiler-maker at Harland & Wolf and Rolls-Royce.

'I don't remember much about Alf Wight,' William Crawford told me. 'He was a quiet boy, kept himself to himself. I don't mean he was standoffish but we didn't mix much, really, just at school. We never went round together. I don't think he had any special friends at the school.'

In fact Alf did make one very special lifelong friend at Yoker: classmate Alex ('Sandy') Taylor, who appears in the class photograph wearing a sailor suit. The two boys were soon inseparable, and their friendship became so firm that decades later Taylor and his wife moved to Yorkshire to be near Alf.

'Alf was a clever boy,' said Mr Crawford. 'He'd have to be to go on to Hillhead. You passed your Qualifying when you were twelve and went to Victoria Drive but very few went there.

'Yoker was a good school. Boys and girls were separated in class and in the playground. We didn't mix – which is the right way. In those days you obeyed your teacher, there was no carry-on like there is now. We didn't get beaten but we got the strap on the hand, one or two. One was enough! We'd get two maybe for arguing in class. We did algebra, English, writing, reading and arithmetic, geography, very little history. The teachers were strict. If you behaved yourself you were all right but if you stepped out of line you got a telling-off.'

As the tenement children sang in the streets in those days:

> *Oor wee school's the best wee school,*
> *The best wee school in Glesca.*
> *The only thing that's wrang wi' it*
> *Is the baldy-headed maister.*
> *He goes tae the pub on a Saturday night,*
> *He goes tae church on Sunday,*
> *An' prays tae God tae gie him strength*
> *Tae belt the weans on Monday.*

While they sang and chanted such songs and rhymes, says Maureen Sinclair in her collection of Glasgow street songs and games, *Murder, Murder, Polis!*, they would form a circle, clapping and singing, while one child stood in the middle acting out the words. Or they would jump over a skipping rope in time to the words, or chant and sing while bouncing a ball against a wall and catching it.

> *Kilty kilty cauld bum*
> *Couldnae play a drum.*
> *He lifted up his petticoat*
> *An' showed his dirty bum.*
> *His dirty bum was dirty.*
> *He showed it tae the Queen.*
> *The Queen wis disappointed*
> *An' jabbed it wi' a pin.*

'The only proper game we played was football,' Mr Crawford told me, 'but there was no school team, we just played in the playground. But we also played Kick the Can and Lah We, which was a made-up name: you would stand with your eyes shut and everybody scattered and you had to look for them.' To decide who was 'het' (or 'it') when they played Kick the Can or Lah We, one child would recite an elimination rhyme while pointing at all the others in turn:

> *Eeeny meeny macka racka*
> *Em oh dominacka*
> *Alla backa sugaracka*
> *Om pom push.*

Or, if they were feeling particularly cheeky:

> *Eeeny meeny miny mo,*
> *Sit the baby on the po.*
> *When he's done, clean his bum.*
> *Eeeny meeny miny mo.*

'The boys also played Moshie,' said Mr Crawford. 'You

dug three holes in the ground about four feet apart and you played marbles into the hole. On a Saturday we went to a penny matinée, a penny for the stalls and 2d for the gallery. There were three picture halls in Clydebank and they played the piano as the words came up. The nearest picture house was a mile down the road there on the right-hand side, the Gaiety Picture House. And the Empire Picture House was just past it. And there was the Pavilion Picture House about two miles away. They were the three.

'I also went to Sunday school for a while and I was in the Boys' Brigade – I was just a private – but Alf wasn't in it.

'I never saw Alf in later life. He never came back. Once he went to Hillhead we lost touch. I didn't discover that he was James Herriot until ten year ago when an old school friend, Adam McCallum, said, "you know who that James Herriot is?" I said no. He said, "Alf Wight!" People round here didn't know. I never thought any of us would be famous. Nobody else from Yoker has been famous except John Logie Baird.'

Mr Crawford recalled that in the 1920s Yoker stood right on the edge of rolling countryside: 'Just at the top of Kelso Street there all the land was farmland and it was not built on until the 1930s.' As Alf grew up the Wights would catch, on summer Saturday afternoons, one of the crowded open-upper-deck trams out towards Loch Lomond or one of the Paisley and District trams across the river with their notices reading: 'Gentlemen Do Not Spit. Others Must Not.' Or they would go into the city on one of the new omnibuses that were threatening the old tram companies and each other by waging a fiercely competitive business war. There were ten different bus companies plying the Yoker route, and their drivers raced each other between stops in the hope of being the first to pick up the waiting passengers. The fastest drivers could career the entire four miles from Ferry Road into the centre of Glasgow in just ten minutes.

Alf was always closer to his father than he was to his mother. They both loved books and it was Jim who first encouraged his reading. From a very early age Alf devoured children's comics and adventure stories, soon progressing to the short stories of H.G. Wells and then to Conan Doyle, O. Henry, Scott, Dickens and Thackeray. Later he claimed to have read the entire works of Dickens by the time he was thirteen. 'My father was such a quiet, unobtrusive little man,' he told Lynda Lee-Potter of the *Daily Mail* in 1992, 'but he was a great influence. He was very humorous, didn't throw his weight about, and a bit of me is like that. We got on like a house on fire.'

In winter Jim would take Alf to watch football, perhaps at Partick Thistle or maybe at Yoker Athletic, which had a magical season in 1924–5, winning twenty-seven consecutive matches, playing thirty-four without defeat, carrying off the Scottish Intermediate Cup and the Elder Cup, and becoming finalists in both the County Cup and the Glasgow and District Cup. During football matches Yoker Athletic fans would cry 'Whe Ho' – nobody seems to know why – and the magic battle cry worked well enough for the club to win the Scottish Junior Cup in 1932–3. Whenever possible Jim would cheer Alf on when he played football in the Glasgow Junior League, and now and then he would scrape enough money together to travel to Sunderland to watch his favourite club. Alf was eight when he had a glimpse of his first Sunderland match. The club had a policy of encouraging youngsters to become interested in the game by letting them into the ground free for the last ten minutes of every match. The Wights were visiting Sunderland for a family party one weekend in the winter of 1924–5 and the boy sneaked away to Roker Park, where he saw the centre forward Dave Halliday score a stunning goal. Halliday was to score forty-two goals that season, and Alfie Wight was hooked for life.

Most Glasgow boys played football in those days. 'In the evenings after school I would play football with my chums on ash and cinder pitches – because there were no such things as grass ones,' wrote John Junor in his memoirs, *Listening For a Midnight Tram*. 'On Saturday afternoons from the age of eleven onwards I would go alone to watch my favourite football team, Partick Thistle. Even today, so many years later, the Thistle result is the first I look for on a Saturday night.'

Like Junor, Alf was also a great football fan from an early age. He played for the Yoker Fernlea Football Club, a team for teenagers, and he often stood on the terraces at Ibrox stadium in Govan to watch Glasgow Rangers. Decades later he was able to recall the names of the great Rangers team of the 1930s – Dawson, Gray, McDonald, Meiklejohn, Simpson, Brown, Archibald, Marshall, English, McPhail, Morton. The Partick Thistle ground was not far from Yoker either. Did the two young Glasgow boys, Wight and Junor, grin at each other on Saturday afternoons, yelling for their team and dreaming of greater glories of their own – these two boys whose backgrounds were so similar and whose careers were destined to cross nearly half a century later?

Alf himself was a good enough footballer to play in the Glasgow Veterinary College XI in his early twenties, and one of his Yoker School contemporaries, Jackie Husband, who was three years younger, became a professional, signing for Partick Thistle in 1937, going on to play three times for Scotland, and in 1965 becoming manager of the Queen of the South team and then of Partick itself.

*

In 1923 or 1924 the Wights left 750 Yoker Road – which by now was crammed with twenty-two adult voters, not to mention all the children and the women under thirty who were still not allowed to vote – and moved into another tenement apartment in the same building, in number 746, which they rented from a Mrs Mary Anderson of 1 Moss Street, Dennistoun, Glasgow. They were to live there for the next twelve years. It was still pretty crowded, with eighteen voters living there in 1925, but it may well have been a little cheaper than the old place, for by now Jim Wight must certainly have begun to feel the pressures of unemployment and an erratic income as the shipyard slump gripped Clydeside. Indeed, it was in 1926 that he began to call himself a joiner rather than a ship plater, and perhaps it was also now that he started to play the piano in the cinema to boost his flagging income from the shipyards.

The Wights' musical careers are difficult to pin down.

In later life Alf always insisted that his father played in an orchestra and his mother was an opera singer, but there is no record of either in the Glasgow University Library Special Collections Department's Theatrical Archive. 'Orchestras' pianists are impossible to track down,' the archivist Elizabeth Watson told me, 'and there is no sign of Hannah Bell or Hannah Wight on the list of opera singers, so she certainly wasn't famous. She could have been a music-hall or pub singer, or perhaps she sang at shipyard concerts. There were hundreds of small places in Glasgow and along the coast where they would have employed singers for small amounts.'

Jim was determined to turn Alf into a pianist too, and the boy started having piano lessons when he was six. It was the beginning of a lifelong love affair with music. His father made him play a lot of Scarlatti's sonatas, but many years later Alf admitted that he never really enjoyed the piano until he started playing popular music, especially jazz, by ear when he was a teenager. 'My parents were professional musicians and that gave me a great love of music,' he told Paul Vallely of the *Sunday Telegraph Magazine* in 1981, 'though when they put me to the piano at the age of six they found that though I had the technique I did not have any real feel for it. I didn't show any promise until I learned to play by ear. That made me in great demand at the college smokers.'

In 1925 Yoker was incorporated as a part of the city of Glasgow, Yoker Road was renamed Dumbarton Road, and number 746 was renumbered 2172. Today the dull-red building of 2172 Dumbarton Road, which faces the River Clyde right on the edge of the docks, is still a depressing place surrounded by deserted, boarded-up buildings and an atmosphere of neglect and decay. In the dock across the road a grey ship looms tall over the street. The empty, echoing hallway of number 2172 has a bare cement floor, and the hall and stairwell are decorated with grubby tiles in white, green and ochre that give them the feeling of a public lavatory or city subway. The stairs and hallway are littered with rubbish; the small communal yard at the back is overgrown with weeds. It is only too easy to imagine what it must have been like during the desperate poverty and unemployment of the 1920s and 1930s, yet for Alfie Wight this cramped, seedy, sorry place was home for a dozen years. Perhaps the bustling, crowded, fetid nature of his boyhood surroundings goes some way to explaining his later exuberant delight in the high, wide, open spaces of the Yorkshire Dales. When at last he came to work there as a vet he could never quite believe his luck in being able to live in a place as beautiful as Yorkshire, surrounded by acres and acres of space and wild emptiness and God's own high blue heaven.

CHAPTER FOUR

Beaumont, the Belt and Barbirolli

ALF WIGHT was a month short of his twelfth birthday when he took the tram three miles across the city to the leafy, middle-class, residential suburb of Hillhead to start his first term at the fee-paying, co-educational Hillhead High School. Hillhead was such a quiet, old-world area that even twenty years later, after the Second World War, horses would still be clip-clopping through the streets, drawing behind them delivery carts, bread vans and hearses. Henry Brougham Morton, who had been a pupil at the school during the First World War, described those 'dusty days of slow time' in his book *A Hillhead Album*: 'the hush of the cathedral city setting . . . the lush foliage of ancient trees clustered and drooped above the but-tressed red brick garden wall . . . the modest elegance . . . the old villas nestle in their cosy gardens while still preserving an air of being country retreats afar from Glasgow. Apart from the rustle of leaves under a quiet sky that knows only the delicate sweep of feathered wings, few are the sounds to be heard. Between long intervals perhaps the creak of cart wheels and the measured slap of a Clydesdale gelding straining in the shafts, or the whirr of a private brougham accompanied by the staccato dig of hoofs on gritty road metal.' It was a highly salubrious district, with substantial houses owned by business and professional people, and because it was close to Glasgow University it had 'more IQ to the square inch than anywhere in Scotland', according to Joe Fisher in *The Glasgow Encyclopaedia*. The contrast with raucous, working-class Yoker could hardly have been more pronounced.

The building that housed Hillhead High School in those days is now a primary school in Cecil Street, three roads away from the high school's present site in Oakfield Avenue. It is a solid four-storey building as staunch as the God-fearing Scottish education it promised to purvey. The classrooms were poky and overcrowded, the playground at the back was far too tiny for sixty let alone all six hundred pupils, and the inside of the building was such a warren of corridors that the new headmaster, Frank Beaumont, had the rooms numbered because he kept getting lost. But the school had a strong reputation for academic excellence. Ten days before the beginning of Alf's first term the Scottish Education Department gave Hillhead a glowing report: its teaching of English was 'thoroughly sound'; Latin 'excellent'; maths of a 'very high standard'; and the head of the modern languages department, Miss Margaret Kennedy, was 'one of the outstanding Modern Language Teachers in the West of Scotland', though unhappily she had just left Hillhead to take up a headmistress-ship elsewhere.

The school's motto was *Je Maintiendrai* – 'I Shall Maintain' – and the pupils were certainly expected to uphold a fine tradition of excellence and hard work. From that September term of 1928 the staff all dressed in

King George V on a visit during the First World War to the Sunderland
shipyards, where Alf Wight's father was working when Alf was born in 1916.
(Press Association/Topham)

Left: Alf's birthplace: 111 Brandling Street, Sunderland.

Below: Ragged Edwardian urchins in the Gorbals. Poverty was still rife in Glasgow when the Wights moved to the city at the end of 1916 and the picture was taken in Govan Street, where Alf's father is said to have played the piano in the Picturedrome cinema. *(Glasgow City Archives)*

Clydeside shipbuilders at work on the *Queen Mary*. (*The Herald*)

Yoker Primary School, where Alf Wight was a pupil from 1921 to 1928.
(*Glasgow City Archives*)

Alf Wight's primary school class: in the third row back Alf is third from the left, Wullie Crawford sixth from the left and Alex ('Sandy') Taylor far right, wearing a sailor suit. *(William McInnes)*

Alf's classmate William Crawford in 1996, aged eighty-one.
'Alf was a clever boy,' he remembered.

The old Hillhead High School in Cecil Street, Glasgow. Now Hillhead
Primary, the building has changed little since the days when Alf was a pupil
there from 1928 to 1931. *(Glasgow City Archives)*

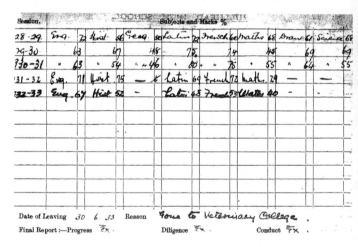

HILLHEAD HIGH SCHOOL.

Name *James Alfred Wight* Date of Birth *3 . X . 1916* Last School *Yoker P.S.*

Date of Enrolment *3.9.28*   Admission No. (a) Primary   (b) Secondary *5986*

Father's Name *James*   Address *2172 Dumbarton Road, Yoker.*

Session.	Class or Form.	Progress.	School Activities.	School Honours.
1928-29	Form I C.	S.	Rugby Cricket	
1929-30.	Form IIa.	VG.	-do-	
1930-31	Form III A.	VG.	-do-	Intersch. prize. Intermediate Champion
1931-32	Form IV b.	V.G	Rugby, Cricket, Tennis	Medal Inter-Scholastic. Prize in English
1932-33	Form V B.	V.G.	Rugby, Cricket, Tennis	Leaving Cert.

Session.		Subjects and Marks %							
28-29	Eng. 72	Hist. 56	Geog. 50	Latin 72	French 60	Maths 68	Draw 61	Science 68	
29-30	63	67	48	78	74	45	69	69	
30-31	" 63	" 54	" " 46	" 80	" " 75	" 55	" 64	" 55	
31-32	Eng. 71	Hist. 75	—	Latin 69	French 72	Math. 29	—	—	
32-33	Eng. 67	Hist. 52	—	Latin 45	French 53	Maths 40	—	—	

Date of Leaving *30 6 33*   Reason *Gone to Veterinary College .*

Final Report :—Progress *Ex .*   Diligence *Ex .*   Conduct *Ex .*

Alf's school record card, which notes clearly his reason for leaving:
'Gone to Veterinary College'.

The genteel Hillhead suburb of Glasgow in 1929. Alf's journey to school each day may well have taken him past this toy shop in Byres Road.
(Glasgow City Archives)

Left: Professor A. W. 'Old Doc' Whitehouse, former principal of Glasgow Veterinary College and the man who persuaded Alf to become a vet. *(The Herald)*

Below: The Glasgow Veterinary College soccer team in Dublin in 1939. Alf Wight is standing far left; Eddie Straiton is kneeling, second from left.

black academic gowns, the male teachers were addressed as 'sir' and the head janitor, Mr Stratton, wore a uniform of black trousers, top hat and burgundy tailcoat. Although Hillhead's reputation was not quite as impressive as that of Glasgow High School, which was generally considered to be the best in the city, it was high enough to attract many more applications than could be accepted, so Alfie Wight must have been extremely bright to have won himself a place there. It was the sort of academy where the school magazine carried Latin jokes – 'Who was the bright young spark who translated "*missus est Hannibal*" as "*Hannibal's wife*"?' – and the editor could be confident that his readers would understand them.

Hillhead pupils won ten university bursaries in 1928, and many of them went on to build distinguished careers as professors, churchmen, diplomats, surgeons, lawyers, newspaper editors and actors – like the comedian Stanley Baxter, and Gordon Jackson, who was to find fame as the butler in the long-running television series *Upstairs, Downstairs*. 'WHAT ARE YOU GOING TO BE?' asked the regular advertisements for the Nelson-Abbott College in the school magazine, suggesting a wide variety of jobs from accountancy and dentistry to banking and the law. Several Hillhead pupils went on, like Alf Wight, to become writers – most notably Robert Service, 'the Canadian Kipling', who had been at the school in the 1880s. Service too had known poverty and privation while he was at Hillhead. 'It was a gallant struggle to bring up a family of ten on £200 a year, and Papa and Mama should be given all credit,' he wrote in his book *Ploughman of the Moon*. 'Especially as they kept up a front of *bourgeois* respectability. Behind the scenes our standards were proletarian. We boys slept in the flannelette shirts we wore during the day and would have considered serviettes at table a form of swank. I was fifteen before I bought my first toothbrush. But we were clean and healthy, for we had a bath with soap every Saturday night. I believe we all used the same hot water. At home it was a struggle to make frayed ends meet, yet each day we trooped off to what was then the Finest School in Scotland.'

Life was probably not all that different for Alf Wight forty years later. He did not have nine brothers and sisters but then his father was not earning nearly as much as Service's, who was paid £4 a week. Where Alf and Service did differ utterly was in the fact that Service was, by his own admission, lazy, bloody-minded, resentful of authority and eventually expelled. Alf, on the other hand, was quiet, submissive, hard-working and very well behaved.

Service's parents struggled to send him to Hillhead, and it must have been a great sacrifice too for Jim and Hannah Wight to send Alf there, especially if Jim was still out of work most of the time. 'They must have scrimped and scraped to send him to Hillhead,' his old friend Eddie Straiton told me in 1996, 'but his mother would have made some money out of her singing.'

Even if Jim were still working in a shipyard he would not have been earning much more than £2 a week, and although the fees at Hillhead were only £2-10s-0d a term there were all the extras to think of: uniform, books, sports equipment. The regulation navy-blue blazer with 'HHS' and the motto embroidered on the pocket cost twenty-one shillings (just over £1), the navy cap 3/6d, the navy-blue shorts 10/6d, the cream shirt, the belt and the navy-blue tie with brown and gold stripes 3/6d each, the shoes five shillings a pair. A boy's Braemar jersey cost 10/6d, The Varsity Fountain Pen ('at a price to meet the need of the times') five shillings, a new pair of 'Annies-land' rugby boots (as 'Worn by International Players') 19/6d, and 'Copland's Wonderful Guinea Suits for Grow-ing Boys' another twenty-one shillings. And for Christ-mas that year the Scottish publishers Collins were advertising in the school magazine books ranging in price from *The Bumper Book of Grimms' Fairy Tales* at one shilling to *The Bumper Book of Animals* at 2/6d. Alf, however, had far outgrown such childish reading. Already he was haunting the second-hand book barrows of Renfield Street in the hope of picking up a bargain classic for a few pence. He loved the feel of a new book, the crispness of the paper, its heady smell.

But he was not by any means a stuffy bookworm. He had just been given his first pet dog, an Irish red setter called Don, which ensured that he did not just sit and read all day. From his bedroom in Dumbarton Road he could see the distant hills outside the city and it was Don who was to fire the passions for small animals and for walking that would eventually lead him to become a country vet.

It is possible that Jim Wight paid for all this sudden extra expense by playing the piano in the cinema – where in theory he could have earned between £3 and £4 a week – but by 1929, with the arrival of the talkies, the day of the cinema musician was coming to an end. It seems more likely that Jim spent far too many of these years in desperate unemployment, whether as a plater, a joiner or a fishmonger. His patchy record of employment is one of the great mysteries of his son's life, especially since Alf always pretended that his father had earned his living as a musician. By the time Jim started describing himself thus in the Glasgow valuation rolls in 1936–7, Alf was twenty years old and must have been aware that his father was not a proper musician. Perhaps his mother, for reasons of snobbery or pride, insisted that this was how Jim's profession should be described. Or perhaps Alf himself was ashamed of his father's struggles to make ends meet and decided to soften the edges of the hard truth. Whatever the explanation, when Jim Wight died in 1960 Alf described him on the death certificate not as a musician but as a retired shipyard clerk. Perhaps Jim's musical career had been nothing more than a part-time hobby all along.

To tighten the pressures on the family finances even more, in April 1930 the fees at Hillhead were suddenly increased by 12 per cent (six shillings a term) so that the school could build up a School Clubs and Societies Fund. A term's fees were now £2-16s-0d – more than the weekly national uniform plain rate of wages for tradesmen, which had fallen from £4-18s-0d for a forty-seven-hour week in 1919 to £2-4s-0d, and which took until 1939 to struggle back to £3-15s-0d. On top of that, Hillhead parents were expected to spend an average of £2-2s-0d a year on books and stationery, and in just two years the cost of a new blazer had jumped from £1-1s-0d to £1-10s-0d and a cap from 3/6d to 4/6d, so that keeping Alfie at just the most basic level was costing his parents as much as an average tradesman earned in two months.

How did they manage to do it? By now the shipyards had slumped into a deep depression and would stay that way until the late 1930s. Every Clydeside yard was hit severely. In his pamphlet *Making Ships Making Men* Alan McKinlay quotes one John Brown's worker, Jim Martin, as telling him that no fewer than five adult men in his family were unemployed for five terrible years – himself, three brothers and his father: 'The entire house was idle. Things just got worse and worse over the years.' Unemployed workers had to sign on at the Labour Exchange three times a week to collect their dole benefit. 'I used to go to the Labour Exchange every day,' said Martin. 'What a terrible place: always packed to the door. There used to be fifteen different queues to get to the counter, sign your name and get your money. The place was that packed you didn't know where to stand. You were sometimes hours and hours before you got out.' Idle men had nothing to do but stand around on street corners, steeped in hopelessness, or play football day after day, or go walking in the hills while their lives shrank with every step. Did Jim Wight suffer all this misery and degradation? Undoubtedly. And what must it have done to his clever, imaginative teenage son to see his father in such a state?

'For people in a working-class shipbuilding area it would have been a great achievement to send their only son to Hillhead,' I was told by Ian McColl, the future editor of the London *Daily Express*, who was already a pupil at Hillhead when Alf arrived in 1928 and who went right through the school in the same class as him. McColl, now eighty-one, recalled in 1996 that Alf's mother was by then a piano teacher giving lessons at home in Dumbarton Road, where, unlikely as it sounds, the family had a grand piano. 'When I learned the piano just before then the cost was two guineas for ten one-hour lessons,' said McColl.

Nell Clark, whose late husband Fergus was in the same class as Alf and lived not far from him in Scotstounhill, told me in 1996 that Alf's mother taught the piano 'and other instruments' at 2172 Dumbarton Road, so it seems quite likely that by now, with Jim Wight struggling to find work, Hannah was the family's main breadwinner. 'I had the impression that Alf didn't have a father,' said Mrs Clark revealingly. She remembered too that one day in 1931 or 1932, when Alf was fifteen or sixteen, his dog caused havoc in the tiny apartment. When Alf and Fergus Clark went into the house after school they discovered that the dog had 'gone mad and had destroyed the whole room', jumping on and over everything including the grand piano. The Wights also had several cats. 'Alfie was mad about animals even then,' said Mrs Clark. 'He couldn't resist them.'

Apart from its academic standards, Hillhead High was also renowned in the 1930s for the excellence of its sportsmen: pupils from the school went on to represent Scotland internationally at rugby, tennis, cricket, golf, swimming, athletics, hockey, badminton and bowls. The standard of rugby at Hillhead was so high when Alf Wight was there – with players of the calibre of Jimmy Cotter and Copey Murdoch, both of whom went on to play for

Scotland – that he never managed to make it into the 1st XV, though he did eventually win a place in the second team.

Not everyone was impressed by Hillhead High. The thriller writer Alistair Maclean was a pupil there from 1937 to 1939 and even though he did well – winning a bursary and a special science prize and coming third in English when he passed his Higher Leaving Certificate in five subjects – he was later scathing about the place, describing it as 'a snooty establishment in the West End which had the misfortune to model itself on an English public school, either ignorant of or ignoring the fact that English public schools, like numerous Italian red wines, do not travel well'.

Not surprisingly, not one of Maclean's books can be found in the Hillhead school library today, although there are two by James Herriot.

Despite Maclean's grumbling, Hillhead was by common consent an excellent school in every way and Alfie Wight was extremely lucky that his parents cared enough about him and his future to pay the fees each term despite their own straitened circumstances. What it was like for a poor boy like Alfie to find himself suddenly thrust among much richer children, however, is another matter. He would, for instance, have had to take a packed lunch with him to school each day because while most of the other pupils went home for lunch, it was much too far for him to traipse all the way back to Yoker in the seventy minutes set aside for the lunch break. There *was* a refectory where pupils could buy lunch, but few of the children used it and in any case Alfie would probably not have been able to afford it. For a boy of twelve years old it is small things like that which can set him apart from his contemporaries and make him wary of being different. Was this partly why Alf Wight always made such a huge effort in later life to be modest and self-effacing? Perhaps this sense of not wanting to be different from the other boys at Hillhead made him so level-headed that when in later years he became immensely rich he was never seduced or corrupted by his wealth. Certainly when he became a multimillionaire he chose to live as he had always done and never allowed his fortune to come between himself and his friends or the life he had always loved.

It seems that Hillhead was generally a warm, friendly place and most former pupils remember the school with immense affection. Some in their seventies and eighties still call themselves The Hillhead Family and younger alumni organise regular reunion dinners, dances and sports days. The Former Pupils even had their own club song, which was sung to the tune of 'The End of the Road' and had a chorus that began 'Keep right on to the head of the hill,/Keep on forging ahead':

> *The School, unchanged as the years roll by,*
> *Still stands on the same old spot.*
> *Is there any other stands as high*
> *As the school where we were taught?*
> *The answer rings out, 'No!'*
> *All other Schools are Low.*

'Hillhead was hard work,' said Ian McColl, 'but I was never *un*happy. There was a very active school literary society and OTC and quite a glittering debating society and dramatic club – I was a member of both – and we were taken to watch plays like *The Merchant of Venice*.'

When Alfie Wight arrived at Hillhead in September 1928 the headmaster was Frank Beaumont, a former head of English at Glasgow High School who had been appointed to the headmastership seven months earlier. Beaumont was a Yorkshireman who was – according to Alastair Campbell in the school's official history, *Hillhead High School, 1885–1961* – 'genial and kindly, approachable and encouraging, urbane and serene'. Even his pupils agreed. In an article in the *Glasgow Herald* on 4 July 1985 to mark the school's centenary, Ian McColl remembered Beaumont as being quiet and 'deceptively benign' and wrote: 'Mr Beaumont wore a black academic gown over his lounge suit. I never heard him raise his voice. Nor did he fuss.'

The school was not, however, soft. Pupils were expected to work hard, the rules were strictly enforced by teachers and prefects, and Mr Beaumont was a firm believer in corporal punishment as an aid to study.

'Stories of the Belt in Hillhead are legion,' wrote Ian McColl, adding impishly: 'It must have been assumed that every Hillhead pupil was a genius, because they certainly had the capacity for taking pains. Up to six staggering cross-handers was the penalty in some classes for failure in exams.'

Alf Wight himself was once given six of the best with the Belt by his maths master, a Mr Filshie, just before he left Hillhead. For years Filshie, a pleasant man who was not at all renowned for being a brute, had merely shrugged and sighed at Alf's lamentable standard in maths. Somehow he managed to remain tolerant even when Alf scored a derisory 5 per cent in one trigonometry exam. Alf always swore in later life that he really was utterly incompetent at maths and that tangents, sines and cosines left him completely baffled, but Filshie's tolerance finally broke. 'Wight,' he announced one day, 'I have always thought you were just an amiable idiot and have treated you accordingly, but now I see that you have come out top of the class in your English paper, so I can only conclude that you have not been trying for me. Hold out your hands.'

'Another name for the Belt was the tawse, or the Lochgelly, because it was supposed to be manufactured in Lochgelly in Fife and presumably distributed to schools around Scotland,' McColl told me. 'It was leather, about a quarter of an inch thick, two feet in length and about an inch and a half broad, with three thongs. It was the three thongs that you got the force of. You were struck three times with each blow. The Belt was very painful. It drew blood on the wrist. The teacher would raise his arm above the shoulder, oh, very much. It was used for failure in exams and for inattention.'

The strict regime seemed to work. 'We were all very well behaved,' said Maisie Cessford, who was at Hillhead (junior and senior schools) from 1927 to 1939. 'I remember only one case of stealing when I was there and everyone was shattered by it.'

When Alfie arrived at the school he was placed in Form IC and started lessons in eight subjects – English, history, geography, Latin, French, maths, drawing and science. His first English teacher was 'Wee Ned' Berry and his history master 'Big Bill' Barclay. His French mistress was the legendary Hetty Wilson, who had herself been a Hillhead pupil when the school had opened in 1885, and a Miss Milligan taught him Latin. Another English master, who taught Shakespeare and produced the school plays, was C.R.M. (Charlie) Brooks, an actor who took part in a radio series called *The McFlannels*. 'He was a really theatrical character,' said Ian McColl. 'He looked eccentric, with ginger hair, and he looked like a monkey, so they called him Monkey Brand because that was a doorstep cleaner.' In fact the theatre was one of Hillhead's strongest points: twice in that first term the school was closed at 1 p.m., to allow the children to go to see a Shakespeare matinée at the Theatre Royal and a matinée of *The Barber of Seville*.

Another Hillhead newcomer when Alf arrived, Miss J. Walker, lasted just one day as a part-time art assistant, walking out of the school just as Alfie Wight walked in. Another newcomer was the new principal maths teacher, James Filshie, who was later to distinguish himself by thrashing Alf Wight for not working hard enough. Other new arrivals that term included the unfortunate William Rae, BSc, an assistant in the science department – of whom more later – and thirty-three-year-old Fred Luke, VC. Luke, a Royal Field Artillery driver, had won his Victoria Cross during the retreat from Mons in August 1914, when he had volunteered to help rescue a British gun under lethal enemy fire from only a hundred yards away. He joined the school as temporary assistant janitor on 8 October, and his heroic presence must have caused quite a stir among the young boys, but he was there only as a stopgap and left less than a month later when the full-time assistant janitor, Allan McCallum, arrived. Luke's brief stay no doubt helped to boost Hillhead's Earl Haig Fund collection to the impressive figure of £23-2s-1d that year.

On Monday 12 November, the first school day after Remembrance Sunday, the entire school marched as usual past the War Memorial. Two days later there was a brief health scare when one of the masters, Mr Wright, was sent home because he had been in contact with a scarlet fever victim, but he returned five days later and the school was able to stay open until the Christmas holidays, which began on 21 December.

Alf returned on 7 January 1929 for his second term. As was usual at that time of year, a large number of teachers and pupils were absent with colds and influenza. In January alone fifteen teachers, including the headmaster, went down with flu, and the epidemic continued right through February too – though that did not stop the rest of the school enjoying a half-day holiday on 17 February to go skating on the boating pond in Great Western Road.

Alf's first examinations at Hillhead did not take place until his third term, when all the first four forms were examined in maths by one of His Majesty's Inspectors of Schools, a Dr Stokes. Either Dr Stokes terrified Alf into performing brilliantly or the exam was incredibly easy, because one way or another he achieved 68 per cent – a much higher score than he was ever to achieve in maths again. His third term was also notable because the school was closed for an entire day on 30 May due to the General Election – and when the election was won by the Scottish leader of the Labour Party, Ramsay MacDonald, the first ever British Labour Prime Minister, the celebrations probably went on until Hillhead's annual summer garden party and half-holiday on 14 June, a fortnight before the end-of-year prizegiving and closing ceremony in the Woodside Halls.

In that first year at Hillhead Alf also played rugby and cricket and at the end of his third term his record card shows that his progress was judged to be 'Good'. Right from the start he was excellent at English, despite his regular claims when he started writing the James Herriot books that he was just a humble vet who didn't know much about words. He read Macaulay, whom he later described as 'the master of the balanced sentence, all florid adjectives', and he was so good at composition that he decided at a very young age that he was going to be a journalist. What is more, from an early age he kept a diary, a habit which was to prove invaluable when he came to write his books. 'Alf said his mother made him write a diary every day as a child,' I was told by Mrs Heulwen Campbell, who was a friend and neighbour of the Wights in later years in Thirsk and whose late husband Douglas was a regular golfing partner of Alf's. 'He wrote all the time. He wrote in it every day.' Apart from English, he did best in that first year at Latin, achieving 72 per cent in both subjects. He even managed 68 per cent in science.

When Alf returned from the summer holidays on 2 September 1929 he was moved up to Form IIA and plunged into the usual annual cycle of school activities: the Armistice Day service in Belmont Church on 11 November with The Last Post played by buglers; the fire drill in November, when the whole school was cleared in just two minutes; the Christmas holidays from 20 December to 6 January; the bout of colds and flu again in January and February; the holiday on 26 May to mark the King's birthday; and in June the garden party half-holiday and the prizegiving and closing ceremony in the Woodside Halls. Each year was so different and yet in truth was very much the same.

In that second year he did best in Latin, achieving 75 per cent. Throughout his career at Hillhead, Latin was his favourite subject. Night after night he would spend hours at home in Dumbarton Road reading writers such as Cicero, Ovid and Virgil, and he became so proficient in the language that towards the end of his school career, he said later, he reckoned he could have carried on an intelligent conversation with an Ancient Roman. He also did well in French (74 per cent), though by now his weakness at maths was showing itself and he managed to achieve a mark of only 45 per cent. Still, his progress in that second year at Hillhead was considered to be 'Very Good', an assessment level that he maintained until he left the school three years later. He was obviously a very bright boy, hard-working and diligent and a source of pride for his parents and teachers.

It was during this time, when Alf was thirteen, that he first started dreaming of becoming a vet. Even though they lived in a cramped tenement building, the Wights were within easy reach of the countryside to the west of

Yoker, where the city filtered itself away into the hills. As often as possible, especially during the summer holidays, he would take Don, his Irish setter, and walk as far as thirty miles a day to the summits of the Kilpatrick Hills or the Campsie Fells, from where he would gaze with longing at the mountains of Argyll. Often a couple of school friends would join him, bringing their own dogs. Alf became so fascinated by the animals' different characters, and by canine behaviour in general, that when one day he read an article in *Meccano Magazine* headed 'VETERINARY SURGERY AS A CAREER', he suddenly knew that he wanted to become a vet specialising in dogs. His ambition was cemented when the principal of Glasgow Veterinary College, Dr Whitehouse, came to Hillhead to give a talk about veterinary surgery as a career. He told his young audience that though they would never be rich if they became vets, they would have varied and fulfilling lives. Alf was hooked – but worried that he would never become a vet unless he could pass exams in science. He went to the Veterinary College to see Dr Whitehouse, who reassured him that he did not need any scientific qualifications: he had merely to pass at least two subjects at Higher Level and two at Lower. He could always catch up on physics, chemistry and biology in his first year at the college. But Alf was still worried. What about maths? Wouldn't he need maths to be a vet? Whitehouse chuckled. 'Only to add up your day's takings,' he said. In that moment 'James Herriot' was born.

Alf had a definite goal now. He was only thirteen but he knew exactly what he wanted to do with his life and how to do it: two Higher passes and two Lowers, and that was it. He was going to be a dog doctor.

The following year, in Form IIIA, halfway up the school and fuelled by his fierce new ambition, he proved his worth beyond doubt not only by achieving his Intermediate Certificate (the equivalent of the modern O-level exams) – excelling in Latin (80 per cent) and French (75 per cent) – but also by becoming the school's Intermediate Champion, which meant that he was both academically and sportingly the best mid-way pupil of them all. Alf Wight's modesty and self-effacement in later years was a mask: he was in fact very clever and well educated. Indeed, in his fourth year, 1931–2, he won not only a prize for English but also an athletics medal in the Interscholastic Sports for coming second in the under-16 broad jump event. The English prize was the award that finally alerted his mathematics master, Mr Filshie, to the fact that he was a very clever boy who must have been slacking disgracefully to end up with a mark as paltry as 29 per cent.

In Form IV, for the first time, Alf found himself in a mixed-sex class but the sudden proximity of girls did not inspire him to ask any of them out, not after the experience of his first proper date a year earlier. That had been a disaster. Late in 1930, just after his four-teenth birthday, he had plucked up the courage to invite a girl to the cinema. On the tram from Yoker into town he asked for a penny ticket and handed over a half-crown coin – 2/6d, the equivalent of thirty pennies. The conductor was so furious at being given such a large coin that he searched his bag for the smallest change he could find and handed Alf fifty-eight halfpennies. With a clanking pocketful of coins Alf met the girl at the cinema and then embarrassed her and himself by holding up the entire queue while he paid for two shilling tickets entirely in halfpennies. That was the end of his first romance. He claimed later that he was so mortified by the experience that it took him four years to summon up the courage to invite another girl out.

When Alf first arrived at Hillhead, music was barely taught – a visiting music teacher dropped by once every three weeks – but one of the masters, Douglas Berry, had set up a school orchestra, and Beaumont soon ensured that every child in the first three years was given two periods of musical study a week. Alf came to love music – not just popular music, though he did enjoy Highland dancing, but also classical. One day when he was at a schools concert given by the Scottish Orchestra in St Andrew's Hall, he went out to the lavatory in the interval and was astonished to discover that the tiny man in white tie and tails relieving himself in the next stall was none other than the conductor John Barbirolli, later Sir John. Barbirolli was immensely kind and gracious to the awkward young Scots boy, asking him about himself and his musical preferences.

By now Alf was playing tennis as well as rugby and cricket, and although he had dropped geography, drawing and science to concentrate on his main Higher Certificate subjects of English, history, Latin, French and maths, life was as full for him as it ought to be for any fit, lively fifteen-year-old.

And yet there is something of a mystery here, for despite Alf's achievements at Hillhead few of his contemporaries can remember him at all. Here he was winning prizes, excelling at sport and even becoming Intermediate Champion – yet for most of his fellow pupils he was utterly faceless.

'I knew about him but he didn't make any real impact,' said Harry Locke, who was at Hillhead in the thirties. Eddie McSween, who was only a year behind Alf, told me: 'I've absolutely no recollection of him. I think he must have been a very shy boy. It would have been difficult for a boy to come to Hillhead from another school like Yoker and to get into things. He just didn't register.'

Maisie Cessford, whose late husband Jim played rugby with Alf at Hillhead, told me: 'Everyone who knew Alf at school says he was very nice but he was also a very reticent person. He was just a nice fellow, a good bloke, quite reserved – not shy, just reserved. He didn't push himself forward or excel in anything in particular, though he was a good rugby player and he did play rugby once or twice for the Former Pupils' XV after he left the school and was studying to be a vet in Glasgow.'

Even Ian McColl, who was in the same class as Alf, told me: 'I have no real memories of Alf except I can remember seeing him. He was about my height, 5 ft 8 ins, and he had a nice, honest, open face and was fair-haired. He was neat – there weren't any scruffs at Hillhead – and polite, reticent, courteous. He was liked by the other boys.'

McColl's slightly younger brother Neil, who was also in the same class as Alf Wight, told me that he too had little recollection of him. 'He was a wee bit older than me but he must have been a very quiet lad,' said Neil McColl. 'I only really remember him in his fifth year. I can visualise him then: he was tall, I was particularly small. I do remember that his great friend was Jimmy Risk, who became a professor of economics.'

'Alfie hadn't got time to lark around,' said Nell Clark. 'He had to keep his head down and work to get through veterinary college.'

Hillhead was certainly still the right school for a boy who wanted to work hard and improve himself. In August 1931 a report by the Scottish Education Department found that even though there were now 708 pupils in the senior school – more than a hundred more than when Alf had joined it three years previously – 'the reports of the individual examiners bear testimony to a solid measure of achievement in the session's work. Tone and discipline are excellent, and a happy spirit of co-operation between teachers and pupils prevails. The school owes much to the unsparing efforts of a competent staff and to the person-ality of the Head Master.' The report found that in English 'the teaching is thoroughly competent', in mod-ern languages 'thoroughly sound', and that maths was 'taught with skill and vigour by a conscientious and hard-working staff'. Class IIID was given a special men-tion because it 'made an outstandingly good appearance in all branches of its work, a noteworthy feature being its admirable rendering of French songs'. Though Alf Wight was in IIIA, not IIID, the comment gives a good indication of the high standards and broad base of the education he received at Hillhead.

*

On 1 September 1931 the school escaped the overcrowded site in Cecil Street when all 736 senior pupils – 398 boys and

338 girls – were moved into the present high school building in Oakfield Avenue, an ugly, double-Y-shaped red-brick monstrosity with vast, echoing balconies that make it resemble a multi-storey car park rather than a haven of education. The building, which was officially opened in front of a large audience of parents on Tuesday 15 September by Councillor Malcolm Macrae, the convener of Glasgow Corporation's Education Committee, eventually cost only half of the original estimate – £75,000 rather than £183,000 – and it looks like it. It did, however, have some major advantages, among them two gymnasia, art rooms, laboratories, a hall with a stage where morning services were held, and a kitchen and lunch rooms. There was even a proper library: in Cecil Street books had simply been stored on open shelves in classrooms and corridors.

A month later, however, disaster struck in one of the new laboratories. On 21 October 1931, William Rae, the science teacher who had joined the staff the same term as Alf, 'met with a serious accident in the laboratory and was removed to the Eye Infirmary', according to the school's official record in the Glasgow City Archives. It must have been a bad accident – probably an explosion – because the unfortunate Rae did not return until eleven months later. When news of the incident spread around the school Alf Wight must have been more grateful than ever that he was no longer studying science: he had given it up at the end of the previous term. Seven months later another science master, Mr W.H. Brown, went absent for two days after an accident in the chemistry lab that damaged his right eye. The subject certainly seemed to be jinxed: just before the school was moved from Cecil

Street, the head science master, John Faichney, collapsed and died of a heart attack as he was walking along a corridor. Ian McColl was just behind him when it happened. 'I can see him yet with his tongue hanging out as he died,' McColl told me. 'I saw him fall over as he was walking along but people just continued to walk past.' Strangely there is no mention of this tragedy in the official school record: death was obviously not considered part of the curriculum.

Most writers can look back at their schooldays and remember one teacher who seemed to fire their interest in words and literature. In Alf's case he found his inspiration when he moved into the new senior school and began to be taught by Johnny Gibb. English had always been Alf's favourite subject but Gibb threw new light on it for him and in later years Alf acknowledged his debt to the teacher. His new enthusiasm resulted in what may have been the very first piece of his writing ever to be published – a schoolboyish spoof of Gray's *Elegy Written in a Country Churchyard*. The original begins:

> *The curfew tolls the knell of parting day,*
> *The lowing herd winds slowly o'er the lea,*
> *The ploughman homeward plods his weary way,*
> *And leaves the world to darkness and to me.*

Alf's spoof – if indeed it was written by him – was about Hillhead's teachers and janitors. Entitled 'Four o'Clock', it was written in collaboration with a classmate and appeared in the December 1932 issue of the school magazine above the initials J.A.W. and D.M.M.:

The buzzing bell doth screech the ended day;
The toil-worn herd winds slowly home to tea;
The teachers homeward wend their weary way,
And leave the School to 'jannies' big and wee.

Now fades the fog-bound landscape from the sight,
And all the School a solemn stillness holds,
Save where the cleaners sweep with all their might
And clanging pail the hidden dirt enfolds.

Save that from yonder smoothly swinging doors
The moping 'jan' doth audibly complain
To such as playing football after hours,
Infest his all too desolate domain.

• • •

The icy blast of cold and frosty morn,
The ringing of alarms beside their head,
The milk-boy's skirl, the matutinal horn
Will tear them, on the morrow, from their bed.

It was the typically facetious sort of spoof verse that could
have been written by any bright sixteen-year-old with a
love of English literature and a facility for words, but a
sixteen-year-old who can scan so accurately and who
knows the meaning of 'matutinal' is hardly the simple oaf
that Alf liked to suggest he was when he started publishing the James Herriot books.

Looking at the advertisement from publisher John
Smith & Son (Glasgow) Ltd in the same issue of the
Hillhead school magazine – *'The Enjoyment of Books is the
Enjoyment of Friends'* – it is fun to speculate as to which of

the titles Jim and Hannah might have bought to give their son as a present that Christmas, the last of his childhood. *Let's Talk of Dogs* by Rowland Jones (3/6d), perhaps, or *Everybody's Dog Book* by Major A.J. Dawson (5/-), both of which had just been published. Did Alf read them, decide he could do very much better himself, and vow to write one day a series of animal books?

In Alf's last year at Hillhead, 1932–3, his general academic level fell dramatically and although he reached 67 per cent in English when he sat his final exams in May he could manage only 52 per cent in history, 53 per cent in French and 40 per cent in maths. Even in his beloved Latin he scraped only 48 per cent, despite the fact that one Douglas Herd, MA had been appointed an assistant classics master at the start of the year. Herd lasted just thirty-one days. Was there some scandal? The record, sadly, is silent.

Alf's comparatively poor showing in his last year may well have been caused by illness since his school record card shows that he attended only 312 out of the year's 389 half-day sessions: in other words he was absent from school for 38 days. 'That's quite a lot,' I was told by Mary Roger, who was for many years the Hillhead school secretary. 'He must have had an illness. He doesn't sound like a shirker or the sort of boy who would play truant.' His absence may well have been caused by the anal fistula that gave him a great deal of trouble in his early years and eventually caused him to be invalided out of the RAF in the Second World War. Perhaps it was then that he had to go into hospital for the first of several anal operations. Or perhaps he was simply fed up with school and eager to escape into the outside world. Like many other boys of real ability, he may suddenly have felt constricted by the petty rules and regulations of school and bored by the endless regime of academic study. At sixteen there suddenly seems to be much more to life than books, chalk and the smells of wintergreen and linseed oil. Alf was probably raring to get out and start healing his beloved dogs.

His love of literature, words and writing, however, lasted right to the end of his final term. Throughout his entire career at Hillhead there was never any mention of him in the school magazine's notes about the Literary and Debating Society, but during his last term the magazine published in its June 1933 issue another spoof verse, 'Words', that may well have been written by him – this time a parody of Hamlet's 'Angels and ministers of grace defend us!' soliloquy. In the parody a horrified student, who is just as terrified as ever Hamlet was on seeing his father's ghost, encounters a strange new word in his Latin examination paper. It is impossible now to be absolutely certain that Alf was the author of this little verse but it was printed over the initials J.A.W. and was typical of the man who was later to write the Herriot books, with its cheeky humour and wry self-deprecation:

> *Angels and ministers of grace defend us!*
> *Be thou a verb, a noun, an adjective,*
> *Come thou from Virgil, Livy, Cicero –*
> *Thy object, or to help or hinder me –*
> *Thou comest in such a questionable shape*
> *That I will guess at thee: I'll call thee Noun,*
> *Pronoun, Conjunction – anything! Oh! answer me!*

Let me not burst in ignorance; but tell
Why the examiners, fiends e'en though they be
Do thus maltreat me; why the dictionary,
In which thou hast been quietly inurn'd
Hath ope'd his ponderous and gilt-edged jaws
To cast thee up at me. What may this mean
That thou, foul word, so tangled, and unreal,
Revisit'st thus the examination room,
Making day hideous; and me befooled,
So horridly to shake my disposition
With thoughts beyond the reaches of my soul?
Say, why is this? wherefore? what should I do?

Despite his disappointing showing in his final year, Alf left Hillhead after the annual prizegiving on 30 June 1933 – presided over by Councillor and Mrs W. McKernon – with Leaving Certificate number 46; creditable Higher passes in English, French and Latin; and Lower passes in history and, somehow, even the dreaded mathematics. Though he had quite enough passes to go on to veterinary college, his father tried to dissuade him from becoming a vet, arguing correctly and sensibly that since horses were being replaced by cars there might soon not be enough work to make a decent living. Jim Wight thought Alf should become a doctor instead, but the young man's heart was set on a veterinary career.

In later years Alf acknowledged how good his teachers had been at Hillhead and said that he would always be grateful for what they had done for him. Unlike most of his contemporaries, however, he did not join the Hillhead Former Pupils' Club, and the school's headmaster in

1996, Ken Cunningham, told me that he had had no contact at all with Hillhead in his later years.

His final report was marked 'Excellent' for Progress, 'Excellent' for Diligence and 'Excellent' for Conduct. He had been a model pupil – yet still hardly anyone had heard of him or knew anything about him. He was to try to keep it like that for the next forty years.

CHAPTER FIVE

Beer and Stardust

GLASGOW VETERINARY COLLEGE was in a terrible mess when Alf Wight started the first of his six years there on 25 September 1933, a week before his seventeenth birthday. The college was housed on the cobbled corner of 83/87 Buccleuch Street and 38/42 Garnethill Street, in the Cowcaddens district of Glasgow, in a dilapidated three-storey building that had once been a pumping station. Its finances and academic standards were also distinctly shaky. The college had been desperately short of funds for eight years, ever since the Board of Agriculture for Scotland had withdrawn its £600-a-year Government grant. It had been decided that because of the decline in the demand for vets, Scotland did not need two veterinary colleges and there was already an excellent one in Edinburgh, the Royal College ('The Dick'). Consequently the Glasgow college was broke and most of the lecturing was done by ancient, retired or part-time teachers, or by veterinary surgeons who had been cajoled into lecturing for nothing. Some were deaf, most were bored and the Professor of Botany and Zoology simply read to his class from a textbook, often missing a page or two without noticing until the students shouted at him. At one point the aged principal, Professor A.W. 'Old Doc' Whitehouse – a former American Wild West rancher and Yukon gold prospector – was the only full-time member of the teaching staff, and although he had been there for eleven years and was highly qualified – with an Oxford MA as well as British, Canadian and American veterinary degrees – he could hardly run the entire college single-handed.

Glasgow Veterinary College was so ramshackle it did not even have a clinic and the students had to try to scrounge their practical experience by attaching themselves to outside veterinary practices. At one particularly low point some of the students were reduced to trying to raise funds for the college by rattling collecting tins at point-to-point races and the Scottish Stallion Show, as though their place of learning were some shabby charity for tired old donkeys.

'It was without doubt the worst veterinary college in the *world*, make no mistake about that,' I was told in 1996 by Eddie Straiton, who joined it in 1935. 'They taught you *nothing*,' he went on vehemently. 'You had to learn the textbooks virtually off by heart to get through. A hundred and twenty-seven students started with me and only five of us went through in five years, and only two of us went through without getting a subject wrong. The only reason I went through was because I couldn't *afford* to get a subject wrong because I was on a Carnegie Bursary that paid the £33–18s–0d a year fees, and if I failed, that was it.'

The college 'was a grim seat of learning', Straiton told me. 'You could not imagine a dirtier, filthier stinking hole than the Glasgow Veterinary College. If the public health department visited it now they would close the place down. It was terrible, and the tuition was absolutely non-existent.' Buccleuch Street itself was 'most disreputable', according to Straiton. 'Prostitutes lived in the old flats opposite and we could see them in the windows having a bath or on the loo.' There was just one great advantage in going to the college: it was so dreadful that any student who did somehow qualify had to have the makings of an excellent vet if he had managed to survive so long. 'The odd jobs that *were* advertised in the *Veterinary Record* said "only Glasgow graduates need apply" because if you could get a Glasgow graduate you knew he had initiative!' said Straiton. Or, as the college's own official history put it guardedly in 1941: 'Glasgow graduates have the reputation of entering the profession better fitted and less "spoon-fed" . . . than most others. That is because in its studies practical knowledge is never submerged by theory.'

Jimmy Steele, another student who joined the college in 1935 and became a lifelong friend of Alf Wight, was as scathing about the place as Eddie Straiton. 'It was the worst vet college in the world,' Steele told me. 'It was just a struggle to keep going all the time. There was no money to do anything. There was hardly one good teacher. But the good thing about it was that you really had to work and see a lot of practice and actually Glasgow graduates were very successful. You attached yourself to a local vet and went the rounds with him all over Glasgow. I think that's why we were in such demand. Even though it wasn't a good college you had to work hard.'

Miss Dorothy Campbell, who became a student in

1938, told me the same story. 'We only had about one class a day,' she said, 'so we'd help practising vets with operations, making up drugs, et cetera. It was crazy. But you saw a lot of practice, so there were these advertisements that said "Glasgow Graduates Preferred" because they knew we could do it.'

Even the college history itself, *Records of 80 Years' Progress*, which was published in 1941, admitted that 'the College premises are far from inspiring' but complained that since the withdrawal of the Government grant, much of the money received from students as fees and from local authorities as grants was spent immediately on repairing the buildings.

The college was built in a quadrangle around a central yard covered by a glass roof. Its premises had been reconstructed to provide classrooms, laboratories, stables and a shoeing forge. On the ground floor there was the general office, board room, staff room, library, pharmacy, Old Doc Whitehouse's anatomy department, some lavatories and a ladies' room. On the first floor was the students' common room, housing the grand piano and ping-pong table that Alf was to use often during his years there, along with a coal stove, brick fireplace and pine bench. Gazing morosely down from the wall, along with some group photographs of past students, was a moose's antlered head. On the landing outside, which was covered with brown linoleum, were two notice boards and a coin-box telephone, and leading off it the four rooms that made up the chemistry department, as well as the students' dining room with its lockers and pine table. The top floor housed the botany, zoology, parasitology, physiology, pathology and bacteriology departments, as well as two lecture rooms, the caretaker's room and the examination room, with its circular oak clock hanging on the wall. According to the old college inventory, the exam room clock was 'defective'. It seems inevitable that in such a shambolic establishment the clock should be broken in the one room where it was vital for the students to know the exact time.

Among the forty-eight students who enrolled at the same time as Alf were David Stewart from Millport, John Hepburn from Helensburgh, Qasuria Ashiq Mohd (who already had a BA from Punjab University) and George Irvine from Whitecrook, who was to drop out after three years, returning ten years later (after the Second World War) and finally qualifying in 1949. Only one of the forty-eight was a woman, Margaret Stevenson from Aberdeen High School. 'Alfie was very friendly with her,' I was told by Miss Campbell. 'We always called him Alfie and she was always known as Stevie. He mentions her in one of his books as the only girl in his class.' Despite Alf's long-held conviction that vetting was too rough and heavy for a woman, Stevie managed to complete the course in exactly the same time as he did, qualifying in the same term at the end of 1939. In fact Alf's year was to fare a great deal better than Eddie Straiton's: two-thirds of them (thirty-three students) eventually qualified as MRCVS (Member of the Royal College of Veterinary Surgeons), and only sixteen failed, among them the unfortunate James Paton from West Kilbride, who left after just one year. John Queen of Glasgow survived his first year but then, seduced perhaps by the arrival of spring and summer, went absent for two entire terms in 1935 and left that July. So did Banytine Maclean from the distant western island of Harris. Some had their studies interrupted by the war, like James Jarron from Giffnock, who left in December 1939 to join up. Saddest of all was the case of Edward Gorman, who was two months older than Alf but spent ten years at the college, failing examination after examination, until finally he gave up and left in December 1943.

Alf himself was to fail several examinations along the way, and although he would claim in Chapter 2 of his first book that he had qualified in four years, and then in Chapters 5 and 18 that he had done so in five years, he did in fact eventually take six years and a term to complete the five-year course. Luckily, like Eddie Straiton, he also had an £18 grant from the magnificent Carnegie Trust, which contributed to the fees of every Scottish boy going on to higher education, as well as a £10 grant from the Glasgow Education Authority, but his parents would still have been making heavy sacrifices to meet the fees of £33-18s-0d a year and to pay for his upkeep during his time at the veterinary college. It was not until he was twenty-four that Alf would at last be able to support himself. Until then he was heavily dependent on his parents, not only for his fees but also because he was still living with them even after he left college, until in 1940 he managed at last to find a job.

When Alf joined the college in 1933 the length of the MRCVS course had just been increased from four to five years. He began his veterinary career by studying animal husbandry, chemistry and biology. In his very first term he became a victim of the chemistry jinx that had felled at least three of his science teachers at Hillhead: while taking his first chemistry exam he had some sort of accident in the laboratory and had to leave the room for treatment, and consequently his chemistry tutor was unable to assess him at the end of term. His other tutors, however, were pleased with the start he had made. 'I think this lad has the makings of quite a good student,' wrote his biology teacher in his report. 'Doing fairly well and attends regularly,' said his animal husbandry teacher with a hint of amazement.

Attending regularly was in fact decidedly rare at the college. Although there were nearly three hundred students, from India and the colonies as well as from all over Scotland, few of them were renowned for their dedication to their studies. Many were simple Gaelic-speaking farmers' sons from the wild Highlands and islands who 'were coming in to the college,' according to Eddie Straiton, 'with a sack of oatmeal over their shoulders to keep them in porridge for the whole term'. One student, whose surname was McAloon, had spent fourteen years at the college and had still managed to complete no more than the first year of the curriculum. Eventually it dawned on him that he was unlikely to qualify as a veterinary surgeon before reaching pensionable age and he left to become a traffic policeman, which was just as well for the equine and bovine population of Scotland but much regretted by Old Doc Whitehouse, who was heard to remark sadly during one of his anatomy lessons: 'Mr McAloon has sat on that stool for eleven years. It is going to be very strange without him.' Many other students had been at the college for ten years or more, failing their exams over and over again, and although they seemed to spend most of their time playing poker on top of the grand piano in the common room, they were allowed to stay on for as long as their parents continued to pay their fees because the college, needing their money desperately, simply could not afford to expel them. Sometimes the card games even continued in class, with the mumbling of the old teachers inaudible above the racket of clinking coins, as Alf himself recalled fifty years later in his introduction to *James Herriot's Dog Stories*.

'There were some real characters in the college,' Jimmy Steele told me, 'like "The Count", who was an aristocrat, and Jack Coleman, who'd go shooting boar in France and come back with great tales of imagination. He was very, very funny. He did qualify eventually. And Gerry Anderson, who took fourteen years to qualify. One term he didn't attend at all except to play cards: there was an exhibition on in Glasgow where he had a job demonstrating washing machines and his mother and sister were in the audience. He was supposed to be in college and here he was demonstrating washing machines! And he also had a great line in selling encyclopaedias round the doors.' Students even took part-time jobs driving trams, Miss Campbell told me, and several ended up as vacuum cleaner salesmen.

After all the strict rules, regulations and high standards of Hillhead High School, Alf was amazed to discover that at the veterinary college no one seemed to give a damn whether he did any work or not. Lectures themselves tended to be riotous shambles, with the students laughing, yelling, throwing missiles and playing practical jokes on the aged teachers, one of whom was so deaf that he would burble on without realising that there was an almighty racket all around him. 'Some daft things went on,' Jimmy Steele told me. 'One of the lecturers simply read from a book, and we got a boy to play the pipes outside the window and we'd all hum to the tune of it, and this guy went on reading, pretending he didn't hear it! Another time Alf's year were in a lecture with this guy and they tied a rope to the door handle and to the banister and he couldn't get in.'

Miss Campbell too remembered the humming: 'It was the old deaf professor who taught us parasitology. Someone fixed a notice under his desk that said "Hum while he's talking" and we would and he'd say "There's a strange noise in the room." Another time someone tied a pail to the skylight and let it drop.'

The 'old, deaf professor' was in fact a retired vet called Hugh Begg. He spent each lesson reading out extracts from *Monnig's Parasitology* and was so bad at controlling his classes that they would generally be conducted in an uproar, with rubbers and pencils being hurled around the room. He did, however, come up with a remark that Eddie Straiton considered so astute that he always quoted it himself to other young vets. 'Aye,' bellowed the ancient Begg helplessly as the chaos eddied around him, 'ye aw think you're very clever but ah'll tell ye this, and I want ye tae listen carefully: *ye'll never be a veterinary surgeon till ye've strewn the fields wi' carcasses.*'

Unlike Eddie Straiton and Jimmy Steele, Alf claimed years later that after Hillhead he found the chaos of the college 'wonderfully beguiling' and always remembered his time there with great affection. But Straiton was adamant that this had to be untrue. 'You *couldn't* say you were happy there,' he said. 'The place was bloody awful.' Alf even claimed that he joined the card school and lost so much money that he only managed to repay his creditors by walking part of the five miles to and from Dumbarton Road every day, and by rationing himself to a lunch of no more than one penny piece of apple cake from the canteen. Eddie Straiton and Jimmy Steele both told me that the story was highly unlikely. 'Alf exaggerated terribly,' said Straiton. 'There was a lot of gambling went on in the college but I never saw Alf gamble.' Steele agreed: 'There was a permanent card school but it was not high gambling and I don't think Alf was a gambler.'

Eddie Straiton remembered Alf then as 'a well-built athlete with fair, curly hair, laughing eyes, good teeth and the tanned complexion of one who has spent most of his available time outdoors. Invariably dressed in a well-worn Harris tweed sports jacket and grey flannels, he could tan the hide of most of the lads at table tennis. He was also adept on the keyboard of the ancient out-of-tune piano stuck in the corner of our far from clean common room. His signature tune, 'Stardust', was a great favourite at the Freshers' Night dances.'

When it came to misbehaving in college, Jimmy Steele told me, 'Alf was not especially mischievous.' Another contemporary, John Morrison, agreed. 'Alf was a very quiet, well-mannered lad by college standards,' he told me in 1997 from his home in Australia.

'He wasn't rumbustious or anything like that,' said Jimmy Steele, 'and I wouldn't say he was the ringleader. I was a couple of years behind him. I was late in going to college – I didn't go till I was twenty-one – but my great pal Aubrey Melville, who is dead now, was in the same year as him and they were pals and I became one too. Alf was a very correct student, quiet and hard-working. A good brain, Alf, and he worked hard. Mind you, he liked his beer as a student although he wasn't a heavy drinker. At college we didn't have much money. We went to the Royal Bar where the heavy beer was sixpence a pint and the whisky was eightpence – a lot of money in those days. But he always had a great sense of humour and we had a lot of fun together. One thing that comes to mind was that we passed an exam and we all went out for a few drinks with girlfriends with us and we were going to go to the ballroom. We got there eventually and found it was closed that night but the security lights were on and the door open, so Alf sat down at the piano and played some quickstep. He played the piano beautifully as long as I knew him, popular stuff, the tunes of the day, what was then pop music. "Moon River" comes to mind. He wasn't especially keen on classical music then. We were all dancing away in this deserted ballroom and suddenly the caretaker and another man appeared at the door and the caretaker said, "Tony, send for the polis! Send for the polis!" We were all out of there very quickly! I can still see Alf down there and the chap who was the janitor – Porter was his name, Porter the porter!'

When Eddie Straiton came to compose Alf's obituary in the *Veterinary Record* sixty-one years later he wrote: 'My earliest recollections of Alf are of his Harris-jacketed stocky fair-haired figure gently extracting the strains of the melody "Stardust" from the shabby piano in the dusty common room of the Glasgow college in Buccleuch Street, of his dexterity at table tennis, and of his "party-piece" after our first professional examinations. The pass mark was 40 per cent. When the marks were declared Alf would go round the lads asking what mark they'd had, and if they said "41", he would shake his head and solemnly declare, "You've been working too hard." '

'At first I used to watch him playing table tennis in the common room,' Straiton told me, 'and soon I became his best friend. Another of his friends was Aubrey Melville, who was in the same year as Alf, and his best friend of all was Sandy Taylor, a very nice chap who had been very friendly with Alf at Yoker School and later became a surveyor. He was Alf's best friend of all but of the college crowd I was. I really got to know Alf when we played together in the college football team. I was captain and president of the athletic club and Alf was in that too. I'd been playing professional football in Scotland in the Central League and I got reinstated as an amateur and started playing in the West of Scotland amateur league, and I got Alf into the team. He was a good soccer player, casual but a natural. He played at left half or inside left, anywhere on the left side.'

It seems quite extraordinary that even at college Alf never had any enemies, rows or bust-ups; right from his earliest days, it appears, he showed the gentle, kind, likeable traits he was later renowned for as 'James Herriot'. 'Alf was exactly like his father,' said Eddie Straiton, 'the sort who would *never* upset anyone. He always said to me, "The big difference between you and I is if you think something you say it, no matter: if *I* think something I'll sleep on it and I might sleep on it for a fortnight and I might decide not to say anything at all." '

Was Alf a bit of a goody-goody? Even, perhaps, too good to be true?

'No, no, no!' said Straiton. 'Alf was very fond of a double whisky and very fond of his beer, and I remember when we went to play football against the veterinary college in Dublin, at Dalyneux Park, he and most of the lads got drunk. Since none of us had any money we raised the fares for the trip by running a successful dance in the college the previous week, which actually produced the magnificent sum of £16-15s-0d – more than enough to take us all there and back. This was the first Glasgow Veterinary College dance ever to record a profit.' The twelve footballers and four supporters made the journey in such high spirits that one of the team managed to lower the suitcase containing all their jerseys and shorts into the Irish Sea on the way over. Once they reached Dublin they all, except the teetotal, fitness-fanatic Straiton, proceeded to get so drunk that most of them, including Alf, lost their voices. Yet the following day they still managed to give a good account of themselves for ninety minutes on the soccer field, even though their kit looked decidedly bedraggled after its immersion in the sea. 'At full time we were winning by 3 goals to 1,' said Straiton. 'By that time all our team were knackered after a night with no sleep, so the Irish referee, the Professor of Parasitology, kept the game going for an extra twenty minutes till the Dublin team had equalised – to ensure (as he admitted afterwards) "that there would be no ill-feeling during the 'banquet' planned for that evening". Alf lost his voice that weekend and wrote a super story about it. I read it and thought it was bloody marvellous.'

Straiton was so impressed by the story that he remembered it vividly for many years afterwards and reproduced it for me – almost word-for-word, he claimed – in 1996. It reads more like a newspaper report than a short story – it was indeed absolutely true, said Straiton – and if his memory was accurate it was an extraordinarily revealing tale for the twenty-three-year-old Alf to have written, for it reported how he and Straiton had rounded up the whores in the tawdry flats opposite the college to attend the fund-raising dance and how he had then planned to sleep with Johnnie Morrison's 'right smasher' of a blonde sister, Kathleen, during the overnight boat journey. According to Straiton, Alf's version of the 'seduction' scene, which apparently took place well after midnight after a heavy evening of boozing, read something like this:

'It took ages to find her cabin – a similar slot in the boat's side to our sleeping quarters but narrower, with only one bunk. She was asleep, with her gorgeous fair hair covering her pillow. The boat rolled over on one side – my head hit the iron baulk and I spewed my guts up. My retching, not unnaturally, wakened the fair lady. She took one look and started screaming – "Get out! Get out!" I lurched forward, garrulously protesting "It's all right, I'm Alf Wight, a friend of Johnnie's." The sylph-like maiden rolled out of bed and came at me like a tiger. Bang! A tough little fist thumped against one cheek – then another – and another – and another. Talk about an Irish terrier – this was an Irish terrier bitch in full flow. I turned and ran, or rather staggered, for my life. I never saw the dear girl again.'

In 1997 Kathleen Morrison was still living in Glasgow and remembered that she had been travelling on the boat that weekend to see her fiancé in Belfast. Time, however, has softened her memory of her ardent would-be lover. She remembered Alf only as 'a nice lad' and recalled that occasionally in Glasgow they travelled home together on the tram to Broomhill.

Like many other students of his age, Alf seems to have developed an early taste for heavy drinking, especially at dances and particularly on the annual Freshers' Night. 'Alf and his friend Aubrey Melville drank to excess,' said Straiton, 'and they used to give me their addresses in case they flaked out so as I could see them safely home because I didn't smoke or drink – I was a fitness fanatic. There was a row of loos in the college – there must have been a dozen – and I remember one night when they were so drunk that I had Alf in one of them and someone in every other loo and I was going round sticking my fingers down their throats to make them sick. Alf had a bit of go about him. He was really great.'

Alf was certainly far from being po-faced. One of his favourite party songs began 'My name is Sammy Hall and I've only got one ball' and he could be just as lewd as the next student. In his last year, said Straiton, they went to Edinburgh to play football against the rival veterinary college there, The Dick – 'Dick was the professor who started the college'. The Edinburgh college nearly always won the match, but this year Glasgow won for the first time in nine years and they celebrated in style. 'I was persuaded by Alf to have a small whisky and ginger,' Straiton confessed, 'and we went into a dance hall – the Plaza Ballroom – and all the boys were tight and Alf grabbed the microphone in this dance hall and said, "Ladies and gentlemen, I've fondled every breast in the hall!" and we were thrown out. Alf had a great sense of humour.'

It was not until Alf's second year at college that he summoned up the courage to ask a girl out. It was his first date since the cinema-outing disaster of 1930. This time he was eighteen and his new girlfriend was Nan Elliot.

'Nan was a lovely girl,' said Eddie Straiton. 'Tall for a girl, 5 ft 7 ins, slim, very, very beautiful. Alf had met her at school. She lived in Knightswood and they were going together for years – all the time he was at college. He had just the one girl even though he was always very attractive to women, very handsome. He taught me how to chat up the girls. His technique was charm and flattery but very gentle flattery. But nobody in our college could really afford a girlfriend. We didn't even have bicycles and I used to walk nine miles every day from Clydebank to the college or took a bus for 2½d. It was a primitive life. Things were tough and people very, very poor.'

Jimmy Steele could not remember Nan Elliot or any other girlfriend of Alf's. 'He had no particular girlfriend,' he said. 'I don't think he was specially a ladies' man. He'd turn up at a dance at the vets' school with a girl now and again but never with anybody steady. But Eddie probably knew him better than I did.'

Alf himself later claimed – in an article he wrote in

1979 for the Christmas catalogue of the Chicago bookstore Kroch's and Brentano's – that he often took 'a girl'
out in those years at college, and that he could only afford
to do so by selling his textbooks and buying them back
later.

★

Right at the start of his time at Glasgow Veterinary
College Alf had to abandon his dream of becoming a vet
specialising solely in dogs. Dogs came a very poor fifth in
the veterinary hierarchy of those days. In the eyes of his
teachers the most important animal was the horse, followed by the cow, the sheep, the pig and – only then –
the dog. To make matters worse, he had been at the
college only three days when he made the mistake of
approaching a coalman's horse in the street and patting its
neck. The beast bit him on the shoulder, gripped his new
mackintosh in its big teeth and lifted him off the ground.
Much to his embarrassment a small crowd gathered and
started laughing at his predicament. The horse refused to
let Alf go until the coalman returned and bellowed '*Drop
him!*', a command which the horse obeyed immediately,
dumping Alf suddenly into the gutter. The coalman bent
over the figure of the prostrate student and snarled: 'Keep
your hands off my bloody horse. Dinna meddle wi' things
ye ken nuthin' aboot!'

Right from the start the students were taught by
blacksmiths how to shoe and de-shoe horses, and they
also learned how to ride, handle, groom, clip, saddle and
harness them properly and how to manage a stable. In
anatomy classes in his second year Alf even learned how

to dissect a horse. Once a week his class was transported out of town to Motherwell to learn to ride and on one occasion Alf, unhelmeted, fell off and was so badly concussed that he lost his memory for several days.

Despite the college's lackadaisical approach, a student's studies were relentless if he chose to work properly. During his six years Alf read again and again Sissons' vast volume *The Anatomy of the Domestic Animals*, and *Common Colics of the Horse* by Caulton Reeks. He learned how to administer various medicines and drugs in different doses to different animals. He studied plants, physics, chemistry, anatomy, physiology, animal management, pharmacology, hygiene, pathology, parasitology, medicine and surgery. He even tried to read Immanuel Kant's *Critique of Pure Reason* but could barely understand a word of it. One of the teachers, at least, was excellent: big, brooding, bad-tempered Professor Emslie, who taught pathology. He was young and energetic enough to hold his own in class and not be messed about by the inevitable jokers, idlers and hooligans. Most of the students were terrified of him and because of that most of them learned more pathology than any other subject.

Knowing as we do that Alf was destined to go on to become the most famous vet in the world, his record sheet at the college makes compulsive reading. His chemistry tutor said of him during his second and third terms: 'Has done fairly well, is pleasant and works quite well in Lab . . . is quite a fair average, not likely to be brilliant but I expect him to be steady.' His biology teacher was confident in the second term – 'A good student, with results very satisfactory' – but not after the third term: 'At the Professional he just managed to scrape thro' in Biology.'

Despite this warning, Alf seems to have allowed himself to coast during his second year (1934–5). It was a mistake. Old Doc Whitehouse was teaching him junior anatomy by now and seemed to become increasingly disillusioned as the year went by: 'a fair student, good appearance and manner' in the first term became 'average results' in the second and 'slightly worse than last term' in the third. Alf, like so many of his fellow students, was obviously beginning to toy with laziness: 'attendance irregular', reported his physiology teacher in the first term; 'inclined to be careless', he said after the second; 'a pleasant manner and capable, but does not sufficiently apply himself' after the third. The animal husbandry teacher was brusque: 'Did very poor xam,' he reported, and 'not too good yet'.

That year must have given Alf a fright. When he sat the Professional examination on 16 July 1935 he failed miserably, scoring just 37 per cent in animal husbandry, 36 per cent in physiology and only 25 per cent in histology. He was forced to retake the examinations in December, failed again in animal husbandry, was 'referred' twice in animal management and had to repeat part of his second-year studies. He was not able to move up to the third year until the start of 1936, and immediately received a devastating assessment from his new tutor in senior anatomy, who wrote brutally on his report: 'Does not work. Results very poor.' The following term he seemed to be floundering. 'Not too well up yet,' sniffed his pharmacology teacher. 'Very modest,' said Old Doc Whitehouse in senior anatomy. 'Very moderate so far,' reported the hygiene tutor.

It is not difficult to imagine the effect of such poor reports back at the Wight family home, where Jim and Hannah may have begun to wonder whether it was worth making such sacrifices for their son to swan about playing Jack the Lad. By now, 1936, the Wights had finally managed to save enough to allow them to move away from the tenement flat in Dumbarton Road and into a much more refined area. Their new home was a semi-detached, bow-windowed stone house a mile and a half away, in a quiet middle-class area at 724 Anniesland Road. It was rented from a John White and the trustees of a John Gardner and its rateable value was nearly three times that of the flat in Dumbarton Road (£70 a year rather than £26-5s-0d). The Wights had the house all to themselves and the sudden extra space and privacy must have been blissful after twenty years in a cramped tenement. Jim, Hannah and Alf could play the grand piano all day now without worrying about the neighbours.

The Wights had certainly moved up noticeably in the world. When they left Dumbarton Road Jim was still calling himself a fishmonger and the neighbours were a seaman, a shipwright, a joiner, a salesman, a draper and two engineers. Number 724 Anniesland Road was in a different class altogether. The previous tenant had been a dentist and the neighbours included a civil servant, a solicitor, two doctors and a civil engineer. The Scotstounhill Bowling and Tennis Club was just down the road at number 633, doubtless echoing with genteel cries of 'jolly good shot!' and 'well played, old man'. Although they had no car, the Wights even rented a garage around the corner in Cairntoul Drive, perhaps for storage.

Jim and Hannah were able to escape the crowded tenement and move to such a choice suburb because his father had recently died and left him some money as well as a house in Sunderland: number 65/66 Fulwell Road. This inheritance allowed Jim to escape the shipyards at last, to become a fishmonger with his own fish and chip shop in Glasgow and to rent a much smarter house. His father, who had himself once been a ship plater, had done very well for himself in the shipyards as a frame turner during the First World War – a highly paid job that allowed him to buy several small houses, to become a landlord and eventually to leave one house to each of his five surviving children. 'He owned on his death nine houses,' I was told by Alf's cousin Harold Summers in 1998. 'They were all terraced cottages – bungalows – in Sunderland. My grandfather Wight was quite a rich man.'

Another possible explanation for Jim and Hannah's rise in the world could be that Jim had finally found regular, full-time employment as a musician. If so, he would have been able to earn about £3 a week, though by this time it is unlikely that he would have been working in the cinema. Some cinemas, it is true, still hired organists to play before and between films, and did so for many years afterwards, but the arrival of the talkies and the demise of the silent movies generally meant the disappearance of the cinema pianist.

'The introduction of sound to movies put a large number of smaller, more primitive picture houses out of business,' says Bruce Peter in *100 Years of Glasgow's Amazing Cinemas*. 'Talkie apparatus was expensive and the new generation of more comfortable and efficient cinemas that emerged around the same time made the competition tougher than ever. By the late thirties there were sleek tiled "super" cinemas, boldly outlined at night in vividly coloured neon, on most of the main roads into the city, their advertising hoardings carefully placed to attract the attention of passing tram passengers. A greater contrast to the grimy ashlar-faced tenements whose streetscene they shared would be hard to imagine.'

Perhaps Jim Wight had found work in a hotel, restaurant or dance hall, or maybe Hannah was getting more regular singing engagements. 'She could have been singing in places like the Theatre Royal or the King's Theatre near Central Station,' suggested Miss Campbell. Certainly it was now that Jim started describing himself as 'musician' in the city valuation rolls. Perhaps he did so for reasons of snobbery – or Hannah's snobbery – to match his new status as an inhabitant of genteel Anniesland Road. Whatever the explanation for the sudden improvement in the family's fortunes, the move to Anniesland Road and up into the middle classes would have been enough to underline Alf's poor results and apparent slacking at the veterinary college. The formidable Hannah would doubtless have been forthright in her warnings to Alf that it was time he got a grip and pulled himself together. She might well have pointed out that he was nearly twenty and that most men of his age were not only earning their own livings, if they were lucky, but were dying on both sides in the Spanish Civil War. Others were joining armies to resist the threat of Hitler. It was no time to be backsliding.

Whatever was said, and however it was done, Alf seems to have returned to college in September 1936 with a sudden new sense of purpose about him. 'Has worked much harder with quite satisfactory results', said one tutor at the end of that term. 'Doing quite well now', commented another. By the end of the spring term of 1937 his hygiene teacher was seriously impressed. 'He has improved very considerably during this term.' Old Doc Whitehouse, too, was much happier with Alf, who had managed to score 67 per cent in senior anatomy. 'Has improved greatly from his junior year,' he reported. The following term, when Alf topped 71 per cent in anatomy, was even better. 'Has made very good progress,' said Whitehouse. 'Doing quite well now,' said pharmacology. 'Has made excellent progress this term,' said hygiene. The corner had been turned. Alf was not going to fail like so many of his contemporaries at the college. He was going to be a success.

*

As a rest from all these labours, Alf was increasingly escaping from the city into the country to breathe fresh air and to listen to the silence. From April to October every year he began to develop the love of remote countryside and wide-open spaces that was to become so important to him in later years and to be such a trademark of the James Herriot books. Every weekend he would escape from the noise, crowds and stench of Glasgow to go camping with his childhood friends Alex Taylor and Eddie Hutchison in the countryside at Rosneath, at the mouth of the Gare Loch, or beside a stream up in the Campsie Fells near Fintry. In later years he would often reminisce nostalgically about those idyllic weekends. 'Alf used to say that one of them used to do fuck-all, one used to say fuck-all, and one was good at farting,' laughed Eddie Straiton. The empty countryside, the fresh air, the smells of pine trees and crushed grass gave him a glimpse of what was possible, of the country life he was eventually to choose for himself.

At the same time his veterinary work at last seemed to be coming together. In those days – before the Veterinary Surgeons Act of 1948 – there was nothing to stop students practising on animals if they wanted to, and by 1936 Alf had had so much experience outside the college, helping vets in their surgeries at weekends, that even though he was still only nineteen one vet with whom he had been working regularly went off on holiday and left him to run his practice for a fortnight. The practical, hands-on experience was invaluable. During one vacation he managed to wangle a job in a veterinary practice near Sunderland, where he was not only able to sneak away to watch his heroes play soccer at Roker Park but also managed to stun the local farmers with his vast knowledge of Sunderland games and players, all delivered in a neat Glaswegian brogue.

In his fourth year, 1937–8, he started returning results of 64 per cent in medicine and 68 per cent in surgery, and even 100 per cent in parasitology. In his final year he was not expected to attend many lectures, so he attached himself instead to the practices of vets such as Donald Campbell, a Rutherglen practitioner, and Bill Weipers, who worked in the middle of Glasgow, in order to learn more of the practical side of the profession. Now at last he was able to indulge his passion for dogs. The legendary Weipers – later Sir William Weipers, Dean of Glasgow University's veterinary school – specialised in small animals and Alf was delighted to be able to work with dogs and cats from dawn to dusk in his superbly equipped surgery, operating theatre and laboratory. He was so impressed by Weipers' energy, enthusiasm and efficiency that he came almost to worship him and vowed to model himself on him. If Alf Wight went on to become a great vet, Weipers deserves some of the credit.

Although Alf was 'referred' again, twice, and had to resit a couple of exams – pathology in 1938 and surgery in 1939 – he finally passed as MRCVS in December 1939, just as Hitler was preparing to invade France and Norway and the German pocket battleship the *Admiral Graf Spee* was being scuttled by its skipper off Montevideo and the River Plate. For the last-year students at Glasgow Veterinary College, however, their final examinations were much more frightening than the Nazis. They knew that they had to work ferociously hard to make up for the patchy teaching they had received if they were to pass their final exams. After Eddie Straiton's third year only thirty out of his original class of 127 students still survived; after the fourth year only twenty were left. As the final examinations approached some students, desperate not to fail, worked like zombies. Straiton remembered that one young man, Ian Cameron, would rise at four every morning to start swotting, and was rumoured to sleep for only four hours a night – a dogged dedication to study that much amused Alf Wight. 'You'll never guess, lads!' announced Alf in the common room one morning. 'How's this for conscientious swotting? Ian Cameron has cut his lavatory time down to two minutes every third day!'

But the stress of finals was a nightmare, Straiton recalled in his autobiography. 'When we forgathered at the Maclay Hall in Glasgow University where the written part of the examination was to be held,' he wrote, 'we were a "wabbit" looking lot. Harry Donovan had shrunk to under six stones, and another pal, a tall wild red-haired Highlander called Maurice McMorran, hadn't shaved for two months. During the first week we faced two three-hour papers on each of four subjects – surgery, obstetrics, medicine and meat inspection – in all forty-eight questions covering the whole of our last two years' work and a considerable portion of the other three. The papers were tricky and very difficult; it seemed obvious they were out to plough as many of us as possible. But the worst was yet to come: ten days of orals and practical tests. In the words of the "referred" students (those who had previously sat and failed), "The examiners tore you to shreds in the first five minutes of the oral." We had to endure one hour of intensive interrogation on each subject. As we waited our turn the loos were overworked; some lads were sick. How we managed to survive is a mystery. I moved automatically from one examiner to another in a mental haze as I tried to answer the endless stream of questions.' Although Straiton was one of only five successful students in his year, he felt terrible. 'As I reached home that day,' he said, 'I felt dreadful, the worst reaction after acute stress I have ever known.'

Yet when Alf Wight looked back on his years at college he did so with that rosy, nostalgic gloss that was to suffuse all of his James Herriot books. When he left the college at last, he reported years later in *James Herriot's Dog Stories*, he felt bereft because despite the seediness of the building and the inefficiency of the teaching he had spent some of his happiest, most carefree years there.

*

Today nothing remains of the two main centres of Alf's life during those last years of the 1930s. The veterinary college was taken over by Glasgow University in 1949 and moved in 1969 from Buccleuch Street to Garscube, out in the leafy north-western outskirts of the city, where it still exists today as the university's faculty of veterinary medicine. On 24 February 1995, the day after Alf died, his son Jimmy went to Garscube to keep his father's promise to open the faculty's new James Herriot Library, a big, modern barn of a place with iron girders and cheap shelving that make it seem like a huge warehouse. Outside there is a blue memorial plaque with Glasgow's coat of arms and the motto *Via Veritas Vita*, Christ's description of Himself: the Way, the Truth and the Life. On the wall inside the library is a charming framed colour photograph of Alf with his last beloved dog, the terrier Bodie, and a black-and-white photograph of one Glasgow Veterinary College class during the 1940s posing outside the college wearing suits, stiff collars and smarmed-down hair. They do not look at all like the sort of men who are destined to spend the rest of their lives sticking their arms up cows' backsides.

The old Glasgow Veterinary College building has been demolished and replaced by an ugly block of yellow-brick apartments. Alf's home at 724 Anniesland Road has also gone. In its place is a Ladbrokes betting shop beside a little supermarket. Inside the betting shop television sets show a series of horse and dog races. Television yet again: John Logie Baird's miraculous invention flickering and dancing through every stage of Alf Wight's life.

CHAPTER SIX

A Yorkshire Vet At Last

WHEN ALF GRADUATED from Glasgow Veterinary College just before Christmas 1939 he was seriously worried about his future. He was a Member of the Royal College of Veterinary Surgeons at last – an MRCVS. He was fit and fancy-free and twenty-three. But there seemed no prospect of ever finding a job. Agriculture was in a state of depression, draught horses were being replaced by the thousand as machinery took over from horse-power, and veterinary jobs were so rare that some of his college contemporaries were working as shop assistants, vacuum cleaner salesmen, street cleaners, dustmen – even as labourers in the shipyards, which were booming once again thanks to the demands of the Second World War.

During this period Alf was convinced that he too might have to work in a shipyard, spending his life, like his father, hanging around the gates of Yarrow's or John Brown's in the hope of catching a surly foreman's eye. His worried mother must have felt that history was repeating itself: was it going to be rags to rags in just two generations for the Wight family? Even those students who did manage to find jobs as vets had to work for a pittance: after five or six years of study they were being paid just £1-10s-0d a week. Some vets, advertising their services in the *Veterinary Record*, were so desperate that they were offering to work for nothing more than their bed and board. Alf's dream of spending his life working with dogs, cats and other small animals seemed utterly hopeless. And now there was a war on. Vets were officially categorised as being in a reserved occupation – and therefore exempt from being called up into the armed forces – but unless Alf did manage to find a job he might well be drafted into the army if the rules were changed. In December 1939 his future looked bleak.

For four months he mooched around Glasgow, living uneasily with his parents in Anniesland Road, restless to leave home, anxiously scanning and answering the four or five job advertisements that appeared in the *Veterinary Record* every week, tramping the hills outside the city with his dog.

'When we left college it was impossible to get a job,' said Eddie Straiton, who qualified six months after Alf. 'There were about a hundred and fifty students after every job, and some of the lads who qualified at the same time as Alf got jobs sweeping the streets and things like that. One got a job as a typing teacher. Some of the lads in desperation were going back to college to do a diploma in public health. They wouldn't even take us in the army because by that time they'd made the veterinary profession a reserved occupation. The only thing that would accept us was the RAF, as a member of an aircrew. When I qualified I was absolutely desperate to get out because my parents couldn't afford to keep me any longer at college, but I failed the eye test for the RAF at five different centres in Glasgow. When I begged one of them to let me in, he said, "Listen, laddie, we're not the least worried about you but we're awful short of aeroplanes." '

Those weeks must have been difficult for all three of the Wights as Jim and Hannah worried about Alf's future and he worried about continuing to be a burden on them even now that he was well into his twenties. Jim was as quiet and self-effacing as ever but Hannah's forceful, dominant personality may well have been difficult to live with. Eddie Straiton went so far as to tell me that Alf developed 'a hate complex against his mother' because she was so bossy and tried to rule the whole family. If that were so, the pressures of living together in Anniesland Road might now have become intolerable. Mrs Jean Schreiber, who lived next door to Jim and Hannah Wight in the 1950s and 60s, told me that Hannah 'was rather a madam. My son Graeme and she were the best of enemies because he kept kicking balls into her garden.'

She remembered Hannah as 'a nice-looking woman with fine features, a well-dressed woman, not particularly tall, about 5 ft 3 ins. She was nicely built, slim, not fat like an opera singer. I should imagine she would have been beautiful when she was younger. Alf's father was a very nice, quiet, gentle man, henpecked. She ruled the roost. She was a bit daunting when she chose to be! Children were frightened of her. She was getting older and she couldn't be bothered with children and they would play in the lane and they had a tree house and she didn't like this. My son Graeme made her very angry running up and down the road. It was armed neutrality!'

Mrs Schreiber bought number 698 Anniesland Road in 1955, more than ten years after Jim and Hannah had moved a short distance down the road from 724 to 694. The Wights' new house, which was still rented, was a tall, thin, three-storey, four-bedroom, end-of-terrace Victorian villa in a row known as Haldane Villas. The move may have been caused by Hitler – 'I have a notion they were blitzed in the Clydebank blitz in 1941,' said Mrs Schreiber – but this seems unlikely because there is no official record of any wartime bomb damage at number 724 and it was still standing in 1966. Not only did the terrace have a swanky name, there was also a lane running down the side of the house between the Wights and the Schreibers where number 696 would have been. They were to rent number 694 for many years, Jim dying in the house in 1960 and Hannah living on there until she was moved to a nursing home in 1981. 'As far as I know, Alf eventually bought them the house,' said Mrs Schreiber. 'They were renting until then.' Number 694 Anniesland Road is still there: in 1996 its occupants were a Mr and Mrs Anwar.

Mrs Schreiber was amazed to hear that Jim Wight had ever worked as a ship plater, joiner or fishmonger. 'Oh my, I didn't know all that!' she said. 'I didn't know he'd actually been a ship *builder*.' Such callings were obviously not to be mentioned in a smart street like Anniesland Road. 'I thought Alf's father worked in a shipyard as a *clerk*.' Indeed, Harold Summers says Jim was later a draughtsman at John Brown's shipyard. Nor did she know that Jim had ever played in an orchestra. 'Mrs Wight hardly ever talked about her earlier life, just that Mr Wight had played the piano in cinemas.' This reinforces the theory that Jim Wight was never a proper musician, despite Alf's insistence that he was.

Was the cinema playing just an occasional hobby, or something to be resorted to when times were particularly hard? If Jim really *was* a musician in an orchestra it seems extremely odd that his next-door neighbour did not know about it.

Equally strange, considering that Alf always told people that his mother had been an opera singer, is Mrs Schreiber's evidence that Hannah was in fact a seamstress. 'She took in work as a dressmaker,' Mrs Schreiber told me. 'She altered clothes at home. She had one or two girls to help. I don't think the Wights were well off: they were middling. They didn't have a car and I know that she had to work too to keep them going and to keep Alf at college. I knew she was a singer but I didn't know she was an *opera* singer.' The extended family believed the Wights were 'very affluent', says Summers, and that Hannah 'had a dressmaking business employing some ten women', but he admitted that she may well have been exaggerating.

So life was possibly difficult at 724 Anniesland Road that Christmas of 1939. But then early in 1940 came the lucky break that was to set Alf Wight on the road towards 'James Herriot'. He saw an advertisement for a job with a practice in Thirsk in the Yorkshire Dales, applied, and was asked by the owner of the practice, Donald Sinclair, to go and have tea with him. Alf went to Thirsk and met Sinclair but quickly realised that the job was not at all the one of which he had always dreamed. Sinclair dealt hardly at all with dogs or small animals: his main customers were farmers and their cows, horses, pigs and sheep, and there were not many of them, either, since he had not yet established the practice as a decent going concern. But in 1940 Alf could not afford to be choosy. Much to his amazement, Sinclair offered him the job. Alf had been extremely lucky: although he never said so in his books, he landed the job in Thirsk because Sinclair was due to join the Royal Air Force at any minute and was desperate to find someone to hold the fort while he was away. He grabbed the job, moved to Thirsk and began to lay the foundations of the Herriot legend.

Despite all the poverty and hardships he had suffered during his twenty-three years in Glasgow, Alf left the city with real affection and in later years often returned to see his parents. He always remembered the place with deep nostalgia and dedicated his fourth book, *Vet in Harness*, 'With love to my mother in dear old Glasgow town'. Although he was to live in Yorkshire for more than half a century, he thought of himself all his life as a Glaswegian and never lost his soft Glasgow accent. The teeming old city had branded him with its mark for ever.

*

Thirsk, twenty-five miles north of York, was in those days a quiet market town where nothing much had happened since the early nineteenth century, when its only famous inhabitant, Thomas Lord, left his birthplace at number 16 Kirkgate – just across the road from the vets' surgery at number 23 – to move down to London to become a famous cricketer and found Lord's cricket ground. True, the Norman baron Robert de Mowbray had built a wooden castle there in the eleventh century to control the local Saxons, but a hundred years later the Mowbrays made the mistake of rebelling against Henry II, who ordered the castle to be burned to the ground. In 1580 a certain B. Smith opened a dressmaking and millinery shop in the marketplace that was still trading more than 350 years later, earning it a mention in *The Guinness Book of Records* as 'the oldest draper's in the world'. Sadly B. Smith & Son no longer exists: like so many of the town's old shops it has gone out of business, rendered redundant by modern mass manufacture and marketing. There was also a brief flurry of excitement in 1702 when a boozy local layabout, Thomas Busby, murdered his father-in-law, was hanged and his corpse left dangling in chains from the gibbet at the crossroads. Afterwards a chair that stood in the pub where Busby used to drink was said to be haunted and to bring bad luck to anyone who sat in it — but today it is safely out of the way in Thirsk Museum, hanging from on high like the late Thomas Busby himself.

Later in the eighteenth century the town was a designated halt on the old coaching route from Edinburgh to York until railways and motor cars replaced the coaches and the thundering hooves of the Scottish mails were silenced. Since then the only real activity in Thirsk had been on market days. For centuries farmers had come into town from miles around to sell their animals in the big cobbled marketplace. 'Surrounded by good grazing land,' says the official Thirsk Museum information leaflet, 'Thirsk was a natural centre for the sale of sheep, cattle and horses. The spacious marketplace and the open ground of St James' Green were once crowded with beasts; bulls were baited at the ring set amongst the cobbles, while butchers had their shambles close by. Fell-mongers and curriers traded in skins and hides, tanners, saddlers, bridle-cutters and shoemakers worked in the yards running out from the marketplace. There were smiths and iron-founders, carpenters and joiners, flax-dressers, weavers, dyers and the oldest drapers in the kingdom. Shopkeepers and traders supplied the needs of town and country folk alike, while a score of inns and taverns slaked their thirst.'

For centuries Thirsk had been a magnet for farmers, horses, cattle, pigs and sheep. It was obviously a grand place for a vet to set up shop.

*

It was on a spring afternoon in 1940 that Alf arrived in Thirsk in his best suit and tie for his interview with Donald Sinclair, the man he was later to immortalise in the Herriot books as 'Siegfried Farnon'. Sinclair was only twenty-eight and had himself qualified in Edinburgh just seven years previously. In 1934 he had bought the practice in Thirsk, comparatively cheaply, from an eighty-year-old vet who had allowed it to become run-down. Sinclair's plan now was to find a capable assistant to keep things going while he went off to join the RAF and then, when he returned, to help him and his student brother Brian – the 'Tristan' of the Herriot books – to revive the practice, which was still all but moribund. He was later to confess to Alf that he was making little profit but hoped that before too long the business could become very successful.

The Herriot books give the strong impression that Donald Sinclair was a bachelor when Alf joined the practice, but he was in fact already a widower. His first wife had died tragically young, and although Alf knew this, he never wrote about her, doubtless to spare his partner's feelings. What was really odd, however, was that none of the obituaries that appeared after Sinclair's death in 1995 mentioned his first wife either, even though they discussed at length his second wife, Audrey.

Many commentators have remarked on the fact that when Alf came to write the Herriot books he gave Donald Sinclair an inexplicably German name. Sinclair himself was later distressed by it. The explanation, however, is probably quite simple. When Alf started in the 1950s to write fictionalised short stories loosely based on his life as a vet in and around Thirsk in the 1940s, he obviously decided to disguise Sinclair's identity by giving him a name that was clearly fictional and by turning him into somebody utterly different. By doing so, he would avoid any danger of a suit for libel and would forestall any possible disciplinary complaint to the Royal College of Veterinary Surgeons, which still frowned on vets advertising themselves or using their real names to write books.

Many James Herriot fans are convinced that except for a few minor changes to some of the names – to avoid hurting or embarrassing people who were still alive, or to allow Thirsk to be combined with Richmond, Leyburn and Middleham to create a composite fictional town – the books were all strictly autobiographical. In fact they were heavily fictionalised. Alf liked to pretend that they were 90 per cent fact and only 10 per cent fiction – he told Caroline Moorehead of the *Daily Telegraph* so in 1975 and was still trying to convince me as late as 1988 – and he claimed later, in *James Herriot's Yorkshire*, for instance, that he had adopted fictional names only because he intended originally to write just one book, never realising that it would grow into a series. This is no more true than his claim in the same sentence that he first started to write at the mature age of fifty. In fact, as we know, he started keeping a diary as a boy and was writing for the school magazine as a teenager at Hillhead High. He also wrote at least one short story at Glasgow Veterinary College and by the 1950s, when he was still only just forty, was trying seriously to write short stories for publication – the stories that he was later to combine to make up his first James Herriot book.

Many of those who knew Alf and his work best have agreed that the books were much more fiction than fact. No one would go as far as the old Irish vet who once told me that the Herriot books were just a cunning collection of hoary old anecdotes, shaggy-dog stories and jokes that veterinary students had been telling each other for years, but Dick Douglas-Boyd, who was sales director when the British firm Michael Joseph published the first Herriot books in the 1970s, told me in 1996: 'They were short stories, really, put together with a connecting link. They were mainly fiction.' Eddie Straiton claimed that many of the anecdotes in the books are based on apocryphal veterinary students' stories and that Alf had admitted to him that his stories were 'one part fact and two parts creative writing' – like many novels. Jimmy Steele agreed that about two-thirds of the books are fiction and Professor Sir James Armour, the retired Dean of Glasgow veterinary school and Vice-Principal of Glasgow University, told me that he reckoned the balance was about fifty-fifty. 'Alf's stories were not at all unlikely and most were pretty reasonable,' said Sir James, 'but some might

Scenes from the two Herriot movies, *All Creatures Great and Small* and *It Shouldn't Happen to a Vet*. *(Ronald Grant Archive)*

THIRSK

The fame and popularity of the Herriot stories has turned Thirsk into a major tourist attraction. On the left is the 'Vet's House', top right the market square and bottom right the parish church where Alf and Joan were married in 1941. *(Judges Postcards Ltd, Hastings)*

The picturesque village of Askrigg – or 'Darrowby' to millions of TV viewers. *(Derry Brabbs)*

Cringley House in Askrigg, which was turned into Skeldale House for filming of the TV series. *(Derry Brabbs)*

Alf, Eddie Straiton and Christopher Timothy in 1979 at the launch of
Straiton's autobiography *Animals Are My Life*, to which Alf wrote
a glowing foreword.

The quintessential
Englishness of the television
series made it hugely popular
the world over. Viewers found
its cosy 1930s charm and
gentle nostalgia deeply
appealing. *(BBC)*

Alf always claimed that the view from Sutton Bank, near his home in Thirlby, was the best in England. *(Derry Brabbs)*

Walking the dogs remained one of Alf's greatest pleasures right until the end of his life. *(Julian Calder/Rex Features)*

Typical scenes from 'Herriot Country', with which Alf will always be associated and with which he conducted a fifty-five-year love affair: Winter near Reeth, Swaledale. *(Derry Brabbs)*

Semerwater, Wensleydale. *(Derry Brabbs)*

Live Moor, North Yorkshire Moors. *(Derry Brabbs)*

River Swale, near Reeth. *(Derry Brabbs)*

River Cover, Coverdale. *(Derry Brabbs)*

'Being a vet is 99 per cent of my life. I'm a little country vet.'
(Julian Calder / Rex Features)

have been apocryphal or hyperbolic. About half of Alf's stories would have been genuine.' Mrs Heulwen Campbell, the Wights' friend and neighbour in Thirsk in the 1950s, came up with a similar assessment. 'Alf admitted that his books were half fact, half fiction,' she told me. 'His wife, Joan, wasn't a farmer's daughter, for a start. A lot of the funny stories of his life as a vet were true but he told me himself that the books were at least half fiction. They're *novels*, not autobiography.' Alf himself became at times so confused about what was true and what was not that when in 1979 he came to publish *James Herriot's Yorkshire* – a book that was meant to be entirely factual and autobiographical – he kept referring to real people by the fictional names he had given them, calling his wife Joan 'Helen' and Donald Sinclair 'Siegfried'. Fact may be stranger than fiction but in Alf Wight's books fiction is stronger than fact.

Anyone writing Alf's biography needs to be wary of the Herriot books and should avoid confusing the stories in them with the facts of Alf's real life. The temptation to recycle the books' best stories is strong because many of them are highly entertaining, amusing or poignant, but to do so would be to perpetuate the inaccuracies about Alf's life that have already been broadcast around the world in his books, films and television series. Many of the details in the books are similar to those in his life but many others are brightly embellished, twisted, polished or blurred. In the first Herriot book, for instance, *If Only They Could Talk*, Alf claimed that his job interview with Donald Sinclair was in July 1937: in fact it was in April or May 1940, just before Sinclair went off to join the RAF on 19 May. But for good fictional reasons it was much more effective that 'James Herriot' should first glimpse the glorious Yorkshire countryside on a lovely summer's day in 1937 – one of those idyllic summers before the Second World War – rather than in 1940, when France was surrendering to the Nazis, the British were retreating from Dunkirk and young British pilots were dying in the skies over England as they fought to save the nation from Hitler's invasion. The gentle meanderings of a country vet would have seemed soft and self-indulgent had they started in the middle of the greatest nightmare the world had ever known. The stories would seem much more appealing if they were set in that safe, cosy age before the war began.

The same need to tidy up the facts would explain Alf's claims in his books that he had qualified as a vet in just five years when in fact it had taken him more than six: why complicate matters by having to explain that he had failed some exams and taken much longer over the course than he should have done? That would only have held up the story. Throughout the Herriot books the facts of Alf Wight's life are used only as a foundation upon which to build entertaining and satisfyingly rounded fictionalised short stories.

There is one aspect of the books about which there is no doubt at all: when Alf first arrived in Yorkshire he was surprised and delighted to find that it was not at all the boring, stodgy, charmless sort of place he had expected it to be after hearing about the dour reputation of most Yorkshiremen. After the dirt, noise and bustle of Glasgow he soon fell in love with the clean, fresh air of the

Yorkshire countryside, the sparkling streams, the birds calling in the huge silences, the wide-open spaces, the hills and valleys, the grey-stone farmhouses, the dry-stone walls marching for miles across the horizon. 'I fell for the marvellous Pennines,' he told Caroline Moorehead. 'It suddenly dawned on me that I could spend all my life driving around the Yorkshire Dales. I was smitten.' As for the vets' surgery at number 23 Kirkgate (which is called Trengate in the books), it was indeed similar to the 'Skeldale House' described by 'James Herriot', though the house that was filmed in the television series as the surgery – Cringley House – was quite different, and was more than thirty miles away from Thirsk, in the village of Askrigg in Wensleydale. The real surgery was an elegant two-storey Georgian house with ivy climbing up the front wall, a brass veterinary plate facing the pavement, and a long, walled garden at the back.

In real life Donald Sinclair too was just like his fictional *alter ego* Siegfried Farnon as described in the books – tall, thin, bony and untidy – but not at all like the Siegfried portrayed by Robert Hardy in the television series. When I met Sinclair in 1988 he could hardly have been less like the rounded, smug, short-tempered Hardy portrayal, resembling instead the scrawny, eager, inquisitive, bright-eyed look of the English actor Wilfrid Hyde-White. Alf later claimed that when he called at the surgery that first day the mercurial Sinclair had rudely forgotten their interview appointment altogether, kept him waiting for ages, and after showing him round the surgery drove him erratically round the countryside in a battered, rusty old Hillman car. Sinclair, claimed Alf, tried him out on three tricky cases: a lame Clydesdale horse; a calf with a cut leg; and a cow that was suffering from a blocked teat and that proceeded (according to Alf) to knock him down by kicking him in the chest. When Alf passed Sinclair's test by treating all three animals successfully, Sinclair took him to a pub, plied him with far too much beer and offered him the job as his assistant. Even better, according to the first Herriot book, Sinclair offered Alf the astonishingly generous salary of £4 a week as well as full board and lodging – a princely sum for a newly qualified vet in those days.

The truth may have been very different. At first the practice had barely any business or customers and Sinclair refused to pay Alf any wages at all, according to Eddie Straiton, who wrote in his obituary in the *Veterinary Record* fifty-five years later: 'He got no salary, only his keep.' In 1940 Alf told Straiton he was being paid nothing, even when Sinclair almost immediately joined the RAF and left him in charge of the practice. 'Sinclair's practice was almost non-existent,' said Straiton. 'All Alf had was the money for his keep, which was kept in a tumbler on the mantelpiece. Sinclair was very stingy.' Straiton and Jimmy Steele – who was soon to join a practice only fifteen miles south of Thirsk, in Knaresborough, and who saw Alf often before becoming a Ministry of Agriculture inspector – both insisted that Donald Sinclair never paid Alf a fair salary in all the fifty-four years they worked together. 'Even in 1945 he was being paid only £10 a week,' said Straiton, 'and the most he ever got from Sinclair was £20 a week in wages.'

In 1997 Sinclair's daughter Janet Grey contacted me to

disagree with these claims, stating that Alf was paid £5 a week as a salaried partner in her father's practice within a fortnight of joining it in July 1940. 'He became a full partner in 1945,' she told me, 'and shared the profits with my father on a 50/50 basis from that time onwards. The practice produced good profits and both of them earned a good living from it.' Her husband Rupert Grey told me that Alf's son, Jimmy Wight, insisted that Alf earned 'very generous remuneration for the rest of his life' – a claim that contradicts Jimmy's remark to the *Daily Mail* in 1995 that even after twenty-six years as a vet Alf still had only £20 in the bank and could not afford to take his wife out for dinner on their silver wedding anniversary. It does seem extraordinary, if Alf's salary really was 'very generous', that he should still have been pleading poverty thirty years later to anyone who would listen and telling them that if he had not written the Herriot books he would have been very hard up.

Both Straiton and Steele told me that Sinclair exploited Alf outrageously throughout his career. In all the books and screen adaptations the relationship between Siegfried and James is depicted as being warm and affectionate but according to two of Alf's closest veterinary friends it was nothing of the sort. In the third Herriot book, when James gets married, he notices delightedly as he and his bride drive away from the church that his own veterinary name-plate has been fixed outside the surgery: Siegfried has given him a wonderful wedding present by making him a partner. In fact both Straiton and Alf's Thirsk neighbour Mrs Heulwen Campbell told me that in reality Alf had to buy his partnership from Sinclair. It seems that the jolly, generous Siegfried may have been another of Alf Wight's fictions.

'I felt from what I heard that Sinclair exploited Alf to an extent,' Jimmy Steele told me in 1996. 'Alf told me one night many years later that if it hadn't been for the Herriot books he would have been a poor man. I could never understand that because the Thirsk practice was a great practice, a big practice, and Alf was a good vet, and at that time the Ministry of Agriculture were eradicating tuberculosis and the local vets were employed on that for very big money. There's no way that Alf shouldn't have been in a very comfortable financial situation. If that really was the case, that if it hadn't been for the Herriot books he would have been a poor man — and I remember him saying it — then he was certainly very severely exploited.'

Why would a vet as good as Alf have allowed himself to be taken advantage of for so long?

'He just loved where he was and didn't want to move away,' said Steele. 'That's the only explanation I can think of. But there's no way that practice wouldn't be making very good money. Alf's practice was booming.'

Strangely enough, Sinclair was to acquire in later years a reputation for generosity as a man who would send anonymous donations to people who were in trouble and needed help, and even gave the Queen a horse which was used to draw the royal carriage. But all that was after he had married a rich shipbuilding heiress, Audrey Adamson, in 1943.

When Sinclair left Thirsk to join the RAF soon after hiring Alf, Alf asked Eddie Straiton to join him. 'Alf qualified six months before me,' said Straiton, 'and by this time we were very good mates and I knew him extremely well. When I qualified I was desperate. Then I got a letter from Alf saying he had this job in Thirsk, he was *not* getting any wages and he couldn't afford to pay me, but would I come down and work with him? He said there was enough money in the glass jar on the mantelpiece for – as he put it – food, beer and baccy, and that if I went to work with him I'd have a better chance of getting a job if it looked as though I had one already. So of course I jumped at this and went down to Thirsk, and I was with him for months and of course I got to know him even better because I was living with him.'

Indeed, the two young men became so close that Alf allowed Eddie to perform the most intimate service for him. 'Alf had a fistula in his arse,' said Eddie Straiton. 'He had already had one operation on it to try to clear it up but it had not been successful, and I used to operate on him, open it up for him, get rid of the pus. He'd get in the bath and I used to nick it with a scalpel.' Straiton's surgical efforts turned out to be insufficient, however, and eventually Alf had to go into hospital for another operation.

Although it seems odd that Alf, only just out of college, should be appointing an assistant only a couple of months after he himself had been hired as Sinclair's assistant, it should be remembered that Sinclair was going to be absent from the practice for some time in the RAF, while his brother Brian was about to go into the army. 'Alf was running the practice while Sinclair was away,' explained Straiton. Odd or not, Alf was obviously immensely capable at his job: before he had been in Thirsk for very long he was appointed an official Ministry of Agriculture and Fisheries Local Veterinary Inspector, which meant that he was empowered to carry out official clinical examinations and to conduct tuberculin tests on cattle.

Eddie Straiton stayed with Alf in Thirsk for six months. 'Conditions were primitive,' said Straiton. 'It was the blind leading the blind. We knew nothing, nothing about anything. We had practically no calls at all because it was only the nucleus of a practice at Sinclair's. We used to have to go up in the Dales and tuberculin-test for a guy in Leyburn who couldn't handle his tests. Every morning we'd set off − I used to be the driver − in this little old Ford, with bald tyres and a battery that kept running down, and we used to have to push at the bugger to get it started and once we got it started we dare not stop it till we got to the first farm. We had spare batteries from every garage in the Dales and we became adept at mending punctures, because in those days you couldn't get tyres, and in the blackout we had one little headlamp. But it was great. I was very fit and so was he.'

It was 'one of the happiest years of my life', wrote Straiton in his obituary of Alf in the *Veterinary Record*. 'For night driving (in the blackout) we had one dim masked headlamp. We didn't average more than four or five veterinary calls in a week but spent most days from early morning till late evening driving deep into the Dales tuberculin-testing for a Mr Bingham of Leyburn whose ill health prevented him keeping pace with his Ministry work. Every morning our housekeeper prepared us a fabulous Yorkshire breakfast and each day on the road we shared a lunch of a packet of Digestive biscuits and a pound of Wensleydale cheese – described by Alf as "an admirable balanced meal". We washed it down with the crystal-clear water from one of the many "becks". Needless to say, we got to know each other very well and the mutual respect and affection stayed with us throughout our lives.'

At first Alf was slightly daunted by the job, even though there was not all that much to do. He had always been a city lad, a townie, and had dreamed of dealing with dogs and cats in a warm, hygienic surgery, yet here he was climbing every morning into breeches and leggings to go driving all over the remote Dales in a car with no brakes. He found himself tramping about in the open in the cold and windy wet, in mud and wellington boots, and struggling in dark byres and barns to control huge, smelly animals that kept trying to kick or butt or trample him. Every day he was having to deal with massive shire and Clydesdale farm horses, and vast red shorthorn cattle, yet he knew nothing at all about farming or the countryside. He was also having to deal with dour, cynical Yorkshire farmers and trying to win their respect. It was a rough, hard life in those days before the great discoveries of modern medicine – before penicillin and other magic antibiotics, before sterilised disposable syringes and needles – and the tools of his trade were rough and primitive too: the ferocious de-horning shears, the tooth forceps, the fearsome docking knives. Sometimes he did not know what had hit him. Sometimes he wondered what he thought he was doing. Sometimes he feared that he had made a terrible mistake and would never be a success as a country vet.

But gradually, as the months went by, he came to revel in the contrast between the job he now had and everything he had known up till then in Glasgow. He loved the open air, the huge spaces, the scenery, the loneliness, the freedom. Before long he was hooked, and knew that he would never be able to work in a city again. He had also found another excellent reason to stay in Yorkshire. He had met his future wife, Joan Danbury.

*

Until then, Eddie Straiton told me, Alf was still courting Nan Elliot at a distance: 'Even when he went to Thirsk he kept writing to Nan. She was a lovely girl and he used to write to her nearly every day but he couldn't get up to Glasgow. But then he met Joan and Nan went to Stafford and married a shoe factory executive.'

Straiton was quite open about his opinion of Joan Wight, and made it plain that for some inexplicable reason she had developed a hearty dislike of him. 'She was nothing like the Helen in the books,' he told me bluntly. Straiton believed that 'Helen' may have been based on Nan Elliot rather than Joan and he was not alone in suspecting that Joan was not the inspiration for James Herriot's wife in the books.

In the Herriot books Helen is described as a dark-haired beauty with deep blue eyes and a smiley mouth, the Yorkshire-born-and-bred daughter of a cowman. In real life Joan's father, Horace Danbury, was a retired government official from Gloucestershire, a one-time solicitor's managing clerk who had become the local borough engineer. Helen's father is a widower, but Joan's

mother was still alive. In the Herriot legend James and
Helen met when he went to her father's remote farm to
treat a calf with a broken leg and took a fancy to the
dark-haired girl in green slacks and a checked blouse; in
real life Alf probably first spotted Joan through the
window of her office in Millgate as she sat at her desk
wearing a red sweater.

Joan Danbury was twenty-one, worked as a secretary in
the local mill, lived in Sowerby just outside Thirsk, and
had already caused a small stir by being the first woman in
the village to wear trousers. 'She was very attractive and
quite an outgoing personality,' Jimmy Steele told me. 'She
was quite like Carol Drinkwater in the television series.'
She was also quite like Alf's mother, as forceful and
determined as Alf was kind and gentle. 'She went after Alf
and he had no chance,' said Eddie Straiton.

Friends of Alf and Joan were unanimous in telling me
that Joan was the dominant partner in the marriage.

'Joan was the stronger of the two,' said a woman friend.

Her husband agreed. 'Oh, I think Joan was very strong.'

'Very strong,' repeated his wife.

'Oh, yes.'

'I remember when we were down seeing them in
Thirsk: Alf would say something and Joan would take
over and I was conscious that Joan was really almost a
protective shell round him.'

'I think they were very happy together,' said the
husband.

'Very happy.'

'Alf wasn't henpecked.'

'Oh, no, no,' said the wife. 'I was just conscious of her

taking over when Alf was telling you something. She sort of took over, you know.'

In the second James Herriot book Alf described James's courtship of Helen as being gauche and strewn with embarrassing moments. There was the dinner-dance invitation that went all wrong when he borrowed a dinner jacket that was far too small and old-fashioned, drove the car into a flooded road so that they both got soaked, had a puncture, and finally arrived at the venue to discover that there was no dance after all and that nobody else was wearing a dinner jacket. The next time he met her he was not only with another girl at a dance but was also hopelessly drunk. Then he invited her to go to the cinema but discovered too late that the film that was being screened was a dreadful Western rather than the one he had expected – and in the middle of it a drunk reeled up the aisle, fell into Helen's lap, sprawled across another seat and spent the rest of the programme snoring. It all sounds just a little too contrived. It is much more likely that in reality Alf and Joan did their courting as they walked together for mile after mile in the glorious Yorkshire countryside; and at dances in the villages around Thirsk, in little wooden halls and institutes where there was only a piano and a violin or accordion to play 'Body and Soul' and 'Stardust', and the food was piled on trestle tables at one end of the room; and when she accompanied him on his evening rounds of the outlying farms; and when they took an afternoon off once a week to go and explore the ancient beauties of York, where Joan was eventually to buy her wedding dress. It is probably quite true that he kissed her first in the corridor of the surgery after a dance one night in Thirsk, and again in the dispensary and again in the back garden. For what does not sound at all contrived was Alf's deep affection for the girl in the red sweater: he and Joan were to marry just over a year after meeting, and their marriage would last for fifty-three years, until he died.

*

Donald Sinclair returned to Thirsk from the RAF on New Year's Day 1941 after his vain attempt to join the Second World War.

'I had been there for several months,' Eddie Straiton told me, 'when Alf's boss Sinclair came back from the air force – he'd failed his flying test – and he walked into the dining room and he said "Who the hell are you?" and I said "And who the bloody hell are *you*?" And he said "I own this place" and "There's hardly any room for two of us and there's certainly no room for three of us. You've got to go."'

Straiton landed another temporary job, in Colne and Skipton, 'with the help of a super reference from Alf', returning two months later to Glasgow, to Clydebank. Just before he left Thirsk he told Alf that he should not continue to drive the practice car, which was in an 'atrocious condition', and that his father would sell Sinclair a good second-hand Standard car for £100. 'Consequently Sinclair released Alf for a weekend to survey and pay for the car if he liked it,' Straiton told me. 'Alf phoned me and said he'd like to take Nan Elliot out on the Saturday night – Sinclair had given Alf a few quid for successfully holding the fort – and could I organise a foursome at the Plaza Ballroom in Glasgow? The idea was that I should pick up Alf at his parents' home in Anniesland Road in the car, then Nan Elliot from her place in Knightswood not far from Alf's home, and then collect my partner. We had a super evening at the Plaza and duly delivered the girls back home but about a fortnight later Alf wrote to say Sinclair kept moaning about the £100 car even though it was worth at least double that amount.

'When I returned to my home in Clydebank there was a letter from Alf saying that since work was very slack and since he was sick of seeing and hearing Sinclair acting as "the returned RAF hero" he had decided to volunteer himself for the RAF. He had plenty of courage. There was no mention of Joan [even though Alf was to marry her just eight months later] and he must have met her later on when he was in the RAF. Nan was obviously very much on Alf's mind as the No. 1 girl, since he did say that leave from the RAF would give him more opportunity to see Nan in Glasgow.'

There is in fact no need to attribute any base motive to Alf's decision to volunteer for the RAF. In March 1941 Hitler launched against Glasgow the most vicious bombing raid of the war thus far. On the moonlit nights of 13 and 14 March, Clydebank was devastated by a terrible German blitz. Seven hundred people were killed – thirty-nine of them in Yoker – 4,000 houses completely destroyed, 7,000 badly damaged and 65,000 people made homeless. Only eight houses were left undamaged. Eddie Straiton's own house in Clydebank was blown to pieces and all his possessions and early records destroyed. Most of the population fled and the army moved in to deal with unexploded bombs and derelict buildings. No other British city had been so badly damaged up to then and the dreadful destruction wrought by the German Luft-waffe on the city he loved gave him, if he ever needed it, a stronger incentive to fight back than the mere jealousy attributed to him by Straiton.

Three weeks later, on 8 April 1941, barely a year after he had started working as a vet in Thirsk, Alf Wight left the practice and joined the RAF as AC2 Wight – a second class aircraftman, the lowest form of human life in the Royal Air Force.

CHAPTER SEVEN

The Phoney War

IT SEEMS HIGHLY APPROPRIATE that AC2 Wight should have begun his RAF career at Lord's cricket ground in London, since Lord's had been founded by Thirsk's hitherto most famous son, Thomas Lord. It was particularly appropriate too for a vet that Alf and his hundreds of fellow RAF 'erks' should have been given their meals each day in an enormous dining room at London Zoo amid the constant racket of animals.

The huge cricket ground was where the RAF processed its new airmen and where they were given their medical tests, uniforms and equipment. Alf was quartered in an apartment block nearby and was paid a paltry three shillings a day – just over £1 a week.

In the Herriot books, in order to heighten the dramatic tension of his call-up and his time in the air force, he took huge fictional liberties with the real facts of his military career. In his fourth and fifth books, *Vet in Harness* and *Vets Might Fly*, he claimed that he had already been married for eleven months when he joined the RAF; that his call-up papers arrived poignantly on his twenty-sixth birthday, 3 October 1942, much to the misery of his young wife; and that at the time his wife was five months pregnant with their first baby. At first sight it may seem odd that he felt it necessary to tinker quite so much with the truth – which in turn may later have forced him to make other claims that were absolutely untrue – but so long as his books are seen as collections of fictional short stories rather than as autobiography it becomes perfectly understandable. It was much more effective to tell the poignant story of a young man dragged suddenly from his lovely, pregnant young wife to go off to war than it would have been to describe just another spotty young bachelor's experiences in the RAF. In fact Alf did not marry Joan Danbury until seven months *after* he joined the RAF, in November 1941, but even fifty years later he was still keeping up the pretence that he had been torn from his lovely young bride's arms to go off to fight for his country. In 1992 he told Lynda Lee-Potter of the *Daily Mail* that the episode of the TV series *All Creatures Great and Small* that had affected him and Joan most was the one about the young vet leaving home to join the RAF. 'They acted it so well,' said Alf. 'It was just how it happened. I came out of the house, we had a flat on the top floor. I looked up at the window where my wife was waving and crying at the same time. Seeing that again gave me a great lump in my throat. I was watching it with Joan and she was the same.' It was simply untrue.

His new life was certainly a startling contrast to the one he had enjoyed in the peaceful Yorkshire Dales. Suddenly he was surrounded by noise, bustle, urgency, physical exercise and NCOs yelling at him. Each day – from the first raucous 6 a.m. clanging of dustbin lids that the RAF used to waken their recruits – became a mindless blur of sweat and exhaustion in the middle of a mob of fifty or more other men; of bursting lungs and aching muscles; of sprinting, marching, running, marching, jogging, marching, press-ups; of mucking out the filthy piggeries where the RAF raised its own pork and bacon; of washing mountainous piles of dirty plates and dishes; of pushing himself just beyond what until then he had thought of as his physical limit. As an active country vet he had always considered himself pretty fit but the RAF was determined to make him even fitter – or bust. He was stunned by the endless activity. None of it seemed to have anything at all to do with flying aeroplanes or winning the war. To make matters worse, Alf's fellow airmen were all aged eighteen or nineteen, whereas he was an old man of twenty-four – a vast gap at that age. It is not surprising that he *was* homesick.

The RAF did not merely toughen him up. It also removed one of his teeth, filled five others, subjected him to all sorts of classes and lectures – he even passed an examination in the dreaded subject of mathematics – and then after several months in London dispatched him back north to spend six more months studying navigation, Morse code and all the mysteries of aircraft and flying at the Initial Training Wing in Scarborough. Alf was delighted. He could not believe his luck: Scarborough was no more than forty miles from Thirsk and Joan.

He must have been given some leave that month because he took the opportunity to marry Joan on a bitter, frosty, sunny morning on Wednesday 5 November 1941 in Thirsk's beautiful five-hundred-year-old Anglican parish church, St Mary's. He was twenty-five, she twenty-two. It was not a white wedding – as depicted in the film and TV series *All Creatures Great and Small* – because of wartime rationing. Joan wore an ordinary burgundy-coloured dress. On the marriage certificate Alf's father's profession is given as 'musician'. The service was conducted by the aged vicar, Canon John Young, who shivered throughout the ceremony, and Donald Sinclair was the best man, which suggests that he and Alf were still friends, though it is true that Alf's choice was limited: most of his other friends, such as Alex Taylor and Eddie Hutchison, were fighting overseas, Alex in the Middle East, Eddie in Burma.

Alf's wedding present to his bride was a gold watch – a decided extravagance considering that it left him with just twenty-five shillings, little more than £1, in his bank account. There was certainly not enough money for a proper honeymoon, so after the wedding ceremony they simply drove the twenty-five miles to Richmond and went to the cinema. Afterwards they drove in the dark across the moors to the village of Carperby, where they stayed for a week at a sleepy old pub, the Wheatsheaf Inn. In his books Alf claimed that he and Joan had spent their week-long honeymoon travelling together from farm to farm while Alf tested cattle for tuberculosis and Joan jotted down notes and measurements but Eddie Straiton told me that this was quite untrue – another example of Alf fictionalising his life.

Back in Scarborough he and his fellow airmen were billeted in the enormous old ten-storey Grand Hotel, with its four huge towers like blunt-nosed bullets. The hotel was right on the sea front, where the bracing breezes blew straight in across the sea from the icy wastes of Norway, and despite the bitterness of that winter the rooms had no carpets and the windows were nailed inexplicably open, so that almost everyone in Alf's flight went down with bronchitis. Each day brought more of the same unrelenting programme of physical jerks, drilling, marching on the windy, icy promenade in the depths of winter, running miles along the beach, the cliffs, to Peasholm Park or up Oliver's Mount. Alf learned to shriek with belligerence at the end of each exercise session in order to psych himself up to terrify the enemy. Among the ruins of Scarborough's twelfth-century castle he was taught how to handle all sorts of weapons, from pistols to machine-guns. He learned how to stick a bayonet in a dummy's guts. He was instructed in how to read an Aldis lamp. He was made to scrub and polish and polish and scrub and in the early hours of winter mornings, when the icy wind off the North Sea seemed to cut him in two, he stood with a rifle on sentry duty outside the hotel, saluting the occasional officer who passed through the doors.

Genial though he always was, Alf came to resent the fact that other people were running his life – people who were not nearly as bright as he was. And yet, much as he hated it at the time, he realised that this frighteningly demanding regime was actually good for him. He lost two stone in weight and began to experience an insidious feeling of pride that he was part of the ramrod rows of smart airmen, immaculate in their pressed blue uniforms with the glowing golden buttons and gleaming boots. When in May 1942 his six months' training was finally complete, he admitted to feeling a twitch of regret at leaving Scarborough. Such was his sunny nature that he always looked back on even the most unpleasant periods of his life with a pang of nostalgia. He was later to admit that whenever he looked back on his early days as a vet in Thirsk it was with a rosy glow that may not have been really justified. Gazing up at the Grand Hotel for the last time, he swore that one day after the war he would return with Joan and see it properly, as a pampered guest.

He had another good reason to look back fondly at that month of May 1942: it was then, before the RAF sent him away from Yorkshire again, that Joan became pregnant with their first child.

We now come to a major puzzle in Alf's life, caused perhaps by his pretence in the Herriot books that he did not join the RAF until after he was married, when Joan was expecting their first baby. In his fifth book, *Vets Might Fly*, he told an odd story about how in January 1943 he deliberately went absent without leave from Scarborough to sneak away to see Joan in Thirsk just before the baby was born. The trouble is that it seems he was actually in Scarborough not in January 1943 but in January 1942 – before Joan was even pregnant, let alone about to give birth.

The baffling story begins with Alf revealing in *Vets Might Fly* that late in 1942, when Joan was pregnant with their first baby, he experienced a phantom 'sympathy' pregnancy, suffering a queasy feeling each morning, a general apprehensiveness and unhappiness and eventually, towards the end of Joan's pregnancy, actual labour pains.

In the book he claimed that because of this he decided that he had to see Joan at any cost, even if it meant incurring the wrath of the RAF for going absent without leave. To go AWOL might even be considered to be desertion and could earn him a prison sentence, but Thirsk was only three hours by bus from Scarborough and his need to be with Joan was irresistible, almost a physical hunger. One Friday in January 1943, when he knew he had an afternoon and evening entirely free of classes, he slipped out of the Grand Hotel, dodging the sentries and the military police, and caught an afternoon bus to Thirsk. He spent an hour with an amazed and delighted Joan, ate a plate of her egg and chips, and was back in Scarborough by nine o'clock: six hours' travelling just for one hour with her.

Two weeks later, he claimed, made bold by his success as a truant and knowing that the baby was due at any minute, he did it again. On Saturday 13 February he dodged out of the Grand Hotel and caught a bus to Thirsk. But this time, he reported, Joan was not at home: she was already in the little Sunnyside Maternity Home in Thirsk and had just given birth to a son. Alf reported that he rushed over to the nursing home, kissed Joan, and then stared at the baby, appalled because the infant looked so disgustingly red and bloated. 'My God!' he said with horror. 'Is there anything wrong with him?' The midwife, Nurse Bell, was furious.

What are we to make of this curious, unconvincing tale – even apart from the fact that a qualified vet must surely have known that human babies are born red and wrinkled? Is the story perhaps absolutely true except for the dates? Or did Alf abscond from some other RAF station later in his military career to go and see Joan but was forced by his earlier fibs about his RAF call-up to alter the date and place of the incident? Or is the story complete fiction? It ought to be absolutely true, for he repeated it in his apparently factual book *James Herriot's Yorkshire*. If it *is* true, then Alf did not actually get to Scarborough until the autumn of 1942, which would mean that somehow a year of his life went missing between his first weeks of training in London in the summer of 1941 and his going up to Scarborough in the autumn of 1942. The RAF refused to let me see his records – the records of Second World War airmen who never became officers still being classified as private – but they did give me one possible clue to his 'missing year' when they told me that Alf was 'in and out of various hospitals' throughout his RAF career. Why? Was the anal fistula playing up again? Did he prefer not to write about such a delicate matter in his books, deciding instead to fudge the exact dates? He certainly had to have at least two operations to try to clear up the fistula. Did he perhaps need more? If so, that would certainly solve the problem of the 'missing year' and would explain why it took Alf so absurdly long to complete his training – two years and seven months. It would also absolve him of the charge of deliberately fibbing in the one book that was meant to be absolutely factual, *James Herriot's Yorkshire*.

There is, however, one more little clue that demolishes that explanation: when Alf registered the baby's birth with the Thirsk Registrar, Robert Douglas, on 25 February 1943, he gave his occupation as a pilot under training: U/T Pilot no. 1047279. He was no longer the humble AC2 he had been throughout his time in Scarborough, nor even the leading aircraftman he became immediately afterwards. By the time the baby was born Alf had long left Scarborough, had been promoted yet again and was flying Tiger Moth aircraft at Winkfield, near Windsor. So his story that he twice went absent without leave from the Grand Hotel in Scarborough to be with his pregnant wife is without any doubt complete fiction.

*

After Scarborough the next stop in his long training schedule was Shropshire. By now, after all the training and examinations, he was no longer an AC2 but a leading aircraftman and his wages had more than doubled, from £1-1s-0d to £2-10s-9d a week, but that did not mean any let-up in the demanding RAF programme. In Shropshire Alf and hundreds of other men were subjected to a toughening course, as though they were not by now pretty tough already. They lived in tents, peeled mountains of potatoes, started building a reservoir in the depths of the gentle Shropshire countryside – excavating a huge hole on a stony hillside with spades and pickaxes – and helped the local farmers with the harvest. It was hot, sweaty, exhausting work in that late summer but at least in the evenings they were allowed out of camp to slake their thirsts in the little country pubs.

From Shropshire they were sent – by now as tough as they were ever likely to be – to the flying school at Winkfield airfield, a cluster of wooden huts near Windsor in Berkshire. Alf had been in the air force for well over a year and it was only now that he felt he was about to learn something that might help to win the war. As a pilot under training he was given a flying suit, sheepskin boots, a pair of silk gloves, a pair of gauntlets, a leather helmet and a pair of goggles, and then – strapped into a parachute – was taken up in a tiny Tiger Moth by a young instructor who sat behind him in the double cockpit as they bumped across the grass and puttered up into the sky above the English summer countryside. Alf had suffered all his life from vertigo and was terrified of heights but strangely enough he was quite unaffected by being up in a tiny aeroplane and could look down at the land far beneath him without any fear.

Over the coming months he flew endless circuits of the airfield, landing and taking off over and over again. He learned how to spin, sideslip and pull his aircraft up out of a stall, fly upside down and loop the loop. Eventually he flew solo, excited and exhilarated as he soared alone above the clouds. In one of the Herriot books Alf later claimed that he got lost on that first solo flight and only found his way home when he spotted the main stand at Ascot racecourse beneath him in the distance. I suspect that this is simply another example of how he liked to depict himself as a bit of an idiot so as to add tension to his narrative. He was far too intelligent not to have picked up the rudiments of flying very quickly indeed. Indeed, the truth is that he made his first solo flight after only nine hours of instruction. Out of his flight of fifty men he was the third to go solo.

It was probably while Alf was at Winkfield that Joan gave birth to their first child. After the birth she stayed in the nursing home for two weeks, as was common in those days, and Alf delayed his compassionate leave until just before she came out. Once Joan was up and about again – she was living with her parents in Sowerby while Alf was in the RAF – they spent their brief, precious time together proudly pushing the baby around in his pram and walking for miles across their beloved Yorkshire countryside.

The baby was given the names James Alexander but Alf was always to call him Seamus for no obvious reason except perhaps to distinguish him from all the other Jameses and Jimmies in the family, not least his grandfather in Glasgow and his great-grandfather. Alf asked Donald Sinclair and Alex Taylor to be little Jimmy's godfathers: if there had ever been any real animosity between Alf and Sinclair it had obviously evaporated by now.

After the flying course at Winkfield, Alf was posted to Heaton Park in Manchester and seemed at last to be about to play a full part in the war as a Royal Air Force pilot. Along with the rest of his flight he was told to prepare to be posted overseas. But all those hours cramped into the sweaty seat of a Tiger Moth had exacerbated his old problem. His anal fistula was by now sore, angry and discharging yet again, and he needed another operation. It was to destroy his hopes of ever seeing action in the air.

He spent three weeks in a hospital at Creden Hill, near Hereford, before being sent for two weeks' convalescence to a big old country house at Puddlestone, near Leominster. Then it was back to Manchester, where he was told he was being grounded because he could no longer be classified as completely fit, a prerequisite for a pilot. At first he was devastated that all those months of training had gone to waste but later he came to realise how lucky he was. 'Maybe that fistula saved my life,' he told me in 1988. 'Most of the others in my flight were later killed in bombing raids.'

The Royal Air Force, however, was still not finished with him. Instead of sending him home to get on with his life and pick up his career as a vet, they kept him in for many more months, setting him to work in the clothes stores at Heaton Park, where he handed out items of uniform and laundry to other airmen, before finally dispatching him to a demobilisation camp at Eastchurch on the Isle of Sheppey, where he was discharged on 13 November 1943 – two years and seven months after joining up. It seems extraordinary that he should have been in training for so long but the RAF were so short of aircraft and had so many more volunteers than they could ever send into the air that in most cases they seemed not to know what to do with them all. Alf's pointless training experience was certainly not unique. I was told in 1996 by an official in the records department at the Personnel Management Centre Headquarters at RAF Innsworth, Gloucester: 'Yes, it does seem a long time but it was not at all unusual. The other day I looked up the case of another airman who spent almost the entire war in training.' It is also quite possible, as we know, that Alf spent a great deal of his time not in training at all but in and out of hospitals while they tried to deal with the fistula.

Alf had contributed nothing whatever to the war effort, though that was hardly his fault. The whole experience had been a complete waste of time, apart from the fact that eventually it provided him with some extra material for two of the Herriot books.

The RAF gave him an ugly brown serge 'demob' suit, a small cardboard suitcase and a rail warrant from East-church to Thirsk and he set off on the long, cold train journey back to Joan and little Seamus. From that moment he was officially excused from the Second World War. U/T Pilot 1047279 was once again James Alfred Wight, Esq, MRCVS.

CHAPTER EIGHT

Perfect Peace

IN JUNE 1943 Donald Sinclair married Audrey Adamson,
the daughter of a rich Sunderland ship-owning family
that may well have once employed Alf's father and
grandfather. In fact he married her twice because he was
a Catholic and she an Anglican – once in St Wilfrid's
Roman Catholic church in York and again in Harrogate,
in the parish church of Christ Church. The two wedding
certificates offer a couple of mysteries, suggesting that
Sinclair had picked up something of Alf's taste for
fictionalising his life: on one Audrey's age is given as
thirty-five, on the other thirty-two; on one Donald's
father is said to have been a leather manufacturer, on the
other he is not only retired but also deceased; on one the
bride and groom give addresses in York, on the other they
mention an address in Harrogate as well as the surgery in
Thirsk. As for the best man, Donald's brother Brian, the
'Tristan' of the Herriot books, we learn that his first name
was in fact decidedly un-Wagnerian: it was Wallace.

Donald Sinclair's new wife could be just as forthright
and rude as he was, yet they became so devoted to each
other that they were to stay married for nearly fifty-two
years and later claimed to have spent hardly one night apart.
Audrey's arrival at 23 Kirkgate must have underlined

cruelly the hugely different financial circumstances of the
two young vets. She had already enjoyed a gilded life,
launching her late father's ships on Wearside, playing tennis
for the county and acquiring a pilot's licence, which must
have been galling for her new husband considering that he
had failed his RAF flying test and been sent home.
Although at first the newlyweds lived at the surgery – the
first of their two children, Alan, was born there in 1944 –
Audrey was rich enough to own racehorses and her own
aircraft, which she flew herself between racecourses, and it
was not long before the Sinclairs moved out of the surgery
into a big house in the country.

By now Donald Sinclair had become Thirsk Racecourse's resident vet, a job he was to retain for fifty years.
Later he was also to become one of the Queen's official
northern advisers on horsy matters, which led to him
presenting her with a horse, a Cleveland Bay gelding
called St David, that went on to draw the royal carriage.
Typically, Sinclair was not impressed when the royal
household planned to reciprocate, as was usual when Her
Majesty accepted a gift, by giving him a valuable piece of
china. Sinclair protested: he might break it, he said. So
Buckingham Palace sent him instead two silver toast
racks, which pleased him even less. He was so incensed by
the gift (though one wonders what he expected – a
knighthood?) that he wrote an angry letter to the Palace,
but was luckily dissuaded by his wife from posting it. In
contrast with such aristocratic pastimes and connections,
Sinclair was equally keen on racing pigeons, a sport that
has always been associated with northern working-class
men rather than veterinary surgeons who have married

well and are on their way to making a million, as Sinclair was. He became a renowned pigeon fancier, advised other pigeon fanatics about the veterinary aspects of their birds, and won a great many international races.

Alf's life was decidedly threadbare by comparison. When he returned to Thirsk in November 1943 after his phoney war he, Joan and nine-month-old Jimmy moved into three small rooms on the attic floor of the surgery. They bought a few cheap bits of furniture to make it seem like home: a table, some chairs, some pieces of cutlery and crockery, a pair of candlesticks, a stuffed owl. They were very poor. The floors were bare boards without mats, carpets or even linoleum, the wardrobe door would stay shut only if a sock was jammed into it, the 'kitchen' contained just a bench and a gas ring, and there was no water supply: when they needed water they had to carry it in a jug up four flights of stairs. But Alf revelled in the delicious domesticity of married life after all those long months in the RAF. He relished the regular cooked meals, the clean laundry, the close relationship that he shared with Joan – a togetherness that was remarkable even for a newly married couple. She often joined him when he went out on his veterinary rounds and when one old married farmer saw her for the first time he was highly impressed, whispering enviously to Alf: 'You've done t' right thing, lad: if I 'ad me time over again that's what I'd 'ave done; I'd 'ave got summat t' look at.' Joan's constant companionship must have seemed a joyous revelation to an only child like Alf. Despite their poverty, he said in later years that he had never been happier than he was then.

They settled easily into the cosy, domesticated country life regime that he was to describe so lovingly more than twenty-five years later in the Herriot books. Each morning he pulled on his old corduroy trousers, canvas jacket and wellington boots, collected Donald Sinclair's list of instructions for the day, and went off on his rounds of the Dales farms. Almost every day he drove over to Leyburn, twenty miles west of Thirsk, to help Sinclair's lazy, unambitious Scottish partner Frank Bingham in his practice there, mainly with tuberculin testing. Bingham — Ewan Ross in the Herriot books — was much older than Alf (he was over sixty by then) and a heavy drinker renowned for going on ferocious alcoholic benders. He had had an astonishingly varied life in the Canadian Mounted Police, as a cowboy on an Australian ranch (where he learned how to lasso horses) and in the Australian army during the First World War.

Almost all of Alf's working time was spent out and about but before he left the house every morning, or in the late afternoon, people would bring their dogs and cats for him to treat in the surgery and he was able at last to start building up the small-animal side of the business, just as he had always dreamed of doing. Donald Sinclair much preferred to treat horses and was delighted to leave the small animals to Alf.

On winter evenings Alf and Joan would sit and read, or play bezique; in the summer they would play tennis. Often — too often — he was called out at night to deal with a difficult lambing or calving or some other urgent problem. But all these veterinary activities have been amply described in his own books: there is no point in

repeating them here. For the next twenty-six years, until
the first Herriot book was published, Alf and Joan shared
a slow, quiet, cocooned country existence that some
people might have found humdrum and unexciting but
that seemed to suit them perfectly. Even though many of
the stories in his books were untrue, half-true, highly
embellished or the experiences of other people rather
than himself, many other tales were genuine memories
and give a vivid whiff of the essence and flavour of his life
at the time. Jimmy Steele – Alf's old Glasgow Veterinary
College friend who was working in the 1940s in a
practice about fifteen miles south of Thirsk, at Knaresborough, and who saw a lot of Alf in those years – told me in
1996 that the Herriot books and television series both
gave an accurate reflection of the tenor of Alf's life at the
time. 'I saw a lot of Joan and Alf then,' said Steele, 'when
they were living in the flat above the surgery. We were
both pretty busy but I used to go and see them and Joan
would make some lovely ham and egg. The food was
rationed but I think they'd killed a pig somewhere. We
just sat and talked about vet things, or football. The books
and the TV series were both pretty good. There's a great
relationship between a practising vet and a farmer, a very
close relationship, and I think a lot of the family stuff that
came out in the books *would* come out in a lot of
practices.'

What helped to add authenticity to the books, and to
make them so convincingly detailed, was that Alf was
keeping a regular diary, just as his mother had urged him
to do from childhood. When he became famous he
pretended that he had never kept any diaries but this was

apparently not true. 'He *was* keeping diaries,' said Jimmy Steele. 'I think he started writing his diaries right from his first day in the practice, in the 1940s. You know, his day was a most exhausting day. A country practice is very physical work and Alf showed tremendous character to come in after a day like that and write up his diaries.'

It may have helped that Joan insisted from early in their marriage that Alf should go to bed for two hours every afternoon. Eddie Straiton was startled when Joan asked him whether he rested after lunch. No, said Straiton. 'I make sure that Alf does,' said Joan.

Even though conditions in the veterinary profession improved immensely after the war with the invention of new drugs and methods and the widespread advances in farm hygiene, it was still, by comparison with modern times, a life of real hardship and hard work, of struggling with disease armed only with crude, old-fashioned equipment and medicines. There were no tranquillisers or metal crushes to control the big animals and treating them was often an exhausting battle. Alf had no operating theatre or nurse and if he needed help in the surgery Joan would have to abandon her housework and come in to give him a hand. Sometimes he would find himself operating on a sick animal on an ordinary kitchen table and in winter his hands became so chapped and ingrained with dirt that in the evenings Joan would try to soften them with a mixture of glycerine and rosewater. Even so, he was so deeply dedicated to the job that in the exceptionally harsh winter of 1947, when remote farms were completely cut off by blizzards, he took to skiing across the snow to ensure that he could reach them and their suffering animals – though he frightened himself more than once when he became completely lost on the unfriendly moors, blundering about without a clue as to which way to go.

You would not guess it from the Herriot books but sometimes Alf found the strain of working for Donald Sinclair intolerable. At one time in the 1940s he became so disillusioned with Sinclair that he decided to leave Thirsk and go into partnership with Eddie Straiton in the practice Straiton had set up a hundred miles away in Stafford. 'Without a doubt "Siegfried" was exploiting Alf,' said Straiton, 'because Alf was only a salaried partner and at the time when he mooted coming to me he was only on about £15 a week. "Siegfried" was also arrogant – he married money – and he hated work. I told him so once and his wife said "You can say that again!" So Alf came down to Stafford, did a locum for me one weekend, gave Donald Sinclair his notice and it was all arranged for him to come. Then Alf's mother, who was a very strong personality, met *my* mother in Glasgow, and his mother said to my mother "Isn't it nice of Alf taking your son into partnership?" As soon as I heard this I thought "We can't start like this" so I told Alf and he had to go back to Thirsk and I got another guy to take his place.'

Yet eventually, despite Alf's disagreements with Donald Sinclair and despite his poverty, he came to relish Thirsk and the life he and Joan were building there. It was a life with a timeless, unchanging rhythm that Alf came to love so deeply that even when his books made him a multi-millionaire he refused to relax or go into tax exile as so many people urged him to do. Instead he carried on practising until he was over seventy. He loved being a vet and he was proud to be a member of what he saw as a fine, worthwhile profession.

*

After the war, when Donald and Audrey Sinclair left 23 Kirkgate to live in their mansion in the countryside outside Thirsk, Alf and Joan moved down into the main part of the house. It was far too big for them, and icy in winter, but they were to live there happily for eight years amid all the bustle and noise of a busy veterinary surgery. On 9 May 1947 their daughter Rosemary Beatrice was born – in the same room as Seamus in the Sunnyside Maternity Home – and it was at 23 Kirkgate that Alf and Joan raised their two children during the earliest years of their marriage.

Alf was a wonderfully loving and active father. By the time his children had reached the age of three he was taking them along with him on his rounds. They would sing at the top of their voices with him between appointments and would help him carry his medicines or hold his torch for him if it was dark. 'The fifties with the kids growing up was the best time of our lives,' he told Lynda Lee-Potter of the *Daily Mail* in 1992. 'I took them everywhere with me when I was working. Little Rosie used to toddle out of the car when she could barely walk and open the gates at all the farms. She'd go red as a beetroot with importance, you know how young girls do.' One job, however, nearly ended in tragedy, when a cow escaped from its pen, charged down a passage towards Rosie and nearly trampled her to death. '*Mama!*' she yelped in a tiny voice as the huge beast thundered towards her. Alf could only watch, horrified, but luckily the animal turned away. On the days when the children were not with him he tried to be home by 5 p.m. so that he could spend some time with them. He would read them their bedtime stories by the fireside despite his own long, exhausting day.

As Seamus and Rosie grew older they started playing practical jokes on him, teasing him with farting cushions, fake ink spots or buzzing envelopes, and whenever he became agitated – he admitted that he could be a bit of a fusspot – they would cluck at him like old hens. He took them paddling and fishing for minnows in Thirsk's little stream, the Codbeck. They went off together on long walks with the dogs – or for picnics or camping – in the remote countryside he loved so much, where they would play games together or just sit and gaze spellbound at some special beauty spot: Wensleydale, perhaps, or Coverdale, or the valley of the Swale river, or the high, windy Pennines, or the view from the top of Sutton Bank, which Alf always insisted was the best view in England. Sometimes he and Joan would take the children to Glasgow to stay with their grandparents in Anniesland Road, and in summer they would go to the beaches fringing the North Sea to paddle, make sand castles and search for fossils along the shoreline. On other outings they would explore together all the towns and villages round about. One of Alf's greatest pleasures was to walk for mile after wild, lonely mile in the open air, far from any town or village, and he passed his joy in the pleasures of fresh air and solitude on to his children. When Seamus was a teenager Alf not only spent a long weekend tramping the Pennines with him and staying in youth hostels but even put up with his playing loud Elvis Presley records before going off to school every morning. 'We had a lovely childhood, Rosie and I,' Jimmy told Noreen Taylor of the *Daily Mail* in 1995. 'He always had a way of making time for us.'

It was a very *English*, protected, parochial childhood that the Wights gave their children. They lived in Thirsk, they went to school in Thirsk, and even their holidays were generally taken within a few miles of Thirsk. Other families might have found it all a little too claustrophobic and hankered after trips to France or Spain or Greece, but the Wights were content to take their holidays right on their own doorstep. One good reason for this was that Alf simply could not afford anywhere more expensive. Throughout the 1940s and most of the 50s he was continually hard up and depended constantly on an overdraft of about £1,000 − a great deal of money in those days when the average wage was less than £1,000 a year. He had just one decent suit, there were holes in his corduroy trousers and his shirt cuffs were frayed. Part of the reason for his continuing poverty was perhaps that he sent his children to a small, fee-paying school in Thirsk, Ivy Dene, in the hope of buying them a better education than the state system could provide. But many other vets and middle-class professionals paid for private education without bankrupting themselves and Alf's children were only day pupils and not boarders, which would have been much more expensive.

By 1951 Donald Sinclair was wealthy enough to be

able to take on a young assistant, John Crooks, after Brian left to work for the Ministry of Agriculture. Even though Crooks could see that the practice was extremely busy and obviously highly profitable, Alf himself was always broke. Sinclair also seemed to have ample funds to spend on the surgery itself and Crooks found during his time there that all the equipment was surprisingly up to date.

Alf himself was baffled that he should always be so hard up. Many years later, in his final book, *Every Living Thing*, he said that he was bewildered by his endless poverty. The practice was extremely successful and he was working seven days a week – yet year after year he seemed to be carrying a constant £1,000 overdraft that he found impossible to reduce. He wondered if the reason might be that he spent a large amount of his time driving from one job to another – which was, of course, unpaid. Eddie Straiton and Jimmy Steele would have disagreed vociferously: they could have told him that Donald Sinclair was simply not paying him what he was worth. It seems extraordinary that Alf allowed himself to be paid so little that he was actually in debt all the time, especially since he must have known how much other vets were earning. Perhaps he was just too gentle and self-effacing to complain. It seems especially odd that a Scotsman, which is how Alf saw himself, should have been so careless about money but maybe he was one of that common type of Scot who hates to make a fuss and much prefers to serve the chieftain of the clan with quiet, almost servile, obedience.

John Crooks also reported later that Alf worked incredibly hard and was keen to learn from him all about the new medicines, anaesthetics, surgical techniques and laboratory procedures. When Crooks went out in the car with Alf he was bombarded with questions about new methods and techniques. 'We used to drive to jobs across the Dales in his Morris Minor with the hood pulled down,' Crooks told *The Times* in 1995. 'His children, Jimmy and Rosie, would be in the back seat and a little dog on my lap in the front. We would sing our hearts out as we drove across country eating our ice-creams. He was such a great family man and when I had my own children I tried to be like him. You could have no better role model.' Crooks worked with Alf and Sinclair for three years before leaving to set up his own practice in Beverley, near Hull, eventually becoming president of the British Veterinary Association.

Crooks' successor was the extraordinary young vet Brian Nettleton, who carried a pet badger called Marilyn on his shoulder wherever he went – even to the pub – and was later to be immortalised as Calum Buchanan in Alf's final book, *Every Living Thing*. In addition to the badger, Nettleton wore a walrus moustache, played the piano, concertina and mouth organ, and drove Sinclair crazy over the next few months by filling 23 Kirkgate with a menagerie of animals, accumulating two more badgers, two huge Dobermann pinschers, an owl, some fox cubs, two rabbits, a hare, a heron and a monkey called Mortimer. Nettleton left after two years to seek his fortune in Nova Scotia, and ended up in Papua New Guinea, where he built up another collection of animals, among them an assortment of water buffaloes and homing pigeons.

In the meantime Alf and Joan escaped the vast, icy spaces of 23 Kirkgate by having a house built on the edge of Thirsk, in Sowerby. 'Rowardennan' cost £3,000 and they told the young architects who designed it that there was only one feature they insisted on having: after tramping all those corridors at 23 Kirkgate they longed for nothing more than a little hatch between kitchen and dining room so that meals could be passed straight through to the table. The building of the house gave them a few nightmares: materials and workmen were still in short supply after the war and one terrible windy night, before the joiners had managed to support the gable facing the road, a 90 mph gale blew the house down and they had to start again with a pile of scattered bricks and wrecked scaffolding.

As the years went by and the children grew up, the family did have an occasional holiday in Spain, and once they went to Switzerland – on a trip that was later to inspire one of Alf's early short stories – but generally even in later years they tended to take their breaks in the little village of West Scrafton, just twenty-five miles west of Thirsk, where they rented a cottage year after year. Once they even went there in the chilly month of October and as usual Alf spent much of the time on long, quiet walks with his dogs. His other favourite holiday spot was the Ardnamurchan peninsula on the west coast of Scotland, the most westerly point of the British mainland, just north of Loch Sunart and the Isle of Mull. Ardnamurchan was often bleak, wet and windy, with rough, stormy seas, but Alf had never minded wet or wind and the place was quiet, remote, wild and stunningly beautiful, the very qualities he always sought in a holiday spot. He could walk for miles on the heaths or through the ancient woods of oak, birch, holly, hazel and rowan trees, and he would revel in trying to spot a rare golden eagle, otter or wildcat, or the more numerous red deer.

Sometimes he would take the family for a break to the Yorkshire coast, to paddle in the cold North Sea, on occasions going with Alex Taylor and his wife Lynne. Often they went to Scarborough, where he delighted in showing the children the Grand Hotel and telling them about the six months he had spent there during the war. He also liked to go to the annual Scarborough cricket festival in September. Unusually for a Scotsman, Alf's love of cricket was such that he listened avidly to the Test match commentaries on his car radio as he drove from farm to farm. One match, between England and Australia at the Old Trafford ground in Manchester at the end of July 1956, was so riveting that he kept dropping the pigs he was supposed to be injecting to rush excitedly over to the radio to hear what was happening. What was happening was that the English spin bowler Jim Laker was in the process of taking nineteen Australian wickets for ninety runs – a Test match record that will probably never be beaten.

And everywhere that Alf went he walked and walked and walked. Perhaps it was a little dull and unadventurous to keep going back year after year to the same places but Seamus and Rosie seemed to be quite content with them all. Alf was so successful in passing on his love of the area to his children that they both settled down to spend the rest of their lives there. In 1996 the two of them were still

living and working near Thirsk, Seamus as a vet and
Rosie as a doctor.

*

One aspect of Alf's life during the 1950s that will come as
a surprise even to those who know his books backwards is
the fact that for many years – even when he was writing
the books – his mother-in-law Laura Danbury was living
with the family in Thirsk. Alf made no mention at all of
old Mrs Danbury in the Herriot books but she 'was a
lovely person, no trouble at all' according to his Thirsk
friend and neighbour Heulwen Campbell. 'She just sat
there and looked at television and she used to teach
Jimmy and Rosie nursery stories. She lived with them for
a long time – oh, twenty years – until she went into a
nursing home in Ripon. Alf got on well with his
mother-in-law and that's how he wrote his novels after
they moved out of the surgery. Alf used to sit on a
window seat and write these stories on his typewriter
with his mother-in-law watching television.'

Novels? Did Alf refer to his books in those days as
novels?

'It was always distorted truth in the books,' said Mrs
Campbell. 'They never lived in a garret – that was
distorted truth. And they always seemed comfortably off
all the time. Rosie went to ballet classes when she was
little. They even built a tennis court at the back of their
house. Alf loved tennis.'

Even if he did get on well with the old lady, any man
whose mother-in-law lives with him needs a respite now
and again and Alf used to escape each Saturday by driving

with a group of male friends to Sunderland to watch his favourite football team, or by playing golf with Mrs Campbell's husband, Douglas, a chartered surveyor. Afterwards he would meet up with friends for a few drinks in their favourite pub in Thirsk. 'There was a funny little pub that they used to go to once a week on a Saturday night,' said Mrs Campbell. 'They used to go to the back room. Alf couldn't stay in at home every night: he liked to go out. And he liked a pint! And he was a wonderful raconteur with a great sense of humour. He was a very happy man, a lovely person, very kind, and would do anything to help you.'

The Campbells lived just a few doors away from Alex and Lynne Taylor, their little daughter went with Rosie Wight to Ivy Dene school, and now and then Joan Wight and Heulwen Campbell would join their men on the golf course for a game of foursomes. 'My husband and Alf were very close,' said Mrs Campbell. 'When Alf wanted to move away from the surgery into a house that was for sale a few doors away from us, he asked Douglas to go with him to the auction because he was a chartered surveyor. He did, but at the auction Alf got carried away and kept going up and up with his bids. Douglas had to restrain him and in the end he didn't buy the house.'

Alf's parents also came down from Glasgow to stay in Thirsk for an occasional holiday. 'Alf's father was very quiet. He didn't have the personality of Alf,' said Mrs Campbell. 'Alf looked more like his mother. He was very attached to his mother.'

According to Mrs Campbell, Alf took up the violin when he was forty. 'He wanted challenges, you see,' she said. 'He was also a brilliant pianist.'

Another couple who were friends of the Wights from the 1950s were May and Douglas Ritchie, who ran a haulage business. 'Alf and Joan were a lovely couple,' Mrs Ritchie told me. 'They were all a very nice family. Our children went to school together, we women were all housewives together and we went around in the same group before he was famous. We went to all the dances together, especially at the Caledonian Society, and he was our vet as well. He was so unassuming.'

Mrs Ritchie also remembered Alf taking up the violin. 'He was a very nice violinist,' she said. 'He played at home quite a lot.'

It was such a peaceful, productive, contented life. Or so it seemed. But then disaster struck. Something sinister had been going on beneath that calm, placid, kindly surface.

Alf had a nervous breakdown.

CHAPTER NINE

The Ex-Hairdresser From Pinner

ONE OF THE GREAT HAZARDS of being a country vet in the 1940s and 50s – before they learned to equip themselves with plastic gowns and gloves – was the serious risk of contracting the highly contagious disease brucellosis from pregnant cows. Time and again Alf Wight had to work in some filthy cattle shed with his bare arm sunk for hour after hour deep inside the vagina of an infected cow as he scraped away the 'cleansings' – stinking, discoloured bits of putrescent afterbirth and yellow discharge crawling with millions of *brucella* bacteria. In cows the disease causes contagious abortion and in those days, because there was no effective vaccine as there is today, brucellosis could devastate an entire herd and bankrupt the farmer. In humans brucellosis causes undulant fever, so called because its symptoms come and go in waves: one minute the victim will feel euphoric, the next, terrible. The disease also affects different people quite differently: one man might suddenly develop arthritis; another might lose an alarming amount of weight; another might become delirious; another might go mad.

Like so many of his colleagues in those days, Alf finally succumbed to the disease in the mid-1950s. 'He contracted it in the forties,' Eddie Straiton told me in 1996.

'As a vet, you couldn't miss: we all got it, and you never get rid of brucellosis; I had a do of it just a couple of days ago. Alf got terrible depressions because of the brucellosis. The high suicide rate in the veterinary profession is due to our generation and the next generation getting brucellosis because depression is one of the main symptoms. Depression is the one thing I never had – I'm not the depressive type – but I've had all the other symptoms: fever, then you feel as though you've been run over by a bus, pains in your joints, apprehension and then instead of depression I feel homicidal.'

At first Alf suffered some inexplicable bouts of depression. Twenty years later he admitted in *James Herriot's Yorkshire* that although he loved his job it could be very stressful, but these depressions could hardly be explained by stress, since they developed into sudden weird fevers with high temperatures that had him alternately shivering and glowing with so much heat that he would shed his clothes even out in the open. As the fever raged he would suddenly feel so wonderfully happy-go-lucky and manic that he would roar with laughter and sing loudly. Eventually, after a couple of days of rest, he would recover and return to normal – until the next time.

At first Alf shrugged off the attacks as being nothing more than bouts of some unusual type of influenza, but one Saturday evening he had a bout that alarmed him so much he went to see the doctor. He and some friends were driving back to Thirsk after spending the afternoon in Sunderland watching football when he suddenly felt deeply depressed. At home, by now trembling, shaking and shivering, he took to his bed with a mountain of hot-water bottles and soon had a ferocious 105° temperature. As the heat increased he became so euphoric and super-confident that he began to sing furiously, then got out of bed to treat a lady customer's dog and proceeded to insult her. The following morning he felt so dreadful, depressed and guilty that he could no longer avoid going to see the doctor, who gave him a blood test and told him the inevitable truth: he had contracted brucellosis.

And yet according to Eddie Straiton it was the trauma of Alf's awful experience of brucellosis that eventually inspired him to write his famous books and to turn himself into 'James Herriot'.

Hitherto it has always been accepted that Alf was finally goaded into writing his first book at the age of fifty, when his wife Joan told him that he would never write a book now because he was too old. That is the version that Alf himself always gave to fans and interviewers but Eddie Straiton told me that the truth was very different. Straiton insisted that the seeds of Alf's first book were sown ten years earlier, after he had suffered one particularly brutal attack of brucellosis. Straiton went to see him and was horrified by the effect it had had.

'In about 1956 or 1957 I was invited to speak to the Yorkshire Veterinary Association,' Straiton told me, 'and I hadn't heard from Alf for some time so I called in to see him on the way up. I was absolutely shocked to find that he was in a dreadful nervous state and his wife said "He can't hold a cup of tea. I'm taking him to York twice a week for shock therapy." Alf had obviously had a very serious nervous breakdown associated with brucellosis – I'm sure of that.'

Straiton decided that Alf desperately needed a long break, preferably somewhere in the sun, and since he himself had recently bought a villa in Majorca he decided to treat Alf and Joan to a proper holiday in the Mediterranean.

'I went back to my practice,' said Straiton, 'and said to my partner "Look after the practice, I'm going off for a month or so, or as long as it takes" and I told my secretary to buy two return tickets from Heathrow to Majorca and two first-class return tickets from Thirsk to London. As soon as I had them I drove right up to Thirsk and walked into Alf's house and gave him the tickets. He said "Who's going to look after the practice? Donald doesn't like work." I said "*I'm* going to look after your bloody practice: I know this area." And of course it was a piece of cake compared to my own practice, where we had a thousand farms on our books and were handling up to 150 cases a day. Jimmy and Rosie were then two little fat kids and I used to play tennis with them every afternoon.

'When Alf came back from Majorca he was completely better and I thought to myself, well, as a therapy Alf ought to start writing some funny stories, so I broached this to him and he said "Oh, I don't think I could" and I said "Listen, Alf, do you remember when we went to play the Dublin college at football? You lost your voice and most of the lads got drunk — I was the only one who didn't drink — and you wrote a story about that weekend and I read it and thought it was bloody marvellous." I said: "You could *do* it, boy." I'd been commissioned by Hutchinson's to write funny books about my veterinary life but I was so busy I never got round to doing it, and I said that with all my other things I haven't got time. I said "This is your therapy, you've got to do it." He said "Right, I'll have a go at it." '

Alf did have a go at it and although he was to meet with numerous disappointments and rejections for more than ten years, he was laying the foundations for his new career as the greatest publishing phenomenon of the 1970s.

'After I got him better after his breakdown,' said Straiton, 'he said that rather than go through that again he'd prefer to have his legs cut off. You can say without any doubt at all that Alf suffered from brucellosis and I would think that probably it was a predisposal cause of his eventual prostate cancer. It could lead to anything because it lowered your resistance.'

Are Eddie Straiton's claims true? For many reasons I believe him. When I met him in August 1996 he was seventy-nine but still a remarkably ebullient, outgoing, combative man – incredibly fit, athletic and active for his age – with an engaging line in forceful opinions, outrageous anecdotes and colourful tastes, like the open-topped sports car he still insisted on driving even in rain or snow. He was a charming, very likeable and generous man. One of his friends warned me with an affectionate smile: 'I shouldn't really say this, but Eddie always exaggerates a bit.' Having said that, Straiton's evidence should always be considered seriously because Alf Wight himself liked and respected him greatly. When Alf came to write the foreword to Straiton's own autobiography, *Animals Are My Life*, he described his friend as being the most dynamic person he had ever known as well as incredibly kind, generous and helpful to those in trouble. As an example of that, Alf confirmed the story of how Straiton had rescued him from serious depression, sending him and Joan to Majorca and looking after the practice for a month for no payment at all. It was by any judgement a wonderfully generous gesture of friendship and compassion.

The radio broadcaster Jimmy Young was also extravagant in his praise of Straiton, who was for many years the popular veterinary adviser on his programme. In his autobiography, *Jimmy Young*, Young described Straiton as 'one of the warmest-hearted, kindest men one could ever wish to meet'.

Eventually Alf's attacks of brucellosis disappeared as mysteriously as they had arrived and after the early 1960s he never suffered another. 'And he never went to pieces again,' said Straiton. But now that he had started writing seriously he was never to stop. The conception of 'James Herriot' had taken place, and the long gestation of 'Helen', 'Siegfried', 'Tristan' and all the others had begun.

*

The 'Swinging Sixties' began unhappily for Alf. On 7 April 1960 his father had a heart attack at home at 694 Anniesland Road and at 4.30 p.m. the following day he died at the age of seventy. Sadly, despite all of Jim Wight's struggles to improve himself, to drag himself out of the working class into the lower reaches of the middle class, to pass himself off as a musician rather than a humble shipyard worker, when Alf reported his father's death to the Partick District Assistant Registrar of Deaths the following day he described him not as a musician but as a shipbuilder's clerk (retired). It seems a poignant postscript to all Jim's frustrated musical ambitions.

Alf's carelessness with dates extended even to his memory of when his father died. In 1992, for instance, he told both Lynda Lee-Potter of the *Daily Mail* and Edward Marriott of the *Sunday Telegraph* that his father died in 1961 rather than 1960. 'When he died in 1961,' he told Miss Lee-Potter, 'something left me, I really did feel it. I used to write regularly to him and he would write to me every week – usually about football. It's funny, there were so many intimate details to exchange and yet we talked about football. I never told him I loved him in so many words, but I loved him a lot and I think he knew. If he'd thought I'd had a book published he would have been absolutely tickled pink.'

Jim Wight and his dreams were buried in Glasgow, leaving his widow, Hannah, to live on alone for twenty more years in the house in Anniesland Road. In her widowhood Alf was as dutiful a son as he had been a father. 'He came to see her quite often,' said her Anniesland Road neighbour Jean Schreiber.

Although the children were growing up, Alf's days seemed on the surface to be as quiet and humdrum as ever. Throughout the 1960s he continued to live the gentle rural life that he had enjoyed now for twenty years. He took Joan back to the Grand Hotel in Scarborough, where they had tea and muffins in the hotel lounge to the strains of a genteel band, and dinner in the long dining room where once he had peered out into the wartime darkness towards the lighthouse to try to decipher the blinking Morse code stuttering across the icy night. Every

Thursday afternoon he took a half-day break from work and he and Joan drove the twenty miles south to Harrogate, the neat, old-fashioned spa town that he called Brawton in his books. There they would stroll around the elegant old streets and parks or sit by the bandstand in the Valley Gardens. Every week in Harrogate they met up with the same couple – another vet, Gordon Rae, and his wife Jean – and the four of them would spend the afternoon lunching together at Betty's or Standing's, then shopping, then taking tea at Betty's, before going to the cinema and having dinner together at Louis' Restaurant. Another couple of special friends were another vet, Denton Pette – who appears in the Herriot books as Granville Bennett – and his wife Eve. 'The Wights and the Pettes ate together every week, taking it in turns to pay,' Eddie Straiton told me. 'Denton was a flamboyant small-animal practitioner and just as Alf described him in the books. He was also one of the kindest and most generous men I knew. He would wine and dine Alf and Joan in expensive restaurants. When their turn came to buy the meal they frequently produced a Chinese takeaway.'

Straiton denied that he was accusing Alf Wight of meanness. 'I don't think Alf was mean, not when I was with him,' he said. 'The trouble was that Joan worried about money a lot. Years later, when Alf and I were making a documentary film together, we were up at Thirsk and I was with Alf in the car going to this farm and he had to stop every half-hour to give his wife a 'phone. I said "What are you doing, Alf? Why don't you relax?" Because of his nature he wouldn't fight. That's the sort of guy he was. He had accepted the situation.'

One cause of friction between Straiton and Joan Wight was the fact that she was suspicious of his influence on her son. Seamus graduated from Glasgow University's Veterinary School in 1966 and went to be trained by Straiton in Stafford after years of living chastely with his grandmother in Anniesland Road. 'The lad was with me for about four years,' said Straiton with a gleam in his eye, 'two years as a student and two years as an assistant, and Joan decided that I was sort of leading him astray. All I wanted to do was to improve his manhood, because when she sent the boy to me I knew he had been molly-coddled. They called my practices in Penkridge and in Stafford "The University of Life", so the first thing I did with Seamus was I put him in the local pub with two randy daughters to introduce him. With every girlfriend he thought he had to ring his mother and his mother would be straight down in three hours from Thirsk to have a look at them.' Eventually Straiton introduced Seamus to 'a nice girl' called Janet, who unfortunately had a broad Walsall accent. 'Seamus fell like a load of bricks for this girl,' said Straiton, 'and eventually decided to get engaged to her, and he said "I'll have to tell my mother now" and that was the end of it. Within a week or two he was gone.'

*

Alf was writing much more than merely veterinary stories as he began to learn how to become a writer throughout the 1960s. He was producing all sorts of very different short stories, like the one he sent me for my new short-story magazine just before he died in 1995.

'La Vie en Rose' is a startling story because although it is not at all explicit in its language it is surprisingly sexy, throbbing with repressed longing and sexual melancholy, and is quite unlike anything else that he ever published. It is certainly very different from his veterinary books. Even though it is no more than 2,500 words long it vibrates with hidden passion. The narrator – a quiet, married, forty-year-old Yorkshire farmer – has brought his young family to Switzerland for their first foreign holiday (just as Alf himself had done a few years earlier) and is treating his wife and two small children to evening ice-creams and lemonade on a darkened hotel terrace. As he sips his beer in the shadows under a full yellow moon and listens to a hotel musician playing the haunting melody 'La Vie en Rose' on the accordion, he suddenly notices that a stunningly beautiful young woman of about thirty, who is sitting at a window table in the brightly lit dining room with two men and another woman, is smiling enticingly at him. She is absolutely gorgeous and at first he cannot believe that she is looking at him but whenever he glances back at her she is smiling at him again with bedroom eyes. He has never been a philanderer or flirt but eventually, of course, he smiles back. Her eyes smoulder in return and his heart pounds with excitement.

Her rich, expensively dressed tycoon husband is obviously not happy with the situation. When the narrator gets up to go to the lavatory the husband follows him and there is a confrontation in the gents. The husband is taller and much heavier than the narrator – who suddenly wishes he had gone on holiday to Scarborough as usual instead of coming to Switzerland – and he pushes him up against the wall and tells him to stop staring at his wife. The narrator is no weed, however – as a cattle farmer from the Yorkshire Dales he has learned how to handle himself – and he grabs his assailant's wrist, twists it and forces him to the ground. After some verbal fencing the narrator lets the husband go, the husband admits that strange men are always staring and smiling at his wife, and both men apologise. The narrator ends up feeling sorry for the husband: perhaps the poor man's stunning wife is constantly unfaithful to him; perhaps she is a nymphomaniac.

Back on the terrace the narrator gathers his family together to leave, but as they do so the accordionist starts playing 'La Vie en Rose' again, so hauntingly that the narrator is overcome by an ache of desire that makes him long to look for one last time at the beautiful young woman. But he manages to resist the temptation by shutting his eyes tightly, which causes him to miss his footing on the last step and sprawl on to the pavement. His good old Yorkshire wife is baffled. Why is her usually placid husband behaving so strangely? Is he ill? He reassures her that he has suffered only a momentary lapse, puts his arm around her waist and they walk away with the children, all four together, a family again. He has stumbled and fallen but come to his senses in time.

Since so much of Alf's writing was semi-autobiographical it is reasonable to ask whether this little parable, like so many of his fictional anecdotes, was based on a similar episode in his own life. Did some beautiful stranger keep giving him the eye one night on one of their rare trips abroad, perhaps on that family holiday when he took Joan, Seamus and Rosie to Switzerland? Was he actually tempted himself – and then appalled by his own vulnerability and weakness? After more than twenty years of marriage, did he suddenly realise, like so many other uxorious middle-aged men, that time was passing and yearn to break out and treat himself to an exciting new passion before it was too late?

What is of greater significance, though, is that 'La Vie en Rose' – and Alf's admission in his accompanying letter that it was only one of many stories he wrote while he was 'practising' to become a professional writer – gives a strong indication of the numerous disappointments he must have suffered at the hands of magazines and publishers who kept rejecting his manuscripts. How many other short stories did he write in those years only to have them returned unwanted, unappreciated or even unread? How often did his heart feel heavy as the fat envelope clattered through the letterbox and fell to the floor with that hollow thud that every author knows and dreads? How many of his typescripts came back so creased and crumpled and covered with marks and stains that they had to be typed out all over again before being sent out to someone else? What sort of stories were they? Did most of them throb with deep feeling, like 'La Vie en Rose'? Did he write about birth and death and love, as well as lust and longing and being a Yorkshire vet? Perhaps he even wrote a couple of full-length novels, and rewrote and changed and polished and rewrote them again in vain before he finally struck lucky with *If Only They Could Talk*.

He always claimed that he could never concentrate on

his writing for much more than half an hour at a time because after that he would become restless. He would tap away at an old Olivetti typewriter in thirty-minute bursts, but somehow even in those short periods he managed to produce plays for the BBC as well as short stories. It is an indication of his remarkable stamina and determination to become a published author that he must have written scores of thousands of words over more than ten years before he finally achieved his ambition. Why else would he refer to his years of 'practising'? His constant pretence that he never really tried to write for publication until his wife goaded him into doing so at the age of fifty did not do him justice. The truth – that he spent year after year after year writing and writing and trying to get it right – is much more impressive. It shows a deep determination and strength of character lurking beneath the placid, humble, self-effacing persona he always preferred to show the world. In 1975 he admitted to Caroline Moorehead of the *Daily Telegraph*: 'I bombarded everybody with short stories and pieces. Everything was turned down.' By 1981 he was confessing to Paul Vallely of the *Sunday Telegraph Magazine*: 'I bombarded newspapers, magazines and the BBC with short stories. They were all sent back by return of post without comment. No one even said: "You show promise." I became a connoisseur of the sick thud that a rejected manuscript makes on the doormat. My style was improving but I realised that the subjects were wrong. They were all adventure stories and not about something I knew. So I returned to the vet subjects.'

'Alf had a drawer absolutely full of his stories,' I was

told by Dick Douglas-Boyd, the sales director of his future publishers, Michael Joseph. 'He told me that his wife kept saying he ought to put these into print. I think they were diaries and fictionalised diaries and he only had to get them out of the drawer and dust them up and put them into order for the first Herriot book.' Victor Morrison, who was managing director of Michael Joseph from 1975 to 1980, agreed: 'I know he'd been writing for a long time. He did write on and off for many years before, so I think his records of these incidents that he managed to turn into these wonderful stories were there.'

Nor was he writing only fiction during the 1960s. He was also regularly keeping his diaries and two of them – for 1961 and 1963 – were especially notable because they recorded his impressions of two unusual trips abroad, one to Russia and one to Istanbul. His veterinary friend John Crooks, who had been an assistant in the practice in Thirsk from 1951 to 1954 and who now frequently travelled abroad accompanying animals being exported from Hull, suggested in 1961 that Alf might like to escort some animals to Russia and see something of that mysterious country, still hidden behind its Iron Curtain at the height of the Cold War. Much as Alf loved his work in the Yorkshire Dales, even he could see that he had sunk into something of a rustic rut and that a foreign trip would do him a lot of good. Taking time off from the practice was no longer a major problem: it was doing well enough by now for him to be able to take Saturday afternoons off whenever Sunderland had a match at Roker Park. From now on, for thirty years, he claimed that he never missed one Sunderland home game. He became so keen on soccer that at one stage he even thought of writing a book about it but in the end realised that he did not know enough about it and decided to stick with writing about what he knew.

He sailed from Hull on the evening of 28 October 1961 on a disconcertingly small, 300-ton Danish ship, the *Iris Clausen*, which was bound for the Lithuanian port of Klaipeda with a cargo of 383 pedigree sheep carried on two decks of straw-filled pens. Before they left harbour Alf inspected the animals and approved their conditions. Two days later they sailed through the Kiel Canal but within twenty-four hours, as they headed up the Baltic, they were tossed about in a violent storm that terrified the sheep so much that Alf had to calm some of them with injections of cortisone. They reached Klaipeda on 1 November, delivered the sheep, and Alf had time for a quick look around the downtrodden town, where he was surprised to see women working as builders' labourers and crane drivers, and saddened by the dingy, under-stocked shops, the public loudspeakers blaring with strident voices all day, and the fact that cameras were forbidden and the soldiers never smiled. He also visited a school where he told the English teacher that she spoke better English than he, with his Glasgow accent, could manage.

On 3 November the *Iris Clausen* set sail for Poland to pick up 800 pigs in Stettin and take them to Lubeck on the return voyage to England. All through the Baltic they battled through another terrifying gale that felled most of the crew with seasickness but affected Alf not at all, although he did spend most of the day in his bunk simply to prevent himself being hurled all over the place. They reached Stettin on 5 November, his twentieth wedding anniversary. The ship's Danish captain offered to send a telegram to Joan for him but he had already left an anniversary card with fourteen-year-old Rosie, who had promised to pass it on to her mother. While the pigs were loaded and formalities completed, Alf spent a couple of hours strolling around the frosty, bomb-damaged town with its little trams, newspaper kiosks and well-stocked shops. The pigs made no great demands on his veterinary skills and it took only a day to sail to Lubeck, where he disembarked, caught a train to Hamburg and flew back to London, his job completed.

The diary he kept on that trip was not particularly vivid or distinguished. In fact it was flat, pedestrian and strangely wooden and his observations were decidedly humdrum. Alf was clearly no Samuel Pepys. But it has to be remembered that this was right at the start of his decade of 'practising' to write, when he was still a novice. The fact that his first veterinary book was immeasurably better when it was published nine years later shows how much his style and skill improved over that long decade of being a literary trainee.

In August 1963 he was off on his travels again, this time as veterinary chaperon for a herd of forty pedigree Jersey cattle that was being flown in a huge, dilapidated old aeroplane from Gatwick airport in Sussex to Istanbul. Because of all the bureaucratic delays when they reached Turkey, however, he had only one night there and saw little of the city.

As the 1960s went by Seamus and Rosie grew up.

Seamus qualified as a vet and joined the practice in 1967 when he was twenty-four. Rosie, meanwhile, was studying to become a doctor, a general practitioner, after Alf had dissuaded her from doing veterinary medicine. 'She was mad keen but I talked her out of it,' he told me many years later. 'It was such a hard and dirty job that I couldn't bear the idea of her doing it.' He must have remembered how his own father had tried to persuade him to become a doctor instead, and how he had followed his own star and had never regretted it. Another aspect of the Wight family's genes had also been passed on to the third generation: Jim and Hannah's musical talents had been inherited by their grandchildren, who both loved to play the piano. Rosie, especially, Alf told me later, was so good that she could have been a concert pianist.

Throughout the Swinging Sixties Alf continued to practise and polish his writing. He later admitted to Caroline Moorehead of the *Daily Telegraph* that his early writings had resembled 'a very amateurish school essay'. Later, he said, his style became 'like Macaulay's essays: beautiful, balanced sentences full of florid adjectives'. But, he told Paul Vallely of the *Sunday Telegraph Magazine*, 'people don't want to read balanced sentences nowadays. Many bestsellers have sentences that don't even contain verbs. I realised that for my sort of story I had to try and create an easy conversational style. For the next year or so I deliberately learned how to write.' He dissected the books of writers he admired to try to see why they had been so successful – Conan Doyle, Dickens, Hemingway, Salinger, Wodehouse – and he even read several instruction books such as *How to Be a Writer* and *Teach Yourself to*

Write. He taught himself to handle flashbacks by reading Budd Schulberg's 1950 novel about Scott Fitzgerald and Hollywood, *The Disenchanted*. He struggled constantly to simplify his style, to iron it out, to make it straight, direct and unadorned.

It should not be forgotten that this long struggle to become a published author was going on at a time when Alf was working incredibly hard as a vet but was still constantly hard up. 'Mum and Dad had little to show for all the hard work he'd put in over the years,' Seamus told Noreen Taylor of the *Daily Mail* in 1995. 'They had £20 in the bank when I was 24. He'd been a partner in the practice but he had no capital and, typically, he rarely chased people for prompt payment of bills. So he was always broke. He couldn't understand why he never had any money, or why on their silver anniversary he couldn't even afford to take Mum out to a restaurant for a meal. I remember how frustrated he was when he realised how little he had to show for all his hard work.'

Unlike most writers, who need solitude and silence, Alf – like Charles Dickens – used to write in the corner of the living room surrounded by his chattering family. Unlike Dickens he had to contend also with the noise of the television set as he tapped away at the typewriter after a long day's work. It was television too that gave him his nom-de-plume. He needed a pseudonym partly to avoid any libel writs from some of the recognisable real people he had depicted and partly because the Royal College of Veterinary Surgeons frowned on any form of advertising or publicity that drew undue attention to its members – and the RCVS had strict disciplinary powers. At first he thought of adopting the name James Walsh but discovered that there was already a real vet of that name in the British veterinary register. Then in February 1969 he was watching a fifth-round FA Cup match between Birmingham City and Manchester United on television. The Birmingham goalkeeper, twenty-nine-year-old Jim Herriot, who was also a Scottish international that year, was playing so brilliantly that even though the Manchester United team included the legendary George Best and Denis Law he managed to restrict them to a 2–2 draw. Alf was so impressed that he felt it must be a good omen and decided to steal Herriot's name.

*

The book that finally made the breakthrough for Alf was *If Only They Could Talk*, a heavily fictionalised light-hearted account of his first year as a vet in Thirsk but set in 1937 rather than 1940. Each episodic, anecdotal chapter was almost a short story in itself and may well have started out in life as precisely that. When twelve years later Alf wrote an introduction to the abridged *Reader's Digest* edition of *The Best of James Herriot* (an introduction that was headed 'The books I almost never wrote'), he said that his first intention had been to write a funny book – the sort of book that Hutchinson had commissioned Eddie Straiton to write but that Straiton had felt he did not have the time to do. 'There is something funny in everything if you look at it the right way,' Alf told Alex Harvey of the *Sun* in 1978.

But as he wrote he found that there was much more to say about the early days of veterinary practice: he wanted to describe the extraordinary contrasts between vetting in the 1960s and the 1940s, when much of the job seemed to have more in common with witchcraft than with science; the moving and tragic moments as well as the funny ones; the quirky, eccentric Yorkshire farming characters who simply no longer existed and had been replaced by highly trained professional farmers; and last, and yet always somehow first, he wanted to glorify the magnificent, sweeping scenery of the Yorkshire Dales. He claimed that as he wrote that first Herriot book he jotted down his memories 'instinctively' in chronological order, but the task was doubtless made a great deal easier by the diaries he had kept ever since childhood: it would, for instance, have been utterly impossible for him to remember so much of the verbatim dialogue from the 1940s that appears in his books unless he had been recording it as it happened. Indeed, he actually admitted in Chapter 9 of *If Only They Could Talk* that he was still keeping a regular diary when he wrote of one particularly unpleasant job that it would make an excellent entry in his diary.

So it came to pass that he wrote what was to become the second chapter of *If Only They Could Talk*, about that first interview with Donald Sinclair. He explained Sinclair's Germanic *alter ego* 'Siegfried Farnon' by saying that Siegfried's father had been a great Wagner fan, and he made Siegfried a man of immense energy and industry, which does not quite fit with descriptions of the real Donald Sinclair. While Alf himself was 'James Herriot', Thirsk, with its cobbled marketplace, was 'Darrowby'. He extolled the beauties of the Yorkshire Dales, and described the surgery at 23 Kirkgate, calling it 'Skeldale House' in

'Trengate', and he also mentioned the sixty-year-old housekeeper 'Mrs Hall'. He wrote about Siegfried's boyish, lazy, practical-joking younger brother 'Tristan', a student at Edinburgh Veterinary College who spent an inexplicable amount of time hanging around the surgery, acting as an incompetent general gofer and Siegfried's whipping boy, and most evenings propping up the bar in the Drovers' Arms and chatting up the barmaid. He wrote about Siegfried's tempestuous rage on discovering that Tristan had failed yet another exam, or made a mess of the accounts, or managed to lose ten pigs and a horse.

He wrote about being called out at two o'clock on a bitter winter morning to drive twelve miles across the frozen, snow-bound moors, trudge half a mile up an icy hillside to a windy barn far out in the wilds, then struggle for hours, stripped to the waist, with his aching arm and hand deep inside a cow's womb, to try and deliver a difficult calf in the light of an oil lamp. He wrote about having to shoot an expensive horse that was supposed to be suffering from nothing more severe than colic but that had in fact developed an agonising twisted bowel. He wrote about the extraordinary old beliefs so rigidly held by some of the old Yorkshire farmers: that cattle could suffer from Worm in t' Tail or Stagnation of t' Lungs, Black Rot, Gastric Ulsters or Golf Stones. He wrote a hilarious knockabout scene – about trying to tuberculin-test a belligerent herd of eighty-five Galloway cattle – that was worthy of some farcical *Carry On* film. He wrote about every other sort of veterinary job he had ever had to face – removing a lipoma from a labrador, treating milk fever in cattle, inoculating lambs against pulpy kidney, castrating colts, even treating a bull for sunstroke – covering a year in the life of a country vet.

Eventually, when the typescript was finished, he sent it to Eddie Straiton, who was one of the few published authors he knew, and asked his opinion of it. Long before Alf became a writer Straiton had himself had several veterinary books published by the Farming Press – mainly picture books about horses and cattle – and by 1996 he had written thirteen volumes with total hardback sales of 786,000 copies. One of the books, about horses, was in its tenth edition.

'I would like to tell you the true facts of Alf Wight's books,' Straiton said to me with the air of a man who was about to correct a great misapprehension. 'Alf phoned and said he'd written his first book and he wanted to send it to me to see what I thought of it. I read it and it was very well written but it was written like an essay, so I said to Alf "Look, now, there's something wrong with this. I don't know what it is, I haven't got enough know-how to know what it is, but there's *something* wrong with this." So I said "I'll arrange a party in the Dolce Vita [an Italian restaurant in Soho, the only place I knew in London, an attractive place where a boy played the guitar] and I'll invite all the people I know in publishing" – there were not very many but by this time I'd been publishing for a couple of years. So I did this and Alf and I went down to London, booked into a hotel and we met John Morrison, who had used to work with Collins the publishers several years before, and as a direct result of that Morrison got Collins's chief reader, a woman, to read this book and tell us what was wrong with it.'

This may well have been Marjorie Villiers, a Collins editor who had made her name in British publishing after working with the Kenyan naturalist Joy Adamson on her book about Elsa the lioness, *Born Free*, which had been published in 1960.

'I was acting as the go-between,' said Straiton, 'so she wrote to me and said "What is wrong with this is that it must be rewritten in the first person." So I took this letter up to Alf and said "Now there you are, get on with it," and Alf says "Oh, I don't think I'll bother. I think I'll get the local printer to print it and I'll put it on the shelf and I'll say to my children *I wrote that*." I says "Listen, Alf, this is the opinion of an *expert* – you've *got* to do it, boy." So he did it and sent the second version to me to read and I thought "This is good."'

Even so, British publishers were in no hurry to buy the book. Collins themselves, after telling him how to improve it, then rejected it. 'I'm surprised,' I was told by the distinguished biographer Philip Ziegler, who was himself an editor at Collins at the time, 'because it was just the sort of book that would have appealed to Billy Collins [the chairman of the company].' Alf posted the typescript off to several publishers, but like a boomerang it kept coming back. One firm even managed to sit on it for eighteen months before returning it. 'I was so pleased they hadn't been sent back by return that I was afraid to ask what they thought of them,' Alf told Paul Vallely of the *Sunday Telegraph Magazine* in 1981 – confirming by his use of the words 'they' and 'them' that this was a collection of short stories rather than an autobiography. Nor were American publishers at first any more enthusiastic when Alf eventually found a literary agent who started sending the book to them for consideration. Several American publishers read and rejected the manuscript, and even the one who was eventually to make such a huge success of Herriot in the USA, Tom McCormack of St Martin's Press, thought the whole idea so dreary and unpromising that it was more than three months before he could force himself to read it.

Depressed by so many rejections, Alf claimed that he gave up, decided he was a failure as a writer and threw the unwanted manuscript into a drawer, where it lay for eighteen months. He said that he would have forgotten all about his writing ambitions had Joan not found the typescript and made him resurrect it and send it to the David Higham literary agency in London.

'By this time,' said Eddie Straiton, 'I was training his son Seamus in my practice and I knew from his son that Alf was getting quite a few refusals when he sent publishers the book. At that time one of my good friends was Lord Barnet – the chairman of IPC, the parent company of the Farming Press – and I dropped a note to Barnet about it and I'm pretty sure it was Barnet who tipped off the agent that took over that book.'

The agent was Jean LeRoy of the David Higham agency, which was eventually to sell Alf's first book to Michael Joseph, the company who were to publish him for the rest of his life. Alf's own story as to how he found an agent was different: he had sent the typescript of *If Only They Could Talk* to two publishers who both turned it down, he said, but then he had borrowed from the library a copy of Jean LeRoy's book entitled *Sell Them a Story* in which naturally she advised would-be writers to find themselves an agent if they wanted to be published. Alf sent her the typescript and legend has it that as soon as she had read it she rushed excitedly into a colleague's office and cried: 'This is a find!'

Considering the impact that Jean LeRoy's reaction was to have on Alf's life it is surprising that he did not mention her at all when, in 1986, Michael Joseph celebrated its fiftieth anniversary by publishing a commemorative volume entitled *At the Sign of the Mermaid* with contributions from its most famous writers, including Alf. In his article he wrote that his literary career had been built and guided entirely by women: his wife; his then literary agent Jacqueline Korn; Anthea Joseph, the chairman of Michael Joseph; and Jenny Dereham, the Michael Joseph editor who handled his books after Anthea Joseph's death. Why did he omit Jean LeRoy? After all, if she had failed to read his typescript properly and just sent it back to him, he might well have given up his literary ambitions for good. Yet he said not a word about her, preferring to run through his old story about Joan shaming him into starting writing. Sadly Jean LeRoy died of cancer in 1970, just as Alf's first book was published.

Anthea Joseph's discovery of the unknown 'James Herriot' was to become part of London publishing folklore. The official version of the story is that when the typescript arrived at the firm's offices at 26 Bloomsbury Street an editor immediately realised that it had the same qualities that had made another Michael Joseph author,

'Richard Gordon', so successful with his medical novels like *Doctor in the House* and *Doctor at Sea*. 'It had the same anecdotal quality,' Jenny Dereham told the *Telegraph Magazine* in 1981, 'with the bonus that it was about animals – which always sell well. It was well written, too, and needed virtually no editing.' Michael Joseph did not, however, take the book on immediately. It was much more chancy than that. According to Peter Day, then a thirty-year-old junior editor who had been with the firm for no more than a year, it was he who first read that dog-eared typescript when it arrived in the office early in 1969. Day, who went on to own the British publishers Allison and Busby, thought that Alf's book – which he took to be a novel rather than autobiography – was very funny.

'The whole thing gripped me very much from the word go,' Day told me in 1996. 'Anthea, who was then in her forties, came into my office in the attic and found me laughing, with my legs up on the desk, and she said "What are you laughing about?" and I said "This vet book." "Oh, we don't want another vet book," she said.'

She was referring to Michael Joseph's series of veterinary books by Alex Duncan, a Viennese woman who also wrote under the pseudonym Marianne Forest. 'Anthea said "The market won't take another vet",' Day remembered, 'and I said "Well, it's really funny, Anthea," and she said "I wouldn't waste your time." But I carried on reading and I really enjoyed it, so I went to her and said "It is *terribly* funny and it's so graphic. We *should* look at this book very seriously." '

Anthea Joseph was still unimpressed.

'I tell you what,' said Peter Day desperately. 'Give it to Jennifer Katz to read.'

Jennifer Katz, Day told me, was an ex-hairdresser from Pinner – an unexciting north-west London suburb – a very tall, elegant woman in her thirties who was now Anthea Joseph's secretary.

'Jennifer *Katz*?' said Mrs Joseph. 'She's never read a book.'

'She's the market for this book,' said Day. 'If you capture her, the book will take off.'

Anthea Joseph shrugged. 'Very well,' she said. 'If you want to waste your time.'

'So I gave the book to Jennifer,' Day told me. 'She was the reader in the street for whom a book like that would be very evocative. If she was captured by it then you had a vast market. I said to her "Now look, on Monday morning we want to know what you think about this book." So she tootles in on Monday morning and I said "Well, what did you think?" and she said "I laughed from beginning to end." So I said to Anthea, "Anthea? She laughed from beginning to end." So Anthea said, "Well, in that case I'd better read it." And so Anthea read it and said "I agree with you" and that was it.' Anthea Joseph agreed to publish the book. In effect 'James Herriot' was really discovered by an ex-hairdresser from Pinner.

Peter Day's story is particularly credible because he later became renowned in British publishing circles for his devotion to the memory of Anthea Joseph, who was to die of cancer in 1982. For many years after that he would go to her grave in Old Basing on her birthday and plant flowers on it for the coming year. 'I loved her,' Day told me simply. 'She was wonderful. I was very close to her all the time. She was just so endearing. When she took on Jimmy Baldwin [the black American novelist] she wandered in with her shopping basket and she had all the shopping for the evening and he said "Well, have you got a contract?" She said "I think I have somewhere," scrabbling down, and there it was amongst the meat – and she said "Oh dear, it's a bit bloody, but there you are"!'

*

Alf Wight's spirits soared when he opened Anthea Joseph's letter of acceptance that morning in 1969. He could hardly believe it. After all these years, after all the hard work and disappointments, he was going to be a published author at last. He was going to have a hardback book of his very own stacked proud on his bookshelf. It was one of the greatest moments of his life. 'Your book is so enjoyable,' wrote Anthea Joseph. 'I hope this will be a lucky day for us both.'

She was prepared to pay him only £500 or so, but that hardly mattered. What was more important was that some proper, genuine publisher actually *liked* what he had written and was prepared to spend good money having it printed and bound and jacketed and put in the shops along with all those books by famous authors he had always so admired. He could hardly believe it.

Mrs Joseph invited him up to London to meet her, gave him lunch at the Garden Restaurant and was so encouraging about his writing that he took to her immediately – so much so that she was to edit his books for the next thirteen years, until she died in 1982.

So it is indeed true that Alf's literary career owed a great deal to a handful of women. But while it was gallant of him to say that he was indebted to four ladies, it was not entirely fair. There is no doubt at all that he owed Eddie Straiton a huge amount, too, otherwise he would not have dedicated that first book:

To

EDDIE STRAITON

with gratitude and affection

If it had really been his wife who had done most to inspire Alf's first book, why did he not dedicate it to her rather than to Straiton? Even his second book, *It Shouldn't Happen to a Vet*, was dedicated to his veterinary colleagues Donald and Brian Sinclair rather than to Joan. It was not until the third volume, *Let Sleeping Vets Lie*, that he dedicated one of his books to his wife.

Straiton himself was more upset that Alf never acknowledged the vital contribution of another man: John Morrison, the one-time Collins executive and charity fund-raiser who first helped to point Alf in the right direction. 'I never really fell out with Alf,' Straiton told me, 'but we did come to cross purposes when he had become famous and the BBC did a fifty-minute documentary film about me in Scotland and Alf was subsequently interviewed by Melvyn Bragg. Afterwards I phoned him and said "Why didn't you tell the *truth*? Why didn't you tell them that the man who is responsible for the success of your books is John Morrison, the man you met in the Dolce Vita and who used to work for Collins, the man who got Collins's reader to read that book and tell you what was wrong with it?" That was the key to Alf's success but he didn't mention it at all on the television. All he said was that his manuscripts kept thudding back through his letter box.'

*

After all those years of practice Alf had become such a polished writer, with a simple, direct style that suited his homely material perfectly, that Anthea Joseph had to do little to his typescript before it was printed and published. 'He didn't need much help with the writing,' Peter Day told me.

The final version of the book demonstrates clearly how far Alf had progressed with his writing skills since the days when he was compiling his listless diaries about his trips to Russia and Istanbul. *If Only They Could Talk* is slick, polished, vividly written and highly readable, and it has about it a spark of magic that was eventually to light a bonfire of acclaim. Right from the start all the ingredients that were to make the Herriot series so popular were there: the warmth of Alf's own homely personality; the delightfully fresh, bumbling, self-conscious nature that he gave his young *alter ego*, James Herriot; the charming descriptions of an extinct society and a lost way of life; the rugged, unforgettable characters living with their ancient ways on their remote farms; the smell of the moors. It is also, above all, very funny. Rereading it, even twenty-six years later, there are several scenes that make you laugh long and loud: when Siegfried loses his temper over 'that bloody swine Holt' and the Epsom salts; when

Tristan telephones James and pretends to be a customer calling him out to a distant Dales farm to deal with a huge, vicious horse late on a Saturday night; when James and Tristan together try to push an entire everted uterus back into a cow; when James meets the elderly widow Mrs Pumphrey and her outrageously pampered little Pekinese dog Tricki Woo – which has just gone 'flop-bott' again – and becomes adopted as the dog's 'Uncle Herriot'; when ten large pigs break loose in the town's crowded square on market day; when Siegfried tries to remove a piece of wire from a cow's stomach and is doused by a jet of foul liquid.

Each story is beautifully paced and Alf had learned by now to choose precisely the right word for each situation. When James plays a practical joke on Tristan, for a change, the three words 'hoarse but resolute' are enough to make me shake with laughter, but when they are followed four lines later by the words 'a wistful quality' I end up convulsed and tear-stained. And he describes a vast stallion as having feet 'like manhole covers'. Perfect. It is all overlaid with a nicely self-deprecating wit so that the reader can laugh at the young vet's nervous apprehensions, lack of confidence and mistakes and yet sympathise and identify with him at the same time.

There are deeply moving moments, too, like the tragic story of the tiny, poverty-stricken old widower who lives in a cold, dank hovel and whose last friend, a cross-bred labrador, is so riddled with cancer that James has to put it down. There is also social comment: describing the old man's poverty and the meagre meal on the table, Alf reminds the reader that this is how pensioners have to live because the state pension is so small. In addition there is a lovely sense of the beauties of the countryside, the miraculous sight of newborn lambs staggering knock-kneed towards their mothers' teats. How do they know exactly what to do, those little lambs? How do they *know*?

Some of the stories are simply slices of life and just peter out pointlessly after a few pages, but all in all it was an astonishingly accomplished achievement for a first book.

If Only They Could Talk by 'James Herriot', a slim little volume of 190 pages, was published at last in April 1970 and went on sale in shops throughout Britain at a price of £1.75. 'When the first cheque came in, about £170,' Jimmy told Noreen Taylor of the *Daily Mail* in 1995, 'I remember Dad showing it to me, with a big grin on his face, saying: "*How about that then?*"'

Publication day was unforgettable for Alf, the climax of all his hopes and dreams over so many years, and like any other first novelist he would have gazed with disbelief at the book and its crude but colourful jacket, fingering it, stroking it, turning it over in his hands. Like so many first-time authors he probably opened it and sniffed the pages, inhaling that heady perfume of freshly cut and printed paper. He probably bought all the national news-papers and scanned their book pages, dreaming in vain of finding huge rave reviews in all of them. Very likely he peered into the local bookshop in Thirsk marketplace to see if they were selling any copies, and hung around for a while, pretending to look at other books, in the hope that he would see someone buying a copy of his. Perhaps he surreptitiously moved one or two copies of his book into a more prominent position – and then drove over to Harrogate, Ripon and York to do the same.

Then, back at home, he could hardly contain himself. He telephoned Eddie Straiton in Stafford. 'You wouldn't believe it!' said Alf excitedly. 'Two little Glasgow guys and we're both bloody authors!'

CHAPTER TEN

The Interior Decorator From New York

Among the many myths that have grown up around the history of 'James Herriot' is the legend that his first two books were completely unsuccessful when they were first published in Britain but that as soon as they were discovered by Tom McCormack of the New York firm St Martin's Press – and were published together in the United States in a bumper edition entitled *All Creatures Great and Small* – they became an overnight sensation, not only in America but also back in Britain. Even Eddie Straiton was always under the impression that Alf owed his initial success to the Americans and that the British did not appreciate him until much later. 'Michael Joseph published the first book but it didn't sell very well,' Straiton told me. 'Alf used to phone me up regularly and say "Eddie, are you going into Wolverhampton or Birmingham? Would you go into Smith's and ask for my book? They've got my book among the *kids*' books!" But when the American publisher joined the first two books together they went off like a bomb in the States long before they went off like a bomb here. Since then Alf never looked back.'

Peter Day, the Michael Joseph editor who discovered that first book, himself confessed in 1996 that Alf owed his great success to the Americans. Yet this version of the truth is not entirely fair. It is of course correct to say that publication in America added a huge new dimension to Alf's sales but not that his early books were disregarded in Britain or underestimated by his British publishers. According to the myth – which Alf himself perpetuated – Michael Joseph printed only 2,000 copies and sold a mere 1,200 of them in the first year, and the book was ignored by the reviewers. It is true that the *Veterinary Record* took seven months to review the book – the paper's reviewer V. Simmons called it 'nostalgic and amusing' – but otherwise even that first book attracted several enthusiastic British reviews, more than most first novels by unknown authors, from papers like the *Yorkshire Evening Post* and the *Northern Echo*. It was spotted too and commended by the immensely influential popular journalist Godfrey Winn, whose views were avidly devoured each week by millions of British women.

It should be remembered that Alf's slim little book was up against some formidable opposition in the shops and on the review pages. Mario Puzo's *The Godfather* was top of the British bestseller lists and among the other books published that month were new novels by such big-selling popular authors as Harold Robbins (*The Inheritors*), Jean Plaidy (*Sweet Lass of Richmond Hill*), Monica Dickens (*The Listeners*), Norah Lofts (*The King's Pleasure*) and Catherine Gaskin (*Fiona*). What is more – according to Michael Joseph's sales director at the time, Dick Douglas-Boyd, *and* according to a letter Alf himself wrote in 1987 – Michael Joseph actually printed a first edition of 3,000 copies and must have sold them all pretty quickly because they reprinted the book nine months later, in December, making a total of 4,000 copies in the first year – more than most publishers would have ordered then for a first novel by an unknown writer. Indeed, that first 3,000 print-run was the same as Michael Joseph ordered for the first highly successful racing thriller by ex-jockey Dick Francis, another MJ author who was destined to go on to become a huge bestseller; and the same as Hamish Hamilton's first edition nineteen years later of Peter Mayle's phenomenally successful *A Year in Provence*. So it is less than fair to suggest that Michael Joseph published *If Only They Could Talk* without much success.

'Anthea was tremendously enthusiastic about the first Herriot book,' I was told by Michael Joseph's production director at the time, Victor Morrison, who went on to become the company's managing director in 1975. 'There were always these tremendous arguments in Michael Joseph as to how Alf took off. I always had some doubts about the American effect and backwash to Britain. I always found that rather strange.'

Dick Douglas-Boyd agreed. 'Anthea Joseph recognised what she'd got right from the start,' he told me, 'and she tried at the board meetings at which I was present to impress upon us that this was not just an ordinary book. My feeling right at the beginning was that we'd got a good author. But they put upon that book the most unappealing jacket – of a horse rearing up – which made it look exactly like a children's book, and it was very difficult as a salesman to promote this book more than by saying "This is a very fine book, read it for yourselves." It wasn't the kind of book that you could spend £5,000 or

£10,000 promoting. It was a book we reckoned had tremendous potential but it was a build-up book. Right from the start we recognised that we had something rather special.'

The jacket illustration by Graham Humphreys – of a young boy trying to control a nervous horse – did indeed make the book look like a children's novel but Alf himself certainly had no complaints about Michael Joseph's treatment of him. Not only did he stay with the firm all his life – at a time when other bestselling authors were chopping and changing their publishers with abandon – but when Douglas-Boyd retired in 1987 Alf wrote him a letter thanking him for all his help and recalling that when the first book was published and he learned that Michael Joseph had printed an initial 3,000 copies he had nearly fallen off his chair with ecstasy.

However, he was less than happy about the apparent lack of copies of his book in the bookshops and he complained to his family and friends that although any bookshop would order a copy for a potential purchaser, there were none actually on display or up on the shelves – a favourite gripe of authors ever since Gutenberg set up shop in Strasbourg in 1439.

Once the publication of *If Only They Could Talk* was under way, Anthea Joseph urged Alf to finish a sequel quickly. She knew that to build up his career as an author he needed to produce a book a year, so that soon there would be a whole series to attract a growing circle of loyal readers. Originally Alf had had no intention at all of producing a series of Herriot books: he had assumed that there would be just the one and that he would then write something completely different. But Mrs Joseph realised that she had a potential hit on her hands.

Publishers and readers alike much prefer it if a favourite author keeps writing the same sort of books – or even the same *book* – over and over again: it makes them feel comfortable and means that they know exactly what to expect each time they pick up a new one. Authors who write a variety of books in various categories are rarely as successful as those who choose one genre and stick to it, and the most successful of all are those who create a popular character or cast of characters about whom they write over and over again. This can be dull for the author – Ian Fleming eventually became heartily fed up with James Bond and Sir Arthur Conan Doyle grew so sick of Sherlock Holmes that he killed him off, only to have to bring him back to life again because of public outrage. Alf Wight, however, set to with a will. Night after night he worked away at concocting more stories about James, Siegfried, Tristan, Tricki Woo *et al.*, and in 1971 he delivered the typescript of *It Shouldn't Happen to a Vet*.

Over the next three years Alf was to publish a new James Herriot book every year and in the six years from 1972 to 1977 he published five new books, a remarkable rate of productivity for an author who was supposed to be a beginner and who was still working full-time as a vet. This was no 'amateur' writer. This was a professional, with a professional sense of discipline and commitment and a fierce ambition. Every year, with the awesome single-mindedness of other determined future bestsellers such as Dick Francis and Ruth Rendell, he worked non-stop on his portable Olivetti to ensure that his publishers had another volume to get into the bookshops in time for Christmas. 'When Alf was writing his books,' Eddie Straiton told me, 'his target was a couple of hundred words a day with *Roget's Thesaurus* on his knee. I wouldn't think the publishers had to change much because his grammar was excellent.' Indeed, Anthea Joseph required very few changes in his books, merely asking an occasional question such as 'What are the "claws" of a cow?' (A cow's claw is in fact one half of its cloven hoof.)

It Shouldn't Happen to a Vet was more of the mixture as before and told of James Herriot's second fictional year in the practice at Thirsk, from the summer of 1938 until mid-1939 – a time when Alf himself had in fact still been at veterinary college in Glasgow. Despite the rumbling of Nazi tanks across Europe in that year, there is no mention anywhere in the book of the looming threat of the war that was about to engulf the whole world. Instead, in the idyllic Yorkshire Dales, young James is still sniffing the fresh country air, gazing at the glorious scenery and loving every minute of his job. At the start of Alf's first book James was exhaustedly delivering a difficult calf in an open cowshed on a bleak moor at 3 a.m. in the middle of winter; at the start of the second he is exhaustedly delivering a foal at 4 a.m. in the middle of summer. As the book progresses he is called out to deal with a cow that has refused to stand up for two days, and to give a full medical check-up to Mrs Pumphrey's new pet piglet, which is named Nugent because it looks just like Mrs Pumphrey's great uncle and which, like Tricki Woo the Pekinese, also calls James 'Uncle Herriot'. He has to treat a dog that has swallowed a rubber ball, another with heart trouble, and a horse that needs its wolf teeth knocked out with a metal rod and a mallet. As a newly appointed Ministry of Agriculture and Fisheries inspector, he also conducts scores of official tuberculin tests on cattle, but despite his official position he still makes the usual amusing mistakes. He tells the farmer with the recumbent cow, for instance, that the beast has a broken pelvis and will never get up again – but the damned thing does get up and is still ambling around years later and being pointed out to passers-by as the cow that Young Herriot said would never stand again. On another occasion he makes the unfortunate mistake of trying to prod a cow's udder only to discover that the animal is in fact a bull. And he is called out one night – to treat a dog 'with a bone in its throat' – by a woman who turns out to be a heavily made-up blonde of a certain age with ferocious perfume, pink lamps, a flickering fire and a glint in her eye.

The whole atmosphere of the second book is just as dreamily timeless as that of the first. The hillside farmers are still convinced that their old-fashioned ways of treating animals are best: that a cow with milk fever can be cured by inflating her udder with a bicycle pump, pouring cold water into her ear, cutting off the end of her tail 'to let the bad out', putting a bloody sheepskin on her back or forcing her to drink beer and Jeyes' Fluid. They have no doubt whatever that sick cows need only to be dosed with eggshells ground in gruel, or blue vitriol and dandelion tea. Other bovine problems, they reckon, can be dealt with by rubbing the cow's tail between two sticks or by massaging the creature's udder with turpentine.

Young James's equipment is also just as primitive as it was in the first volume: he goes about his business with an alarming arsenal of ancient forceps, frightening shears and positively medieval chisels and rasps. Siegfried is of course as infuriatingly contradictory as ever, still yelling at Tristan and regularly sacking him without any effect. Tristan is as feckless as always, drinking too much, chatting up the girls and smashing all three of Siegfried's cars. The other characters, too, are as vivid and vital as their predecessors in the earlier volume: the huge, drunken layabout and hooligan Gobber Newhouse; Sam Broadbent, the village idiot who can do such a brilliant imitation of the vicious warble fly that cattle stampede away from him in terror; the brawny lorry driver who cries for three days when he decides to kill and eat the family pig, sobbing that the animal was almost a Christian. And once again there is a lonely old-age pensioner (a woman this time), who has a beloved old dog that has sadly reached the end of its life. Over the old lady's bed there hangs a poignant card that reads 'God is Near'.

It Shouldn't Happen to a Vet is very much the recipe as before but with one major development: the book introduces us to James's smiling, blue-eyed, dark-haired future wife, Helen Alderson, whom he meets when he goes to treat a lame calf at her widowed father's farm. They discover immediately that they share a deep love for the Yorkshire countryside, and the gormless James pursues her through the pages of the book as doggedly as a mournful English bloodhound. After a succession of disastrous dates, they decide to do their courting simply by walking together in the countryside, since it seems safer that way. By the end of this volume it is obvious that they are heading towards the altar – an enticing way for a book to end when the author is planning to write a whole series about the same characters.

This time Michael Joseph put a light-hearted cartoon on the jacket so that no one could confuse it with a children's book. 'They put a proper jacket on the second book,' said Dick Douglas-Boyd. 'And the first book reprinted twice very quickly in a short space of time before his second came out. It flew out of the shops, selling four or five thousand copies. It's a myth that the first one didn't sell at all. I spoke to the head of St Martin's Press many years later when he was putting it round at the Frankfurt Book Fair that he was the man who discovered Herriot. I sat him down and said "This is untrue" and told him he mustn't go round saying Herriot was an undiscovered, failed author before he'd taken him on. We printed eight thousand copies of the second book and then we upped the print-run for the third one. It's absolutely wrong to say that the Americans discovered him.'

Michael Joseph also made sure that the second book came out at the quietest time of year, in January, when few books were published in Britain and there was more chance of an unknown catching the eye of literary editors and reviewers. On Sunday 16 January 1972 Alf drove into Thirsk, parked his car on the cobbles in the marketplace, walked into the newsagent and bought a pile of Sunday newspapers to see if any of them had reviewed his book. None had – but his heart leapt for a moment when he

turned to the book page of the *Sunday Express* and saw
that my own weekly column was illustrated with a picture
of a goat looking over a wooden fence: for one heady
moment Alf thought that the picture must have been
picked to accompany a review of his second book. It had
not: it was in fact a picture taken from a new collection of
humorous photographs entitled *Cyclists Please Dismount*,
with a foreword by the comedian Spike Milligan.

Four days later, on Thursday 20 January, when most of
the British daily newspapers of those days also published
pages of book reviews, he bought another pile of national
newspapers but there was still no review of his book. By
now he must have begun to despair. Were all the papers
going to ignore his books? Was he never going to be
reviewed or recognised or even mentioned after all those
years of work? Was he destined to be passed over, ignored,
forgotten even before he had properly begun? Were all
the good omens and the praise and hopes of people like
Anthea Joseph no more than that – just idle hopes rather
than canny professional assessments and expectations?

But then that Thursday morning he received a telephone call from the literary editor of the *Sunday Express*
in London – me – asking questions about his background
and writing, and three days later came the magical
morning that Alf said afterwards he would never forget.
When he opened the *Sunday Express* in Thirsk marketplace on Sunday 23 January he saw the headline 'The
blonde in distress called out the vet . . .' and beneath it a
long rave review spread across four columns, the first
review of any decent length that he had ever had. 'James
Herriot is on to a winner,' it said. 'A delightful new

collection of medical stories that would make a marvellous basis for a TV series . . . Lively, vivid, and very funny, they give the medical comedy a completely fresh twist . . . I haven't laughed so much since reading David Niven's best-selling autobiography.' It concluded: 'James Herriot still practises in Yorkshire. He has almost completed a third book and tells me he has enough material to write sequel after sequel. When the telly executives get on to him he is going to need them all.'

Alf sat and stared at that review. He read it again and could hardly believe it. He read it a third time, just to make sure. His dream had come true at last, and the following day he sat down and typed me one of the nicest letters I ever received from an author in all my twenty-three years as a literary editor and books columnist. Whether his claim about my influence was true or not, he stuck firmly to his belief until the end of his life. When he died in 1995 Rosie told Brian Duffy of the *Sunday Express* that my review had 'made all the difference. Until then, you couldn't buy his books in High Street shops. You could get them ordered, but they were not up on the shelves. The *Sunday Express* piece changed all that and really put him on the map. And he always remarked later that it was that review which gave him the invaluable first boost.'

In fact it was the editor of the *Sunday Express*, John Junor — who had been raised like Alf in Glasgow — who played the most important part in publicising and promoting the James Herriot books in Britain. It was he, not I, who decided to serialise *It Shouldn't Happen to a Vet*, thus bringing it for several weeks to the attention of millions of readers. Throughout the 1970s Junor was to serialise each new Herriot book in the *Sunday Express*, a paper with a vast ten-million-strong middle-class, middle-brow readership perfectly suited to Alf's books.

It Shouldn't Happen to a Vet was also serialised at length in the influential London newspaper the *Evening Standard*, and there was a highly enthusiastic review in *Farmers Weekly*, which may well have been read even in some of the remotest farms in the wildest reaches of the Yorkshire Dales. 'His easy and at times excruciatingly funny case history narratives must rate as country classics,' said *Farmers Weekly*, 'and he throws in a stumbling, awkward courtship for good measure.'

'Even before Alf's third book was published,' said Dick Douglas-Boyd, 'I took him up to the Newcastle booksellers' annual meeting, where he made the guest speech, and by that time I was taking him round to signing sessions. He was a success right from the start.'

Michael Joseph did, however, have one major problem in trying to launch Alf's writing career. 'We could not interest the paperback people at all,' said Douglas-Boyd. 'We tried Pan [which was eventually to paperback all the Herriot books] but we couldn't get anyone interested. I also tried the book clubs and they said "They're nice little books, but . . ." We tried everywhere. Anthea was so keen. I suppose they thought they were just little short stories, that it wasn't a novel they could promote very easily. The books were too short for a book club and they didn't know Alf was going to do a whole long string of books. They couldn't foresee the future. Ralph Vernon-Hunt was the head of Pan at the time and he said "Yes, they're lovely books, Dick, but we can't quite see how to do it." They did eventually put him into paperback after the second one but even then Pan didn't do the first paperback until a long time after the second book. I was also the export director and I had to go round selling this very English country vet and no one wanted to know. Trying to flog James Herriot in Australia was very difficult until the Americans took him up and then everyone wanted him, from Hong Kong to Japan. So to some extent the USA claim is true.'

It may be difficult to believe now, but not everyone was a great fan of the early Herriot books. 'Don't quote me,' one of Alf's old veterinary friends said to me, 'but to be honest I thought his books were a bit corny. It was all a bit manufactured and the sentiment was sometimes a bit heavy but they appealed to just the right set of the public at the right time, when they were still fresh and clean.'

*

Tom McCormack may have enjoyed boasting later that it was he who really launched the James Herriot phenomenon but the American side of the story is not quite that simple either. The American discovery of Herriot was in fact made not by a sharp-witted New York publisher but by an interior decorator – McCormack's wife Sandra – who picked Alf's first book off a pile on the bedside table and knew within twenty pages that this could be a winner.

McCormack himself, then aged thirty-eight, had recently been appointed chief executive of the small, ailing New York publishing house St Martin's Press. He had been horrified to discover that the company had just recorded a huge $160,000 loss and had an accumulated deficit of more than $500,000. The figures convinced him that unless he could publish a bestseller or two the company would die, throwing thirty-three employees out of work. In a desperate search for promising new titles, he flew to London in June 1970 – two months after *If Only They Could Talk* had been published in Britain – to do the rounds of the British publishers and literary agents.

'I went around with my beggar's basket to ask them to fill it up with manuscripts and books,' McCormack told me in 1997 in his apartment overlooking Central Park in New York. 'They'd hardly heard of St Martin's and they'd certainly never heard of me but on my very last day I finally got into the David Higham literary agency and I was given an appointment with an agent there called David Bolt. Bolt had never heard of me and was not about to give me anything that seemed to have any promise but he wanted to be courteous. He was thrashing around thinking "What can I *give* this guy?" He reached up and picked off the shelf a bound, jacketed book that he gave to me. I looked at this book. It was a slender thing of 190 pages and on the cover was what looked like a sixteen-year-old in overalls pulling on a horse. And the title of the thing,' said McCormack, affecting a deeply bored voice, 'was *If Only They Could Talk*. Oh, God. "Well, thank you very much, David," I said. "It looks delightful."

'This thing had sold just 1,200 copies and I thought "This thing has been seen by all kinds of visiting firemen from America" and this turned out to be true: I know several other American publishers saw it first and a number of them said quite openly later "You know, I read that book and I didn't see it." But I took it back to the States where it lay unread on the table at home for about three months. One night my wife Sandra – the very best reader I've met in my life – picked the thing off the great stack of stuff from the table and read it and she knew. "This guy is good," she said. "You really oughta read this guy." So I read the thing and knew that it was a wonderful specimen of writing.'

Even so McCormack told me that he felt the book needed to be fatter for an American audience, and also needed love interest and a happy ending. 'There are two kinds of books,' he said. 'There are *caper* books and *milieu* books. A caper book is a book – like a mystery book – that you start tonight and you want to finish tonight. A milieu book is a book that creates a world and you want to stay there: you *don't* want to finish it tonight because all day tomorrow you want to be able to look forward to getting back into it tomorrow night, and at the weekend.'

By this time Alf also had an agent in New York, Claire Smith of the Harold Ober agency. 'I called her,' said McCormack, 'and said "This is a milieu book written at caper length. I need more. And it doesn't have an ending, it just stops." She said "How nice that you should say that because there's another one coming." Eventually I got the next one, *It Shouldn't Happen to a Vet*, and I read that and it was equally good but again it didn't have an ending and it just stopped. But in the second book he'd just met Helen and she was obviously to be the big love of his life.'

McCormack decided to publish the first two books

together in one volume if Alf would add a new upbeat, romantic ending in which James marries Helen. McCormack's version of the story makes it all sound so smooth, but in fact the truth is more complex. The Michael Joseph files show that McCormack was trying to buy the US rights of *If Only They Could Talk* as early as November 1970. It was to take him more than a year to work out just how to package James Herriot for the USA.

By now David Bolt had left the David Higham agency in London to set up on his own – foolishly omitting to take Alf Wight with him – and Alf's new London agent was David Higham's assistant, Jacqueline Korn. McCormack asked her for Herriot's telephone number in Yorkshire, rang the number – which was that of the surgery in Thirsk – and was baffled when nobody there had heard of James Herriot. Nor had the local telephone people. After some confusion and further checking, McCormack was irritated to discover that 'James Herriot' was a pseudonym and that Jacqueline Korn had not thought to tell him. 'I think Jacqueline Korn has a red face,' McCormack wrote sarcastically to Claire Smith. 'They're sorry they forgot to tell us.'

Eventually he managed to speak to Alf – whom he was always to call 'James'. 'Initially I called him Alf,' said McCormack, 'but at one stage in an oral exchange I said "Would you like me to say James or Alf?" and he said "James is fine" – and I made the judgement that I was part of his writing life. It was also the case that somehow or other I picked up from him or some member of his circle that "Alf" has a certain lower-class caste to it in England and I don't think he liked it much.'

McCormack asked him to write three new chapters. 'So I stuck this big cigar in my mouth and eventually spoke to him,' McCormack told me, imitating a Hollywood film producer: ' "I want you should gimme three chapters and you should marry da goil." I thought "Here's this guy living in Thirsk, 400 miles from civilisation: what on earth is he going to make of this crass Madison Avenue American idea?" But he understood immediately and he made more of it than I could ever have dreamed. He knew exactly what I was after and he gave me three chapters and an ending that chimes like *The Sound of Music*. It was a glorious ending and the hills were alive.' The three new chapters describing James and Helen's wedding appeared at the end of *All Creatures Great and Small* and again at the end of the third book, *Let Sleeping Vets Lie*. It was yet another example of Alf's complete professionalism. If his publishers came up with a good commercial idea he was always happy to fit in with what they wanted and produce the goods.

McCormack bought the first two books plus the three new chapters for an amazingly small advance of $1,250, the equivalent then of just £520 – about the sum that Michael Joseph had paid for the first book alone – and he refused to agree to the usual 10 per cent/12½ per cent/15 per cent sliding-scale royalty, insisting instead that Alf's royalties should not exceed 10 per cent no matter how many copies were sold. 'I negotiated a very tough contract on it,' said McCormack, 'because I knew the book was going to be very long and if I ever went to 15 per cent royalties I'd be pricing it out of the market.'

Even so he faced a daunting obstacle in persuading his

colleagues at St Martin's Press that this book could be the company's salvation. 'It seems perfectly likely to us now,' he told me, 'but at that time? Two years in the life of a vet 3,500 miles away? And the two years are 1937 and 1938? I remember trembling. I got up there and said "I'm now about to tell you about a book that will be in print one hundred *years* from now." They all looked at me and I said "It's the memoirs of a doctor. But it's not a *people* doctor, it's an *animal* doctor. And he's not an animal doctor in some place logical like Kansas or Connecticut, it's York-shire, England. And it's not really the *memoirs*, it's only two years. And the two years are 1937 and 1938." And I was then confronted by a vision of a dozen of my best friends walking away from me sideways. Oy-yoy-yoy. "Come back!" I shouted to them. "It's going to be a bestseller! My wife says so!" A publisher at Macmillan in London just sat and laughed at me when I told him this book was going to be a bestseller in America.'

Since McCormack was by now the president of St Martin's as well as the chief executive officer, in reality he could publish anything he chose. He also insisted on a different title for the book. 'Alf's titles were terrible: *If Only They Could Talk*! Absolutely not! *It's a Vet's Life*! Absolutely not! *Let Sleeping Vets Lie*! Ugh! Oh, God! *Vet in a Spin*! I used to make a lot of fun of him on his titles and then when I found he got most of them from Joan I had to stop that! The big candidate title in-house at the time, believe it or not, was *Cow in the Waiting Room*.'

Alf suggested title after title: *They Can't Tell You*; *They Ask No Questions*; *The Animals and I*; *Physician on the Farm*; *Two Years in the Dog-House*; *Two Years in the Cattle-House*;

The Vet Set; *Get the Vet*. They chose eventually *All Creatures Great and Small*, an inspired title derived from a hymn written in 1848 by the Irish poetess Cecil Frances Alexander, who also composed in that same year 'There Is a Green Hill Far Away' and the Christmas carol 'Once in Royal David's City':

> *All things bright and beautiful,*
> *All creatures great and small,*
> *All things wise and wonderful,*
> *The Lord God made them all.*

'We actually had a Brit working at St Martin's who came up with the Alexander doxology,' said McCormack, 'and I looked at it and saw "All creatures great and small" and I said "That's it!" Meantime, by God, James had hit on the same idea and the same line but he suggested *Ill Creatures Great and Small* but we talked him out of it.'

In fact the original suggestion for the *Ill Creatures* title came from twenty-six-year-old Rosie. Alf loved it, but McCormack preferred to play it straight and he was right, for Alf's cosy, old-fashioned writing was not meant to be sharp or clever: it was supposed to be old-fashioned and gentle in contrast to the laid-back, liberal, sex-obsessed permissiveness of the Swinging Sixties (which Alf himself later called 'the horrible Sixties'). It was the book's outdated values, its gentleness and kindness, that appealed so much to so many millions of readers.

'*Ill Creatures* was too clever and jokey,' explained McCormack. 'I actually in the end think this is a very dignified figure, James Herriot. This is an extremely respectable man doing extremely respectable things and experiencing extremely respectable emotions and loves and I said "No no no, this is salt of the earth and I don't want a joke title." ' Michael Joseph, by contrast, always saw the books as funnies, and put cartoon covers on all of them after the first one, a move that McCormack felt was a grave mistake. 'They were not warm enough and I thought the idea of putting cartoons on the cover – at least for the American market – was to trivialise the books. They were saying "Oh, come and laugh at some barnyard humour." That's not what these books were about.'

Did he think that Michael Joseph had let Alf down by publishing his first two books in the way that they did? 'Yeah,' said McCormack, 'I do. I don't think they knew how to publish those goddamn books.' For the jacket of the American edition (and for all the subsequent books) he commissioned an idealised painting showing a handsome young hunk of a vet with an animal.

In 1972 Tom and Sandra McCormack and their four-year-old son Daniel flew to London on another book-shopping expedition and invited Alf and Joan Wight to lunch at their hotel, the Connaught, on 22 June. 'That's where we first met one another,' said McCormack. 'James was a *bon vivant*: he liked good food and good drink and it was always a pleasure to take him out. He mentioned Scott Fitzgerald as being his favourite read at the moment. He was *highly* sophisticated and very widely read. I was just drunk with conviction and enthusiasm about the book. I said "We are going to make this a very very big book." I put a cigar in my mouth and I pointed at him and said "I'm gonna make you a *star*" and he said "Sounds wonderful" and I said to him "You may say wonderful but I'm telling you, James, it is going to change your life" and he said "I'll lap it up" – and for about two years he did lap it up.'

The American omnibus edition of the first two books plus the three new chapters was published in the United States at the end of 1972 – to a silence from the reviewers that was almost as resounding as that which had greeted the first British edition, despite the fact that McCormack had written begging letters to all the most influential critics in America and had backed his gamble with a $25,000 PR campaign to publicise the book. He had taken advertisements in papers across the country, including a two-page advertisement in *Publishers' Weekly*, had told bookshops to offer any disgruntled purchaser his money back, and had sent little ivory animals to booksellers and reviewers to draw their attention to the book. In vain. It was still no go. Not yet. The *New York Times*, for instance, did not review the book until 18 February 1973 – three months after publication and a whole month after the book had appeared on its own bestseller list. The *Los Angeles Times* waited until 4 February, *Time* magazine until the 19th.

'We shipped the book in September for publication date of 14 November 1972,' recalled McCormack, 'but the book did not hit the *New York Times* bestseller list until the third week of January – almost four months after initial release. I committed what was at that time a relatively large amount to the promotion of the books. I printed up 6,000 copies of Chapter 1 of the first book to just give away to librarians, booksellers, reviewers. I said "If I could just get them to *taste* it they're gonna want more." This was the quintessential book where it was "Just get 'em to try it and they'll be hooked." It doesn't matter how small you are – if you have *the* book and if you press press press press just to get people to read the bloody thing it's going to make it. If you've got *the* book and you *realise* you've got the book and if you absolutely put your shoulder to the thundering wheel of a great book, it'll go.

'By publication day we only had 8,500 copies out there in the stores in America but this was going to be the word-of-mouth book. Getting to the reviewers was the trick. There's no way in which you can advertise in any dollar-effective way direct to the consumer. I couldn't get New York interested in the book but out in Chicago a guy I'd never heard of in my life, Alfred Ames, who was reviewing books for the *Chicago Tribune*'s Sunday Book World, had somehow or another been exposed to the shotgun of promotional tricks that I'd conjured up, and he read the book and he flipped. His review [on 12 November] was on the front page and the first line was "If there is any justice, *All Creatures Great and Small* will become a classic of its kind. The publishers call it 'a miracle', not too strong a word." And he goes on up from there. I've never seen a rave like this in my life and it was the beginning. Next thing we know the orders started in Chicago. I took that front page, photographed it in facsimile and I reran that review in the *New York Times* and pushed and pushed and the word-of-mouth began. One of the reviewers, William Argo of the *San Francisco Chronicle*, who raved about it, said "I'd have missed this one but I had two *readers* call me up and say I really ought to look at it and am I glad I did." The reviews were over the moon. There was one bad review in something called *The Library Journal*: somehow or another they had given this damned thing to a reviewer in Brooklyn when they should have given it to someone in Middle America, so this guy in Brooklyn says "Ah, you know, these are barnyard memoirs about funny pigs," but five months later *The Library Journal* ran a second review, the only time they ever did, saying "We blew it." But the book did not hit the bestseller lists until about four months after it was released and that gives a sense of the word-of-mouth effect and the reviewers finally catching up. We were still getting first reviews in January and February. And that was the beginning. If it weren't for a man named Alfred Ames it all might have turned out different.'

As professional about his writing as ever, Alf Wight finished the third book, *Let Sleeping Vets Lie*, delivered the typescript to Anthea Joseph and then, at the end of February 1973, flew with Joan to the United States for a six-day publicity tour that had him giving two or three television, radio and newspaper interviews every day in New York, Philadelphia and Chicago.

'It was his first time in America and we showed him everything,' McCormack told me. 'We took him to Trader Vic's, the Russian Tea Room, Sardi's, Grant's Tomb, Harlem, the Bowery, the Lower East Side. In one day he had five things he had never had in his life, including gefilte fish, caviar blinis and the very best Dom Perignon at the Russian Tea Room and he said "Oh boy." ' Joan, it seems, was less impressed. 'At no time did

Joan ever convey the same capacity for *joie de vivre* that he did,' said McCormack. 'He just loved all these things that we showed him in New York, and his exhilaration more than filled one's bag of hopes, but I don't have any memories of Joan exhilarating in nearly the same way, which is not a criticism, it's a regret for her. It's wonderful to have that capacity to exhilarate: to say "Wow, is this the life!" '

The publicity tour was a triumph. 'The book was just dropping off the bestseller lists when he came over,' said McCormack, 'and his appearances drove it back on and it stayed back on the national lists for another dozen weeks. It was still on the bestseller lists in Chicago eleven *months* after original publication.' Within a year *All Creatures Great and Small* had been selected by two book clubs, serialised in three American magazines and published as a *Reader's Digest* condensed book, the *Digest* paying $30,000 for the privilege. Afterwards McCormack wrote to Alf: 'Sandra and I have never enjoyed an author more than we have you. Absolutely everything we did with you was a pleasure – for us and for everyone else who met you. You are, say I, exactly the kind of man one comes into publishing for.'

McCormack had no doubt as to why the Herriot books became such a huge success in the USA. 'They are warm and they are joyful,' he told me. 'Alf Wight created the wonderfully attractive character named James Herriot that all of us like to be with. This is a man who is not at all a fool – he's quite smart – who clearly loved life and was also doing things that all of us approved of. He saved animals' lives and he was doing the quintessential family man thing and he was a kind of hero that an American could identify with. This guy would have been a great pioneer for us. He loved the land, he was not afraid of work, he loved the outdoors and did things with his hands.'

Alf agreed. 'My stories are not just funny animal tales,' he told the *Saturday Review* in 1986. 'They're about tough pioneering days and hard-bitten old farmers. Because they come from pioneering stock themselves, the Americans saw that at once.'

As for whether the books were mainly fact or mainly fiction, McCormack told me: 'The stories are based on actual events. James told me that he used to keep day books and he'd always put in them a line or two – and sometimes even more – about each visit, so that later he was able to recall cases with high density of detail. He would not claim by any means that every single line of dialogue was verbatim, but sometimes he would. Sometimes I would say something was a weak last line and he'd say "But that's exactly what he said, it's a true story and I don't want to change it." But he was an artist more than he was a reporter and he was more than willing to shape stuff and frequently he would meld things together. There were times when he was quite open to reshaping suggestions. He had to use imagination. Absolutely.'

Back in Britain the third book, *Let Sleeping Vets Lie*, was published in April 1973 to a growing storm of applause, popularity and sales. It became an immediate bestseller in Britain only a couple of months after the success of *All Creatures Great and Small* in America – obviously quite independently of America since it seems most unlikely that an American success would affect British sales so swiftly. 'Our first hardback print was 15,000 copies,' Dick Douglas-Boyd told me, 'and at last the BCA book club agreed to put the first two books together, as they had done in the States, and to launch them in one volume, *All Creatures Great and Small*, so we did an omnibus volume as well under the same title.'

When *Let Sleeping Vets Lie* was published I reviewed it in the *Sunday Express* and the paper also serialised the book over several weeks. An increasing number of other British reviewers were recommending the Herriot books in a wide variety of publications. 'It is a pleasure to be in James Herriot's company,' said the intellectual Sunday paper *The Observer*. 'Enormous pleasure,' said the *Sunday Times*, 'the stories can be read and re-read.' The *Daily Telegraph* agreed: 'He can tell a good story against himself, and his pleasure in the beauty of the countryside in which he works is infectious.' Even the tabloids were smitten. 'James Herriot provides a chuckle, or a lump in your throat, in every chapter,' said the *Daily Mirror*. The specialist country magazines were equally impressed. 'Full of warmth, wit and wisdom,' acknowledged *The Field*. James Herriot was suddenly becoming a household name.

When it came to the American paperback edition of *All Creatures Great and Small*, McCormack decided that the way to sell it by the million was to make it as cheap as possible, so he signed a ferocious $50,000 contract with Bantam under which the books were sold for just $2.50 each. To make matters worse for Alf, he was to be paid only half the usual royalty. 'He was not getting anything like 10 per cent,' said McCormack. 'He was getting just

12 cents a book.' Most authors and agents would have been incensed and insulted by such a paltry deal but it worked: Bantam went on to sell more than ten million Herriot paperbacks in America and Alf was paid the proper royalties for the later books. In fact, despite McCormack's ruthlessness, Alf could not have hoped to find a more attentive and understanding publisher. In numerous letters over the years McCormack flattered, cosseted and guided him, never pushing too hard or demanding too much, and each year at Christmas he paid personally for an expensive Fortnum and Mason hamper, loaded with champagne and caviar, to be sent to Alf and Joan in Thirsk.

To publicise the paperback, Alf returned to the States for a second tour in November 1973. This time the experience was so unhappy that he vowed never to return.

'Bantam blew it,' said McCormack. 'Ahead of time he requested just a couple of things and he didn't get any of them. He was here for three weeks and he got exactly one half-day at the end of the whole trip to do some shopping for the family. And then they put him in the middle seat of a VC10 aircraft with very small seats and he got off the far end with phlebitis and he was miserable. We never got him to the States again. Later I said "Look, I'll fly you in the goddamn *Concorde*" but he wasn't gonna go through that again, and then by the end of the seventies he was world-famous, very rich and did not need it. He was hitting No. 1 with every book.'

During that exhausting Bantam tour Alf was constantly climbing on and off aircraft. He had to rise at dawn in a different city each day to begin the long, exhausting round of interviews and bookshop signing sessions, where his new, devoted transatlantic fans even brought their pets along to be introduced. 'They made me autograph books for their pets,' he told me later. 'They even brought canaries in cages and I remember once signing a book for two hamsters called Herman and Lucius.' He had suddenly found himself swamped by an entire nation of Mrs Pumphreys and Tricki Woos. 'They're even crazier over animals than we are,' he told me. 'On one radio phone-in programme I was asked to give advice about pet skunks. I know nothing about them. And alligators. They buy them by post and when they're small they're quite sweet but when they grow the owners get frightened of them and flush them down the toilet. Apparently the New York sewers are seething with grown alligators.' This urban myth, at least, was quite untrue despite spreading far and wide during the 1970s.

Draining though it was, the publicity tour was another triumph. America, with its warm heart and its taste for sentimentality and nostalgia, took Alf immediately to its bosom. Within days *All Creatures Great and Small* was riding high in the US bestseller lists again. The Herriot bandwagon had started to roll.

'I'm proud of what we did,' admits McCormack. 'We got committed and devised some things that were effective, but the truth of the matter is it was the writing that did it. It was the books. You cannot dupe the public, especially with a total unknown with such an unlikely subject matter. I said to James: "I'm like the guy who runs an art gallery: OK, I mount a nice exhibition but it's the paintings that count, babe." Or "It's like giving the piano the credit for the Beethoven." James was so skilful with such ease. Again and again he saw the right way to write a story. He saw the *centre* of the anecdote wonderfully.'

*

It was a golden year for Alf and Joan in 1973, the year he began to make his big literary breakthrough and to accumulate some serious royalties, the year he was elected president of the Yorkshire Veterinary Society, the year he had a dream come true when he saw Sunderland beat Leeds United in the FA Cup Final at Wembley: he was so delighted and excited that when the final whistle went he hugged the spectator standing next to him – an elderly stranger in a camel coat – and in their euphoria they danced a victory jig together. Nineteen years later, when Sunderland had once again reached the Cup Final, Alf told Tony Hardisty of the *Sunday Express* that his memory of that victory was still so vivid that he could close his eyes and taste the gin he had enjoyed on the train journey back to Thirsk and the iced champagne that Rosie had poured for him when he got back home. 'Being a football fan is something that seeps into your bloodstream and stays for ever,' he said.

And then on 22 September Rosie – by now a qualified doctor – married Christopher John Page, a twenty-seven-year-old ex-airline steward from Haydon Wick, near Swindon in Wiltshire. She had been doing her medical internship at Swindon Hospital and had met Page in the local hi-fi shop where he now worked. They were married in the parish church at Thirsk just as her parents had been thirty-two years previously.

Alf and Joan sorely missed Rosie when she and her husband moved to Wiltshire but thirty-year-old Seamus was still living at home and still working with Alf and Donald Sinclair in the Thirsk practice. Life for Alf was rich and full. He was working hard as a country vet, still loving his work, still tapping away at the Olivetti in the evenings, but now a dozen foreign publishers were also after him, clamouring for the rights to his books. He must have looked at himself in the mirror with bewilderment and wondered if it were all a dream. How had it happened so suddenly, so quickly? After all those years of trial, practice and failure? After all those years of rejections?

But he had not seen anything yet. In the following year, 1974, the Herriot explosion was to become such a massive, volcanic eruption that it made what had gone before seem no more than a nice little tremor. This time the film makers were after him – and so were the Japanese.

CHAPTER ELEVEN

The Reluctant Millionaire

FAME CAME AS A MASSIVE SHOCK to Alf. He had always been a modest, unassuming man and now at the age of nearly sixty he was being fêted wherever he went and treated like some Hollywood film star. Print, radio and television reporters from all over the world wanted to interview him. Thousands of fans wrote to him – sometimes a hundred letters were delivered at a time, tied up in bundles, reaching him even when they were addressed to the non-existent town of Darrowby. One envelope read simply: 'James Herriot, It Shouldn't Happen to a Vet'; underneath someone had added 'It Shouldn't Happen to a Postman, Either.' Unlike most bestselling authors, Alf answered every letter personally, so that some days he was exhausted even before his proper work as a vet had started. Hundreds began to make pilgrimages to Thirsk, queueing outside the surgery door eager to shake his hand and persuade him to sign books for them. One afternoon he opened the door to find two dogs and sixteen Americans waiting. Gingerly he backed blinking into the limelight and was sometimes appalled by his own celebrity.

One day in 1974 he received a letter from Tom McCormack that finally brought it home to him that he could retire tomorrow in luxury and need never work again. He called his dogs, Dan and Hector, and took them out for a long walk. 'I suddenly realised I was successful and rich, and this was only the beginning,' he told Alex Harvey of the *Sun* in 1978. 'I should have felt happy, shouldn't I? But I felt nothing at all.' He was in fact already fed up with writing one veterinary book after another and had told McCormack in February that he would much prefer now to write a straight novel. McCormack encouraged him to do so but the success of the veterinary books was now such that Alf had become their prisoner: he continued to dream about writing the novel and probably even started it but it was never completed.

Alf was still stunned by his astonishing success. In America *All Creatures Great and Small* had by the end of 1974 sold not only 125,000 copies in hardback but also more than a million in paperback and the *Reader's Digest* condensed book edition was on the way to selling *three* million – an all-time *Reader's Digest* record. In Britain *If Only They Could Talk* and *It Shouldn't Happen to a Vet* had already sold 100,000 each in paperback. As each new book was published the first print-run was increased and yet every time the books sold out and had to be reprinted. Book clubs ordered large numbers of copies: when the fourth book, *Vet in Harness*, was published in October 1974, along with *Let Sleeping Vets Lie* in paperback, Michael Joseph printed 80,000 copies in hardback and a further 40,000 for a book club edition. And by the end of the year the books were being published in twelve languages, including Japanese. 'I mean,' Alf said to me at the time, baffled, 'can you imagine it? Yorkshire dialect in Japanese?' In fact the Japanese adored his books, bought them in huge quantities and flocked to make the pilgrimage to Thirsk in almost as large numbers as the American fans did. When I wrote Alf's obituary for the *Daily Mail* in 1995 it was a Japanese publisher, Shuei-sha, that quickly bought the article to use as a foreword for a new edition of James Herriot cat stories that they were about to publish.

It was also in 1974 that the first Herriot film was shot. *All Creatures Great and Small*, sponsored by *Reader's Digest*, was made for American television but was later screened also in cinemas. Simon Ward played the young vet, Ward's old RADA friend and flatmate Anthony Hopkins was Siegfried, Lisa Harrow was Helen, Brian Stirner was Tristan, and there were two splendid cameo performances by Freddie Jones and Brenda Bruce. The producer was David Susskind and the director Claude Whatham, who had previously directed *That'll Be the Day* and *Swallows and Amazons*. Neither Alf nor Joan had ever met an actor before and since most of the film was shot on the North Yorkshire Moors they went along excitedly to meet the cast, watch the filming and see Alf's words and stories conjured into pictures. He was filled with powerful emotion as he watched Hopkins and Ward, dressed like vets of the 1930s and driving an old car, filming James's first encounter with Siegfried thirty-four years before. It was, he said later, exactly how he remembered it.

He watched the scene being shot over and over again, perhaps a dozen times, and then he and Joan were introduced to the actors. Alf felt very shy about meeting them and was amazed when Simon Ward told him later that he had himself been very nervous. 'I didn't meet Alf in advance because there was never any suggestion that my performance should be an impersonation,' Ward told me in 1997. 'He had a Scottish accent, for instance, but in the film I was a Londoner.' In the film, too, Ward appeared not as the son of a Glasgow shipyard worker and musician but as a man whose father was a bank clerk and whose mother was dead. 'Yes, Alf and I were both shy of each other,' he admitted. 'I am very shy anyway and you're especially shy of someone you're actually playing. I mean, it must have been very strange for Alf to talk to a bloke who was playing him with a South London accent.'

Ward played the part with a gentle, boyish, clean-cut English charm. He trained for the role by spending two weeks with an Irish vet in Somerset, following him on his rounds and helping him to perform an embryotomy on a mare. 'They don't teach you that at RADA,' said Ward. 'This was real life.'

His first meeting with Alf was when he and Tony Hopkins were shooting a scene near Pickering. Out of the corner of his eye Ward spotted a group of people being ushered in to watch the filming. 'I thought "Oh no, oh dear" but of course Alf was extremely welcoming and very flattering. He was a lovely man. He made me feel that he was very nervous about meeting me and about the whole experience. He told me he was very flattered that I was playing him after I had just played Winston Churchill.'

Alf would have been most amused to learn that in between impersonating Churchill and himself, Ward had

in fact played the part of a Nazi in Hitler's final bunker –
and that after *All Creatures Great and Small* he was to play
the Devil opposite Kirk Douglas in *Apocalypse 2000*.

'Alf wasn't involved at all in the filming,' said Ward, 'but
he used to pop along sometimes and we went out to
dinner occasionally and I got to know him quite well. He
adored Joan – it was a very, very good marriage – but he
must have been baffled by this totally bizarre world of
sitting down to eat with American film executives where
they used to do something called the Wisconsin Two-
Step, where you're all sitting round a table and for
networking reasons people have got to be shifted around,
so you're made to table-hop just as you're finishing the
avocado and starting to know the people you're talking to.
For Alf this contrast with his life as a real person must
have been extraordinary.

'But for me it was very nearly my happiest experience
as a film actor. Of all the films I've made I've always had a
very special affection for *All Creatures Great and Small*. It
was fun playing Alf and we had an extremely happy crew,
a wonderful cast and I enjoyed it enormously. And Hugh
Whitemore's script was lovely. Unhappily two or three of
the big comic set-pieces – like Tristan driving a car into a
cricket pavilion – were cut because of lack of money. And
at the end of the film, when Lisa and I were married, the
script called for a flight of Spitfires to fly over and wheel
in the sky, and we were both to look up and see them so
that there would have been this shadow of the war to
come. But they got only one Spitfire and in the end they
didn't have the money for the petrol or something so we
didn't have an end to the film at all. Luckily David

Susskind, our producer, was at hand and he said "Lisa, you sit on the five-bar gate and you say 'I love you' and Simon you say 'I love you too.' There, that's great. What the hell do we need writers for? We don't need writers." So that's how we shot it.'

Alf and Joan returned many times to watch the filming and joined the crew when they threw occasional parties at their hotel in Pickering. Simon Ward came to revel so much in the role of Herriot and in the North Riding countryside that he told Alf more than once that he would like to give up acting and become a Yorkshire vet, and Alf told him how good he was in the part.

Donald Sinclair, however, was less than enthusiastic about Anthony Hopkins's portrayal of his *alter ego*, Siegfried. Alf made the mistake of inviting Sinclair along one day to watch the filming, and he was not at all amused. For a start Hopkins was nothing like as tall as the long, gangling Sinclair, but Sinclair was particularly annoyed to see that Hopkins was playing the part as though he were an idiot or a maniac. Hopkins's performance is in fact described by his biographers Quentin Falk and Michael Feeney Callan – in their books *Too Good to Waste* and *Anthony Hopkins: In Darkness and Light* – as being merely 'crusty but benign' and 'gruff', but there are indeed moments when Hopkins is tetchy and manic and portrays Siegfried as being decidedly unstable, screeching wild-eyed and biting on his pipe. Simon Ward told both Falk and Callan that one Hopkins scene was the funniest he had ever been involved in – a classic.

'My favourite all-time scene,' he told Callan, 'is one in which he and I, as the vets, drive up to the wrong farm, ready to perform some gruesome operation on a pig or something. And as the old sweetie opens the door, Tony says, like a maniac, "Give me the carving knife! Let's start cutting!" I've seen that four hundred times and I still roar with laughter . . . it is a moment of classic comedy, the very greatest you'll see.' He commented to Falk: 'You actually got the feeling he was going to go in and chop up everyone in the house.'

During a break in the filming Sinclair approached Hopkins on the set and asked him why he was playing his character in that way. Hopkins told him that that was the way he had been told to play the part and that that was the way the script had been written. Later he told friends that he thought Sinclair was 'barking mad'. Simon Ward told me that he had himself been 'quite nervous' of meeting Donald Sinclair 'because I'd been warned that he was quite eccentric and also a man who was going to speak his mind. But I can't imagine why he objected to Tony's performance: I thought that Tony was absolutely lovely in the film, very funny, terribly amusing.' For most of the film Hopkins is indeed roguishly attractive as well as bloody-minded, inconsistent and exasperating but Sinclair was notoriously thin-skinned about his image.

'Alf and Donald Sinclair had an extraordinary relationship,' I was told by Alf's film and television agent John Rush, who handled his visual rights from 1972 until 1994. 'I was always convinced that Sinclair was the one person who made Alf nervous. When David Susskind was making that first feature film up in Yorkshire I got a call one day from Alf who said "We've got to stop the film, we've got to stop the film" and I said "We can't do that, we've sold the film rights." Alf had seen the screenplay and he said "You've got to come up," so I leapt on a train and met him at York. The whole problem was that in a scene that Alf had seen being shot the Donald character was helping in a kitchen and was wearing an apron. Alf said "Look, that man's never been in a kitchen in his life, he would *never* wear an apron. If he sees that in a film he will go absolutely berserk." Alf was terrified that Donald would be distressed by seeing himself in an apron. We talked to Susskind and there were revisions made. It's interesting how that really distressed Alf. There was always a servant/master relationship there which Alf never quite escaped from, in the sense that he was the junior partner who was taken in by the senior partner. It was deference. Thirsk was an old-fashioned world and that deference was still there.'

Sinclair was certainly furious to read the reviews when the film was released in Britain in May 1975. 'The eccentric bachelor . . . Siegfried's a bit of a trial, with his failure to keep accounts and aptness to suffer from hangovers,' reported Patrick Gibbs in the *Daily Telegraph*. 'Anthony Hopkins, chewing away at a pipe and gesticulating wildly, steadily works up the character of the excitable Siegfried . .' In the *Sunday Telegraph* Tom Hutchinson wrote that Hopkins's performance consisted of 'grunting on a pipe and occasionally letting off steam like an hysterical kettle'.

This was too much for Donald Sinclair. He had always been unhappy about the way that Alf had portrayed him in the books – which may explain why Alf dedicated the second book to him and his brother Brian with the

nervous and somewhat surprised line 'still my friends' –
but now he was being held up to public ridicule on
cinema screens all over the country. He threatened to sue
Alf for defamation of character. Hopkins heard later that
Sinclair had refused to let the matter drop and had taken
some sort of action against Alf, which surprised him
because the two men were meant to be such good
friends. Alf's great veterinary friend Denton Pette later
told Eddie Straiton that Alf had allegedly had to pay
Sinclair £250,000 to mollify him and prevent him suing
for libel. Dick Douglas-Boyd confirmed that there was
tension between Sinclair and the Wights. 'I heard that Alf
had real problems with Donald Sinclair,' said Douglas-
Boyd, 'and I know there was no love lost between Joan
and "Siegfried".' Simon Ward was also aware of friction
between Alf and Sinclair over Hopkins's performance. 'I
knew that was always a very dangerous area,' Ward told
me, 'but I liked Donald too. He was always very charming
to me.'

John Rush thought it was quite possible that Sinclair
might have threatened to sue Alf for libel. 'I know that Alf
was very generous to him and gave a percentage of his
income from all film and television exploitation to
Donald and his brother from the first film onwards,' Rush
told me. 'It was a sop that was never objected to by the
Sinclairs. Brian and Donald received a reasonable percentage, as did Alf's children, out of the films and television
series – not on the books – and subsequently Donald
didn't murmur at all about how he was portrayed. I don't
think it ever came to a situation where Alf made an actual
payment to the Sinclairs. I think that one day he went to

them and said "Look, you are portrayed and I think it
only reasonable that you receive a percentage." We paid
them from 1973 onwards. Certainly they shared all of the
television money.'

Sinclair's son-in-law Rupert Grey told me in 1997 that
Sinclair did make 'a verbal threat in the heat of the
moment' but that 'the threat was never put into writing
and never mentioned again. It was triggered by the
feature films rather than the books. The statement that Alf
Wight paid Donald Sinclair £250,000 to mollify him, or
indeed for any other reason, is fantasy. The arrangement
whereby Donald Sinclair accepted a modest percentage
on royalties from the films was unconnected with that
threat.'

Sinclair was never to be happy about the way Siegfried
was depicted on screen by any of the actors who played
the part, especially when Robert Hardy, in the later
television series, made him out to be a crusty, irascible,
contradictory, unpredictable boss. Right from the very
first book it had also rankled with Sinclair that Alf had
given him the name Siegfried. Sinclair's son Alan told
John Woodcock of the *Daily Mail* that his father had felt
that to be saddled with a Wagnerian name was almost as
bad as being accused of being a Nazi. Brian Sinclair had
never minded being called Tristan in the books, and
indeed had actually revelled in the notoriety, exploiting
his unexpected fame by going on speaking tours to talk
about Alf, Donald and the Thirsk practice. Neither did
Miss Marjorie Warner – the Sowerby woman on whom
Alf had based the character of Mrs Pumphrey, Tricki
Woo's doting mistress – mind that Alf had depicted her in

the books as a spoiled and silly widow with more money than sense. But Donald Sinclair was less thick-skinned. 'I think it hurt Dad all the more,' said his son. 'In a way Siegfried sold him short, and to be landed with a German name, too – that was a bit much for Father to take.' His father had mixed feelings about the books and what they led to, said Alan Sinclair. 'He accepted that Siegfried was a caricature of himself but overall the character wasn't my father. He certainly had a wild unpredictability but he was shy and more generous than the crusty, intolerant man of the books. Father, I think, would have wanted to be identified as more than the image portrayed. He was a very real person but the books didn't reach his humanity somehow. His caring side often went unnoticed. He worked for the Samaritans and on occasions when he heard of someone in financial distress, he would get my sister to send off the cheques so they wouldn't be linked to him.'

Alan's sister Janet Grey, however, admitted to the *Daily Mail* that both her parents had been strong-willed and didn't suffer fools gladly. 'They could be very critical and direct to the point of rudeness,' she said. And when Sinclair died in 1995 the *Daily Telegraph* obituary, though fair and affectionate, was forthright: Sinclair, it said, was 'refreshingly inconsistent and alarmingly direct'. It added, however: 'he was also a man of great warmth and independence of spirit'.

If it is indeed true that Sinclair threatened to sue Alf for libel and took £250,000 off him in the process, it is difficult to see how they could possibly have remained real friends. Jimmy Wight, however, insisted that they

were friends right to the end of their lives. His sister
Rosie agreed. 'They were friends for the best part of fifty
years,' she told the Newcastle Sunday Sun in 1997, 'and
their relationship wasn't simple. Donald was a difficult,
eccentric and demanding man, but he was never a tyrant.'
Rupert Grey concurred. 'Donald and Alf did not fall out
with each other,' he told me. 'They remained the closest
of friends until Alf died in 1995. As Donald often
remarked, he was incredibly fortunate to have both "such
a happy marriage and such a happy partnership". Alf and
Joan only invited fifteen people to the last wedding
anniversary they celebrated in the early 1990s. There were
only two couples invited other than family, one of which
was Donald and Audrey Sinclair. The same fifteen people
were the only persons invited to Alf's funeral service.'
Even so, it must have been a strange friendship, for even
when Alf was famous and much richer than Sinclair,
Sinclair still appears to have treated him with condescen-
sion and Alf seems to have continued to regard Sinclair as
being very much his superior. 'I met Donald at his fairly
grandish place in the early years and he was very lord-of-
the-manorish,' Tom McCormack told me. 'I almost
expected Alf to tug his forelock at certain stages. Donald
could be a crotchety hombre toward Alf. He had great
amour propre and there was the sense of Donald taking the
big chair in front of the fireplace and the rest of us almost
sitting on stools around him. I did have the impression
that something of a show was being put on for us: the
Grand Man At Home with no muck up his fingernails at
all.'

Alf did indeed have great respect and admiration for

Sinclair. 'I can remember Donald telling me one day, "Alf, there is more to be learned up a cow's arse than in many an encyclopaedia",' he told the *Saturday Review* in 1986. He was in fact so nervous of Sinclair and his wrath that for the American edition of the third and fourth books – *All Things Bright and Beautiful* – he made McCormack tone down the character of Siegfried and dispense with some of his less attractive traits. McCormack begged him not to soften Siegfried's character and also made numerous suggestions for editorial changes. 'The truth is,' he wrote in a letter dated 5 March 1974, 'that the toned-down rewrite does lack a delicious liveliness that the *LSVL* [*Let Sleeping Vets Lie*] manuscript has. I think you can honestly tell your partner that the million American readers who have come to know him through *All Creatures* are immensely fond of him. Next to James and Helen he is easily the favorite character in the book. Surprisingly, his combustibility is a much more attractive thing than any blandness and sobriety that might replace it. It is, of course, a decision for you and him to make, but I'd urge strongly that the American edition be allowed to retain the lively and explosive Siegfried we've all grown so fond of.'

Alf was still having none of it. Sinclair had frightened him. On 17 March he replied to McCormack insisting that the Siegfried character had to be toned down. He admitted that the softer version was not as good as the original but said that Sinclair refused to accept that people could be fond of the character even though he had tried time and again to persuade him so. Sinclair was almost obsessive about the subject, said Alf, and had been angry even when a Los Angeles newspaper had described Siegfried as being 'rather daft'. Since Alf had to work with him every day it was vital that the portrait be softened.

'James has in fact been getting a hell of a lot of static from his partner who will no longer stand for what he thinks is the lampooning he gets in the guise of Siegfried,' McCormack wrote to Alf's American agent on April Fool's Day. 'So, all of the Siegfried episodes of *Let Sleeping Vets Lie* have been altered and indeed the printed version that appeared in England is different from the manuscript.' That same day McCormack wrote to Alf to thank him for agreeing to some of his suggestions for extensive cuts and editorial changes: the sequence of chapters was altered, as were many of the 'facts', and fifteen chapters were dropped altogether as being either not good enough or of little interest to American readers. McCormack added: 'I should give you absolute assurance that we will use the revised version of Siegfried throughout . . . We've also run through the manuscript and changed all the "boss" references to "partner" wherever appropriate.'

In 1997 McCormack told me: 'We changed things that demonstrated Sinclair as being more crotchety and blunderous than he wanted to be portrayed as. He and James evidently had some goddamned bad clashing moments about that. I said to James "Make him mild in the British edition but leave it as it is in our edition, because our editions have never been identical with yours anyhow." But James said "No no no, believe it or not, Donald has friends all over the United States and if *anything* appears in the States – bam – it's here within forty-eight hours."

There was something in the *San Francisco Chronicle* – seven or eight thousand miles away – and it was in Donald's mailbox within a matter of hours! And Donald wasn't digging it.'

It did not help at all that in November 1974 *The Smithsonian Magazine* published a photograph of Brian Sinclair wrongly captioned 'Siegfried' and describing him as Alf's assistant.

It is of course possible that Alf was simply becoming so immensely rich by the time of his dispute with Sinclair that he just decided to shrug off a quarter of a million pounds. Or maybe – given his feelings of inferiority – he even felt that Sinclair was justified in his complaint and that he *had* defamed him. Eighteen years later Alf was to make a revealing remark to Stephen Pile of the *Daily Telegraph* when he told him that he had always written about the distant past 'because the people are all dead now and they won't sue. I daren't go beyond 1950.'

Alf was certainly wealthy enough by now for his financial advisers to be urging him to go into tax exile. The Labour government of the 1970s had raised taxation to levels where a rich author could pay 83 per cent tax on income and 98 per cent on investment income – if he managed to build up any savings. Numerous British writers, from Graham Greene to Alistair Maclean, went into exile in France, Jersey, Guernsey, Ireland, Switzerland or Monaco in an attempt to keep a reasonable proportion of their hard-won earnings. Alf did at first seriously consider living in tax exile in Spain – he even started going to night classes to learn Spanish – and he and Joan made a brief foray to the Channel Islands, their first holiday for years, to see what they were like. In a letter to Tom McCormack two months earlier, in August 1974, Alf said that he would have to live wherever his accountants told him. But he was unimpressed by Jersey. They took a quick tour of the island and shook their heads. Joan turned to Alf. 'Give them the money,' she said. He returned to Yorkshire, shrugged his shoulders, and paid his taxes with a genial good grace. 'Although I'm harassed by fame,' he told Lailan Young of the *Sunday Times Magazine* in 1979, 'I'm willing to pay the price. I've only one stomach and there's a limit to what one can do with money. I'll stay here and pay my 83 per cent.' Over the next twenty years the vast amounts he paid in tax – many millions of pounds – must have funded several new hospitals and a couple of fighter planes. 'He said that if he left Yorkshire he wouldn't have been able to write a word,' said Victor Morrison.

Eddie Straiton told a different story, believing that Alf would have loved to have gone to live abroad in luxury if only he could have persuaded Joan to agree. 'Once we asked each other "What would you do if you won the football pools?"' Straiton told me. 'And Alf said "If I won the pools I'd like to go and live in Switzerland." I think he wanted to go and live abroad but he'd never dare mention it. When he started making money I thought he would start travelling the world a bit. They went eventually to Jamaica and Joan said "I'll never go there again, I couldn't go out in the streets without beggars following and begging" so they never went abroad again. He didn't spend his money at all.'

Tom McCormack was also disconcerted by Joan's

JAMES ALFRED WIGHT

Autumn Term 1933-34.   1st Year.

Animal Husbandry
Doing fairly well &
attends regularly,

Chemistry
Absent through accident or became
a I can say nothing so far

Biology
I think this lad has the making
of quite a good student

Spring Term 1933-34.   1st Year.

Animal Husbandry
50% at Xam

Chemistry
Has done fairly well, is pleasant
& works quite well with/to.

Biology
A good student, with results
very satisfactory

Summer Term 1933-34.   1st Year.

Animal Husbandry
Not so good this class
Xam.

Chemistry
Above marks held — is quite a
fair average, not likely to be brilliant
but I caused him to be steady.

Biology
This student did better at the
beginning of the Session than latterly.
At the Professional, he just
managed to scrape thro' in Biology

Autumn Term 1934-35.   2nd Year.

Junior Anatomy
a fair student. Good appearance & manner

Physiology &c.
Attendance irregular

Animal Husbandry
Quite good.

Spring Term 1934-35.   2nd Year.

Junior Anatomy
average result

Physiology &c.
Attendance fair; a good student
but inclined to be careless; exam
results, good, 54%

Animal Husbandry
Attends fairly well, but did very
poor Xam

Summer Term 1934-35.   2nd Year.

Junior Anatomy
Slightly worse than last term

Physiology &c.
Of pleasant manner and
capable but does not
sufficiently apply himself.

Animal Husbandry
Not too good 7th.

Autumn Term 1935-36.   3rd Year.

Junior Anatomy
fair in attendance

Physiology &c.
Capable and of excellent
promise, but a little unsteady
in application.

Animal Management
Not much better 7th.

Spring Term 1935-36.   3rd Year.

Animal Management
Not attending

Alf's first vet college reports. (DC144 Glasgow Veterinary College,
Glasgow University Archives and Business Records Centre)

The students and staff of Glasgow Veterinary College in 1945, a few years after Alf qualified. Professor Whitehouse is in the very centre of the front row. On his right are Professor Lindsay (arms folded), who taught hygiene, and Professor Emslie (wearing spectacles), who taught pathology. In the days of Alf Wight and Eddie Straiton no photographs were taken because few of the students in the 1930s could afford to buy them.

Alf's fellow student and lifelong friend Eddie Straiton (left) with the radio broadcaster Jimmy Young. Straiton became famous himself as 'the TV vet' in the 1960s and 1970s and as the vet on Young's radio programme.

The ivy-clad entrance to the old surgery in Thirsk, where Alf Wight worked from 1940 to 1989.
(Derry Brabbs)

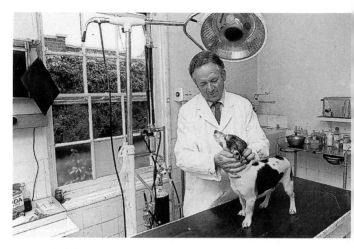

It had always been Alf's dream to work with dogs, cats and other small animals . . . *(The Press Agency (Yorkshire) Ltd)*

. . . but when he joined Donald Sinclair's practice in the market town of Thirsk in Yorkshire most of his work was with farm animals, especially pigs, cattle, horses . . . *(Daily Mail)*

. . . and sheep. *(Daily Mail)*

The real James Herriot, the Birmingham City goalkeeper whose name
Alf Wight borrowed in 1969. *(Colorsport)*

Tom McCormack of St Martin's Press, the New York publisher
responsible for Herriot's massive success in the USA.

Signing autographs in his office: though first and foremost a working vet, Alf always tried to find time for his readers. *(Ian Cook/Us Magazine-NYT)*

Alf with his wife Joan in June 1979 at the height of his fame – a year
after the start of the first television series – when he was feeling the strain
of his huge success and his American publisher, Tom McCormack, was
begging him to relax. *(The Press Agency (Yorkshire) Ltd)*

attitude towards Alf and his writing. 'She never talked much about his writing and certainly never bubbled about it at all,' he said. 'I did not get the impression of a sense of humour from this woman and you said to yourself "Gosh, that's tough." There was never any evidence at all of Joan's participation in his writing. She probably read the early books but did she read them all the way through? She never talked about it. I've been with spouses who will bubble about what their husband did in Chapter 8 – but I never had such a conversation with Joan.'

Even though Alf was by now a millionaire – Bantam had just agreed to pay $650,000 for the American paperback rights of *All Things Bright and Beautiful* – you could almost say that he was a reluctant millionaire. In September 1974 Seamus left home at last, at the age of thirty-one, to marry a twenty-seven-year-old doctor from Prestwich, near Manchester: Gillian Hind, an anaesthetist at the local hospital, who had studied at Cambridge with Rosie. Seamus's very close friend Rod Jenkinson was best man and Alf and Joan were at last free to think about selling Rowardennan, their family home in Sowerby. But instead of moving into a country mansion they built themselves for £28,000 a modest little two-bedroom bungalow in the shadow of Sutton Bank. Mire Beck, in the hamlet of Thirlby, just outside Thirsk, had five acres of hillside woodland beside a stream, and Alf and Joan moved in in 1977. 'When we went there we were surprised by how small the rooms were by American standards,' admitted Tom McCormack. 'They had started building the house when they still were unaware that there were going to be millions of pounds – *millions* – coming in. Over the years I paid him many many millions of dollars. At one period I was sending him a million dollars a year and in one year it was two million. James and Joan just didn't have a grasp on how much money there was and how it was going to continue and snowball. Most people who come into a lot of money later after having led a life of necessary frugality have to learn how to spend it. What is it for but to spend? He was clearing a lot of money by the mid-seventies – it was piling up – and it discomfited him to think that the kids were going to get all this money before he felt they were ready to handle it. He was not sure that this was such a great idea.' Perhaps because of Alf's own early poverty and struggles he was worried that his children might be spoiled by being too rich too soon.

The other explanation for the tiny house, of course, was that Alf was utterly without pretension. 'Being a vet is 99 per cent of my life,' he told Lailan Young. 'I'm a little country vet.' So he continued to drag himself out of bed in the early dark hours to drive for miles in his orange Peugeot across the Dales, with his beloved dogs Hector and Dan, to tend to ewes and bulls and budgerigars, and he continued to work for six or seven days a week. He did briefly splash out by spending £184 on a new hi-fi stereo system – hardly an extravagance for a man who loved music so much – but that trip to the Channel Islands just after Seamus's wedding in 1974 was in fact the first proper holiday that he and Joan had had for three years. They did not, however, go in the height of the warm summer season. They waited until the cheaper out-of-season month of October.

'I'm going on exactly as before,' he told me while he was staying in Jersey, 'and I still only write in my spare time.' He aimed to write a page every night: 'At that rate a book magically appeared about every eighteen months,' he told Lailan Young.

'I'm a vet, and it's very satisfying,' he said to me, 'and I'm fifty-eight, so it'd be silly to change my whole life pattern. The only thing the success has done is to give me security. I made a modest living as a country vet but I don't do anything now that I didn't do before. I haven't bought anything I wouldn't have done. I can't see the point. I like my work and taking the dogs for a walk, drinking a pint of beer with friends, and I don't like high living or high society or expensive things.' He also believed that if he concentrated full-time on writing it might ruin his style. 'I feel that if I stopped it all now and just sat tapping a typewriter all day – at which I'd make a hundred times the money – the effect on me would be bad,' he told Alex Harvey of the *Sun* in 1978. 'I might go to seed and my writing would probably lose its impact. I am lucky that all this has happened to me late in life, when I am already fixed in my ways. If I had been much younger or was just starting as a vet I might have lived an entirely different life and not been nearly as happy.' He gave Harvey a third good reason for not changing his life. 'The great charm of animals is that they don't let you down the way people do,' he said with unusual sourness. 'They don't cheat on you. It is such a contrast to modern living, which is a cut-throat business. The more I look at animals the more faults I see in people.'

Even so Anthea Joseph was disappointed by his decision to continue working as a vet and not become a full-time writer. It was, he said later, the only time in their long relationship that they had a serious disagreement. He had not changed even his weird working pattern and was still writing in front of the television – 'nothing important like football or music,' he told Paul Vallely of the *Sunday Telegraph Magazine* in 1981, 'but if there's one of those plays on, that'll do. It helps when writing if I have my mind half on something else.'

He told me with a chuckle: 'I drive people mad by saying that I write in front of the television but I do, in the bosom of my family. I can take in the television and converse with people and write at the same time, perhaps because I really do the writing in my head as I'm driving on my rounds. It's a lonely life as a country vet: you spend most of it alone in a car, so I think about what I'm going to write that night.'

For some reason he was still keeping up the pretence that he did not write a diary. 'I've never kept a diary,' he fibbed, 'but my wife and my partner and I have joked so often about what happened in the old days that it is all still very vivid. I've also been pretty cunning: when most people write their memoirs they put it all in one book, but each of my books is about just one year of my life and so far I'm only up to 1940. I've got yards of material. As long as they want it I can keep going.' He was being devious: the books were never his 'memoirs', and in 1940 he had not been about to enter his fourth year as a vet but had in fact only just been joining the practice. Despite his huge success he seemed to think it was still necessary to pretend that his books were autobiography rather than fiction, and perhaps he was right to do so: it is certainly possible that they would have been less successful, particularly in America, if his readers had suspected that they were mainly fiction. Who would fly across the Atlantic to visit a fictional town and shake the hand of a fictional country vet? Part of the appeal of characters like James Herriot and Sherlock Holmes – certainly in America – is that so many readers are convinced that the character is a real person. Even today letters arrive regularly in London addressed to Sherlock Holmes Esq at the non-existent '221b Baker Street', and doubtless they will long continue to arrive in Yorkshire addressed to 'James Herriot' in 'Darrowby'.

I asked Alf why he thought his books were so successful in America: his answer was that the Americans liked them because they were so different from their own high-powered, frenetic city lives. Certainly the fourth book, *Vet in Harness*, which came out in Britain – along with the Pan paperback edition of *Let Sleeping Vets Lie* – just after Alf and Joan returned from Jersey in October 1974, was as leisurely, homely and charming as ever, with lyrical descriptions of the Yorkshire countryside that must have made any inhabitant of Manhattan or Minneapolis yearn to sniff the northern air and stride across the moors. He wrote of the old Dales farmers who started coming to the vets' surgery for their own ailments because they did not think the local doctors were any good. He told of a kitten that was raised by a pig; of a pig that had to be bribed with digestive biscuits before it would allow itself to be examined; of the strangely silent dog that was heard to bark only once in its whole life, a single, excited *woof* when its brother won the local sheepdog trials. And he also told a delightful story about a mongrel dog treated with a new drug that suddenly made it irresistible to all the other local dogs, which became convinced by its delicious odour that it had turned into a bitch: packs of lovesick hounds started following the unfortunate mongrel everywhere, much to its alarm. The book also introduced the ebullient, life-loving character of Granville Bennett, the brilliant small-animal vet who was always leading young Herriot astray by persuading him to drink far too much and who was based on Alf's great friend Denton Pette.

On his way home from Jersey to Thirsk Alf stopped off in London to help to publicise the latest book. 'He didn't like coming down to London,' said Dick Douglas-Boyd. 'He would come for publication and I'd take him round the bookshops for signing sessions. He quite liked that, meeting his readers, and he was very good at it. He was a very great success when I took him back to Scotland for signing sessions. He enjoyed meeting his public, like a lot of them do. "These are the people who are reading my books," he would say.' He also still had an abiding love for Glasgow. 'He was very much a Scot,' Victor Morrison told me.

In Glasgow Alf would drop in to see his mother, Hannah. For many years he, Joan and the children spent every Christmas with her but now for her it was like Christmas every day. She was euphoric with happiness and revelling in her son's incredible success. She could barely contain her pride. 'Everybody knew Mrs Wight,

especially when Alf became famous,' said her Anniesland
Road neighbour Jean Schreiber. 'Oh, she was very proud
of Alf's success as a writer. She talked about it on buses, in
shops, and everywhere. She'd say to strangers "*I* am James
Herriot's mother." Once when I was going into town and
I was at the back of the bus and she was at the front of the
bus I could hear her telling people, and this happened
quite often. Some people didn't believe her. Once she
was in a shop with Alf's wife, Joan, looking at some
dresses and she started to tell someone that this was James
Herriot's wife, and Joan was creeping about so that
nobody could see her! Old Mrs Wight was very proud of
Alf and she had every right to be. They must have made
tremendous sacrifices to send him to school and college.
She had a little niche in the corner of her big drawing
room where she kept photos of Alf and all his books and
pictures. She was quite well off in later years, quite
comfortable, though she didn't suddenly seem better off
after he wrote the books. She still went into town by bus.
For holidays she went to visit her niece, who she said had
an estate somewhere, but she was a bit imaginative.'

Almost everyone who met him in these years remarked
how modest and unassuming Alf was. Three days after
Christmas 1974 he wrote a humble letter of thanks to
Tom McCormack telling him that he owed his entire
success to him. In 1975 he won an American award 'for
services to the veterinary world' but told the benefactors
that he was far too busy as a vet to fly to the US to receive
it, so they travelled to Yorkshire instead to give it to him.
He revelled quietly in some aspects of his fame and told
Lailan Young with typical openness: 'I enjoy the luxury of

staying, for instance, in the Beverly Hills Hotel, where no expense was spared, and seeing the famous stars in the Polo Lounge, or staying in a suite at Claridge's. It's exciting.' What other famous star, as he undoubtedly was by now, would admit publicly that he was excited by staying in an expensive hotel and gawping at other famous stars? And he could hardly contain himself when he received a fan letter from one of his own greatest heroes, the legendary Yorkshire and England batsman Sir Len Hutton. One of Alf's stories in *Vet in Harness* was about a hilarious rough-and-ready village cricket match held in a field full of sheep, an event that he described with such affection and humour that Hutton wrote to congratulate him. The great man was probably especially amused that one of the characters in the story, an old fag-smoking batsman with baggy grey trousers held up by braces, was also called Len.

Diana Mackay joined Michael Joseph in 1973 and was rights director from 1975 but although she met Alf several times 'he wasn't the most memorable person. He was always very quiet.' But far from being the simple little country vet, as he liked to pretend, 'he modelled himself on some great writers and he was a very well-read man', according to Douglas-Boyd. Alan Brooke, who was editorial director of Michael Joseph from 1974, agreed: 'He pretended to be a simple countryman, but in fact he was very intelligent and very well read. He was a very gentle man, so polite and charming that one never knew the inner Alf.' Alf himself told Caroline Moorehead of the *Daily Telegraph* revealingly: 'I make myself as colourless as possible. I'm the Damon Runyon character on Broadway, the guy who lives around.' He was talking about the way he portrayed himself in the books but he could just as well have been referring to how he played himself in real life.

'Alf was always delightful, charming, smiling,' said Victor Morrison. 'I never saw a down side, though when he was working as a vet there must have been occasions when he was irritated beyond measure by hundreds of people turning up with their books held out for him to sign them. But I think the way he managed to remain a professional vet was wonderful. A quite remarkable man. He was a wonderful raconteur with this quiet way of telling a story. He was a very appreciative person, very charming. Women liked him very much.' Susan Hill, the British novelist, playwright and critic, agreed. She had met Alf when they had appeared together on a radio programme in 1973. 'He was a lovely man, delightful,' she said. 'He liked women and was incredibly sweet to me, incredibly *respectful.*'

One of Alf's most charming traits was that he wrote people the most flattering letters. A couple that he wrote to me were so outrageously complimentary that for a terrible moment I wondered whether they could possibly be sincere. But of course they were, because he was such a nice man. Alf was in fact so selfless and obliging that in the summer of 1975, when Tom and Sandra McCormack travelled up to Thirsk to spend the day with the Wights, Alf entertained them splendidly without even hinting that he would much rather be watching the Wimbledon men's tennis final, which was being televised that very afternoon. 'James and Joan were wonderful,' McCormack recalled ruefully. 'We got in the car and drove around and did the sightseeing bit, and at the end of the day my son, Sandra, James and I hiked up this rather sharp hill while Joan stayed in the car park down the bottom. Then we were coming back down – it's 4.30 in the afternoon – and Joan comes to the edge of the car park and shouts up "Arthur Ashe won!" My goddamn life passed before my eyes when I realised what we'd done: James loved tennis and he watched it all the time and here this goddamned boorish American calls up and says "We're coming up", totally oblivious of the fact that it was the day of the Wimbledon final, which you *know* that he really would have loved to have seen. But he didn't say a bloody word, he just took us out.'

Alf was proud to be elected an honorary member of the British Veterinary Association that year, but he had started to become deeply irritated by the way some people treated him now that he was A Celebrity. 'Fame didn't change him a bit,' said his old Thirsk friend and neighbour Mrs Heulwen Campbell. 'Alf was always so unassuming. I remember he was attending some animals in a field and a bus full of people came by and they knew who he was and were all pointing and he hated it. He hated people pointing.' As he himself told Caroline Moorehead of the *Daily Telegraph*: 'If a farmer calls me to a sick animal he couldn't care less if I were George Bernard Shaw. If we discuss anything at all other than work it's the fortunes of the Sunderland Football Club.' For all his fame and fortune he liked nothing better than driving out across the Yorkshire Dales with his beloved dogs – Hector the Jack Russell terrier gazing through the windscreen and Dan the black labrador lying beside him on the front passenger seat. Nothing else gave him quite the same pleasure as when he opened the car door on some high moor and let them trot ahead of him across the Yorkshire countryside.

Now and then, though, Alf would let his hair down and revel in the unaccustomed pleasures of his new life, at times almost as though he were a boozy, carefree, football-mad veterinary student again. One year Anthea Joseph, Dick Douglas-Boyd and his wife June took Alf and Joan to the Imperial Hotel, Torquay, where Alf was to be the main guest speaker at the Booksellers' Association conference. Alf noticed that he was expected to make his speech on the day of the FA Cup Final and agreed to go to the conference only after Mrs Joseph promised that he would be left undisturbed in his room with a colour television set to watch the match before he spoke. She was almost as baffled by the request as she had been by Alf's decision to continue to work as a vet instead of becoming a full-time writer. She knew so little about football that she was under the impression that the match was to be played not in London but in Leeds. Alf had become very fond of her by now and thought her ignorance both hilarious and charming.

'At the Imperial that night my wife taught Alf to dance some of the modern dances,' Douglas-Boyd told me, 'and I introduced him to Lowenbrau. He'd never had this strong beer and he had rather too many! After his speech they had a discotheque in the hotel night club and we went down and he had a few Lowenbrau and he was dancing round the room, letting his hair down, marvellous. He liked booze a lot. He could have been a heavy drinker but he wasn't.' In one of Alf's letters to Tom McCormack he wrote that although he knew he ought to hate all the adulation, he was in fact revelling in it.

The vast amounts of money pouring into his bank account by now must have come as a huge relief after years of never quite having enough. In an interview with Peter Lewis of the *Daily Mail* in 1976 Alf said: 'Assistant vets make less than dustmen – about £50 a week. If I hadn't written the books I'd have been right on my uppers.' But eventually there came a time when he began to fear that all this success might be beginning to corrupt him. His wee Scottish conscience started to trouble him, especially after he found himself basking in the praise and laughter of gatherings where he had to make speeches. Dick Douglas-Boyd noticed a huge difference between the diffident Alf when the first two or three books were published and the confident performer that he became when he was a huge bestseller. 'There was one great thing that indicated to me just what Alf was,' Douglas-Boyd told me. 'When he had published just two books I took him up to Newcastle-on-Tyne and he spoke to the booksellers there and he used stories from his book – about approaching a bull from the wrong end, all that sort of story – and they laughed and clapped and they liked it. Years later, in the late seventies, when he spoke that day at the Booksellers' Association Conference in the Imperial Hotel in Torquay, his timing was different – he'd learned how to pace it – and everyone roared out and at the end they all stood and cheered and clapped him because it was a brilliant humorous speech. I met him afterwards and took him off the stage and said "Alf, that was *marvellous*. Remember what it was like in Newcastle all those years ago? You've timed it perfectly. It's absolutely lovely now." And he said – and this is what I've always remembered – he said [in a rich Scots brogue] "Aye, Dick, it's a heady brew and I'm giving it up." He said "It's dangerous, it's bad for my self-esteem. All this input from the public." He never spoke again to my knowledge. "Aye, Dick," he said, "it's a heady *brooo*. And I'm giving it up." That's lovely, isn't it? That indicates the sort of man he was. He knew what he could *do*, but it was not what he wanted to do.'

Alf's confidence now was such that he realised he was no longer beholden to anyone and could do precisely what he wanted. 'I tried to get him to write about his childhood,' said Alan Brooke, 'and he said he would but he never did.' It is in fact extraordinary how little Alf wrote in his books about his early years. He never mentioned Yoker School even once, Hillhead is dismissed in a couple of sentences and never referred to by name, and even his years at Glasgow Veterinary College are covered sparingly. It is almost as though he wanted his readers to believe that he hardly existed until he joined the practice in Thirsk, when he was twenty-four. Such huge omissions could hardly be due to shyness or to a belief in his right to privacy since his books were all supposed to be almost entirely autobiographical. So why the heavy silence about his early years? It seems decidedly odd until you remember that because he had fictionalised the dates in his books any further discussion of his early years would soon have revealed that the dates were all wrong, that since he did not join Sinclair in 1937 but 1940 the books were not about the 1930s at all, and that consequently much else in them was probably not true either.

*

The late 1970s brought Alf great happiness. In 1975 he became an honorary member of the British Veterinary Association; in March of that year he became a grand-father when Rosie gave birth to a girl, Emma, in the Princess Margaret Hospital in Swindon; and once he and Joan had moved into the new bungalow in Thirlby, Mire Beck, his daily routine was invariable and brought him great pleasure.

He would rise at seven o'clock, switch on the radio, and drink two pints of tea while listening to the *Today* programme on BBC Radio 4. He would eat just a piece of toast for breakfast, feed the ducks on his garden pond, then Hector and Dan would scamper ahead of him to jump into the car. He would play a tape of classical music – Mahler's eighth symphony, perhaps – while he drove the four miles into Thirsk to join Donald Sinclair and Seamus in the surgery, where by now the practice had all the latest smart equipment he had dreamed of as a student so long ago, from the operating theatre to the X-ray machine.

In the surgery the telephone would ring almost every minute with calls from worried clients and he would try to check his post and appointments and be out of the building by ten o'clock, driving out into the hills and around the farms where he was needed, always taking the dogs. By one o'clock, after a frugal breakfast and such an energetic morning, he would be starving and would try to be home for lunch with Joan, who would feed him a huge meal of beef and Yorkshire pudding or a simple dish of mince and potatoes before sending him off to bed for his afternoon rest. Later he would be back in the surgery treating small animals, as he had always dreamed of doing. The balance of veterinary work, even in the Yorkshire Dales, had shifted from horses and cows to dogs and cats, and about half of the work in the practice was now with small animals.

Later still he might be out and about again, visiting farms and customers in their homes. Besides the dogs, another constant companion was the radio, particularly when Alf was out in the car. He loved listening to music, especially violin music and tuneful composers like Mozart and Scarlatti, and he always regretted that he had no time to go to concerts: one of his most fervent dreams was to hear the Hallé Orchestra play. He would get an obsession about a particular piece of music and would play it again and again until he was heartily fed up with it. As well as music he would listen to many of the local news programmes, to the Test match commentaries in the summer and football reports in the winter, and on Saturdays he loved tuning in to *Sports Report* on Radio 2.

Alf would go out walking as often as possible with his staunch boyhood friend Alex Taylor, who had now retired from his job as a civil engineer and moved with his wife Lynne to Yorkshire, to the nearby village of Ampleforth, to be near Alf. And when Alf was out and about on his calls he would take every opportunity to stop the car, let the dogs out and have a long walk in the bracing Yorkshire air. He had always kept dogs and once confessed that he was 'soppy' and sentimental about them – the Irish red setter he had had as a boy in Glasgow, the bright little mongrel, the beagle, the Jack Russell, the black labrador. These were the moments of each day that he loved the most – one man and his dogs alone in the high, clean Yorkshire countryside.

In the evenings, while he and Joan drank a couple of gin and tonics, he would glance at all the fan mail that Joan had read and sorted for him during the day. Then they would have supper in front of the television and watch favourite programmes – about soccer, perhaps, or showjumping – and series like *The Professionals*. Or they would read quietly before he went out for one last walk before bed, climbing the nearby hill with the dogs and listening to the ducks and the noises of the night. This was a man in love with life and nature and in glorious harmony with the universe.

One afternoon a week, as usual, he and Joan would drive over to Harrogate for lunch, tea and the cinema. On Saturdays he would watch sport on television and whenever Sunderland had a home fixture he would drive the fifty miles north to watch the game at Roker Park, just yards away from the little house where he had been born. It must have given him a special pleasure to return so often to his roots, to feel so much part of that warm, working-class society from which he had sprung. When Sunderland Football Club hit a bad financial patch he invested a six-figure sum in the club yet refused to accept free director's seats and insisted still on paying for the family's season tickets to the ground. 'In later years,' said Jimmy Steele, 'there was a group of us who always met for lunch in the Royal Restaurant in Glasgow before football matches at Hampden, or in London at the Regent Palace Hotel in Piccadilly when we went down for matches at Wembley.' On Sundays Alf would listen to *Gardeners' Question Time* on Radio 4, even though by now he had little time to do much gardening himself and had to pay others to look after his five acres.

But the 1970s brought him several deep sadnesses as well. It became increasingly obvious that Rosie's marriage to Chris Page was unhappy and only two years after the wedding she had already decided to petition for divorce. On 8 November 1976, after a court hearing before Judge Chapman at the Castle in York, Rosie was granted a Darlington County Court divorce after just three years of marriage on the grounds of her husband's unreasonable behaviour.

Early in 1997 Chris Page, now aged fifty-one and remarried, was still a company director and still living near Swindon, in the village of Wanborough. He owned two tiny companies – Cord Power Parts Ltd and Cord Power Parts (North) Ltd – but unhappily his main business, Consumer Promotions Corporation, had gone into receivership six months earlier with an estimated deficiency of £192,388, of which £105,504 was owed to trade creditors and £24,714 to employees, with further employee claims of £18,726. Page, whose business ventures have included a joke shop and a scratch-card company, would not discuss his business affairs with me but he was surprisingly open about the breakdown of his marriage. 'I was useless as a husband,' he told me. 'I take 90 per cent of the blame. And Rosie was a very Yorkshire girl and wanted to live in Yorkshire.'

Page seems to have been fond of his ex-father-in-law. 'Alf was a very nice guy,' he said, 'but whenever he came here he just sat in the corner and said nothing. He was completely dominated by his wife. I never saw eye to eye with the lady. She was always too domineering for me. I tried to avoid her. Even our daughter's name, Emma, came from Joan. But no, she didn't destroy my marriage: I destroyed that.'

Alf and Joan, who had now been married themselves for thirty-four years, were shocked and upset, and Joan was heard to remark that she hoped Rosie would never marry again because she might catch AIDS if she did. 'Alf asked me if Rosie could borrow my house in Majorca to get over the divorce,' said Straiton. There were a couple of consolations: a month before Rosie's divorce Seamus's wife Gillian gave birth to their first child, Nicholas, in the maternity hospital at Northallerton; and after Rosie had spent a year in New Zealand licking her wounds she returned with three-year-old Emma to Thirsk. Several years later Alf and Joan had a house built for her on land they owned right beside their own house in Thirlby. Rosie became one of the village doctors and with Jimmy still working in the veterinary practice and living in Sowerby, the family was all together once again. Before too long Rosie was happy again with her new boyfriend Richard Whiteley, the Yorkshire Television presenter who was for many years the front man for the afternoon quiz show *Countdown*, who became for two or three years a co-opted member of the family and who often joined them on Sunday nights for family meals out. 'They were a terribly close family,' Whiteley told me, 'and Alf and Joan were devoted to each other and very happy. She was much more sophisticated than him: she used to smoke those gold-coloured Sobranie cigarettes. Alf was the nicest man I've ever interviewed but he was annoyingly modest and self-effacing. I wanted to take him by the neck and shake him and say "Don't you realise how much pleasure you've given to millions?" I remember he told me once that he'd got soft, lady's hands, which was very good for a vet. Rosie and I eventually fell out over something silly. I wish we hadn't. She's a lovely person.'

Finally, to round off the sadnesses of that decade, both Alf's dogs, Hector and Dan, died. For a while he could not bear to replace them, although he knew that that would be the best way to overcome his grief, and for the first time in decades he did not have a dog to walk across the moors.

Alf was himself beginning to run out of steam. For how much longer could he be expected to write another book every year? It had all become too much. Throughout the 1970s the Herriot books rolled off the printing presses in an endless stream and the Herriot bandwagon had started to career out of control. *Vet in Harness* went into paperback in 1975 and was published in a second omnibus edition in America (along with *Let Sleeping Vets Lie*) under the title *All Things Bright and Beautiful* – the first line of the Cecil Frances Alexander hymn. It went on to sell 250,000 in hardback, two million in paperback and nearly three million as a *Reader's Digest* condensed book. In July that year Pan presented Alf with four of their Golden Pan awards in recognition of the fact that every one of his first four books had now sold more than a million copies in paperback in Britain alone – even *Vet in Harness*, which had only just been published in paperback. In 1975 too Michael Joseph followed the example of St Martin's Press and published the first two Herriot books and three chapters of the third in a combined omnibus edition, also entitled *All Creatures Great and Small*, which was published in paperback by Pan in 1976. The fifth book, *Vets Might Fly* – which purported to be about Alf's days in the RAF during the Second World War, but which consisted mainly of flashbacks to his veterinary life in Yorkshire – was published in 1976.

Also in 1976 a second *Reader's Digest*-sponsored feature film, based on the second Herriot book and also entitled *It Shouldn't Happen to a Vet*, was released. Simon Ward was again offered the lead but declined because the fee was no higher than that for the first film, so this time John Alderton played James Herriot, Colin Blakely was Siegfried and Lisa Harrow – who had already played Helen in the first film, *All Creatures Great and Small* – was once again James's wife. The film was again produced by David Susskind, directed by Eric Till, and this time the surgery, Skeldale House, which had been played by a house in Pickering for the first film, was an old house on the corner of the village green in Reeth in Swaledale, just west of Richmond. The screenplay was written by Alan Plater, and once again Donald Sinclair was unhappy about the portrayal of Siegfried. Colin Blakely played the part, according to Tom Hutchinson in the *Sunday Telegraph*, 'with an expression so implacably fierce it could stun a bull'.

John Alderton was far and away the best of the three actors who portrayed Alf on screen, with a boyish but twinkly British charm that managed to make him appear shy and gauche without ever being wet or pathetic. Twenty years on Blakely's portrayal of Siegfried does not seem at all 'implacably fierce' but rather serious, honest, warm and highly professional. It seems extraordinary that Sinclair could have taken any exception at all to Blakely's performance, which was utterly subdued by comparison with that of Tony Hopkins in the previous film and barely eccentric at all. It looks as if all Sinclair's complaints and threats had had their effect.

Today the film still seems quite delightful: engagingly English, endearing and very funny. It is also quite different from the book, in that James and Helen's first baby is born before the Second World War, not in the middle of it, and the ending is affectingly sombre as the Herriots listen to Neville Chamberlain's 1939 radio speech announcing that he has failed to secure peace with Hitler and that consequently Britain is at war with Germany.

'I first met Alf halfway through the filming because I didn't want to meet him too soon,' John Alderton told me in 1997, echoing Simon Ward's wariness about playing a living character. 'To play somebody who is still alive is an extraordinary thing. I didn't know quite what he was like and I didn't want to meet him until I had created my impression of the script and sorted myself out with the character. I knew he was a small guy from Scotland, which is not the best casting for a tall guy from Yorkshire [Alderton came from Hull]. Everybody who met Alf was just totally enchanted. He was such an unassuming guy and so modest about what he did, unaffected by it all, completely untouched. It was delightful to meet someone who was so unchanged from what he was when he was an eighteen-year-old student. And Joan seemed the perfect partner for him – I'm sure they were very much in love – and Rosie adored him.

'I was a bit nervous of meeting him – as he was a bit nervous of meeting me – but we got on so well because he'd lived in Yorkshire all his life and he had the common touch with people. He kept himself out of the filming, he popped in just now and again. He was a bit shy of being where the film unit was because he felt that people were watching to see how he was reacting. He was always astonished that we were making a film about him and perplexed that other people found it so fascinating when he was writing about the ordinary stuff of life. He touched obviously a spot which opened up into that area of the environment and birds and all those things which maybe society's general consciousness was just ready for. There was something quite *collective* about what happened to his writings. There must have been other vets who had thought of writing about country life and animals but they never sparked or took off like Alf did. Maybe it was because of his common touch, his clever eye, his humour – he always had a twinkle in his eye – and he had that facility in his writing where you say "Oh *yes*, I recognise that: I *know* that, I've *seen* that"; but you haven't quite.'

Like John Rush and Tom McCormack, Alderton was

surprised by Alf's subservient attitude towards Donald Sinclair. 'Sinclair threw a party for us,' remembered Alderton, 'and I was looking around the room and couldn't believe my eyes when I saw Alf put a ham sandwich in his pocket. A minute later the sandwiches came round and he took another and surreptitiously put it in his pocket again. So I had to ask him what this was about. I said "Why do you steal ham sandwiches? I must know." And he said "When I first started in the practice I was a bit nervous of Donald – I'm still nervous of him, I'm still frightened of him, I'm still in awe of him – and Donald got the impression that I liked a particular type of York cured ham. I never disabused him of the idea because it was just a mistaken impression but he remembered this about me and always when I come he says 'Now I'll give you that ham, I know you like it.' And Alf said "I hate it, but I've never been able to tell him because it's gone on so long, so when we come here I have to slip it into my pocket and I go outside and throw it to the sheep." '

Alderton chortled. 'And there was this wonderful picture of Alf Wight, still the schoolboy, with the ham sandwiches, throwing them to the sheep, who seemed to be waiting for them. And he'd never been able to say "Actually, I don't like York cured ham." '

Why was Alf so frightened of Sinclair? 'I think there was always that feeling that he was the employee,' said Alderton, 'and he was always in awe of him. I suppose it's like if you meet somebody who was senior to you at school you will always feel inferior. You've been programmed.' It is highly revealing that Alf had just described himself to Peter Lewis as an 'assistant vet' despite the fact that he was meant to be Sinclair's partner and had had his nameplate up outside the surgery for thirty-five years.

Alderton remembered particularly one vivid anecdote Alf told him about his earliest days in the Thirsk practice that was so outrageous it could not be used in the film. 'Alf said he had anaesthetised this cat with chloroform and cotton wool inside a jam jar but the cat had a heart attack and died. He said that he'd learned at veterinary college that one way of kick-starting a heart is actually to swing the cat quickly by its tail – it sounds ridiculous but it can sometimes just shake the cat and start the heart again. Alf said "I went outside and swung this cat round by the tail and unfortunately I let go and this cat disappeared over the garden wall and I didn't know where it had gone and couldn't find it anywhere." A week later the guy who was living three doors down came in to see him and said "Mr Wight, I was in the garden the other day, reading the paper, and this cat jumped at me from the top of the tree and it hit me on the back of the neck and killed itself." And Alf said "Sometimes they do." But we never could use that story.'

Alf's sixth book, *Vet in a Spin*, another volume ostensibly about his RAF career but once again mainly about Yorkshire and animals, was published in 1977. In America it was published along with *Vets Might Fly* under the title *All Things Wise and Wonderful* – the third line of the Alexander hymn – which sold 435,000 in hardback and millions more in paperback and as a *Reader's Digest* condensed book. In 1978 Michael Joseph once again followed the American example and published a British omnibus volume of *All Things Wise and Wonderful*, which Alf dedicated to his dogs Hector and Dan. That too was published in paperback by Pan, the following year, 1979. Alf was number 1 on every American and British best-seller list and had little doubt about the reason: it was because he was a standard-bearer for older and more solid literary traditions than those of the 1970s. 'I think the success of my books may be a backlash against some writers who are trying so hard to be sexy, to find new deviations to interest readers,' he told *Maclean's* magazine in 1978. But he realised that even standard-bearers need to lay down their banners and rest now and then, and that it was time he took a breather. For a start he was beginning to run out of Alexander hymn lines to use as titles: soon he would be reduced to calling one of his books *Each Little Flower That Opens* or *Each Little Bird That Sings*. Enough was enough. It was time to take a break.

He could certainly afford to do so: on 31 January 1978 Tom McCormack wrote to say that he was about to send Alf a cheque for nearly a million dollars – and that was for just six months' royalties. Alf was still dreaming of giving up the veterinary series and writing a straight novel instead but this time McCormack dissuaded him, arguing that he ought to stick to what he could do best. Perhaps McCormack was hoping to encourage Alf to put more effort into the veterinary books, which he was beginning to feel uneasily were nowadays not nearly as good as the first two had been. McCormack had long been Alf's main editor – 'Anthea Joseph was very good in that she gave him support and warmth,' he said, 'but editing, no' – and he had begun to spot signs of weakness in Alf's fifth and sixth books. Some American reviewers, too, had started to mutter that the stories were becoming threadbare. 'Early on he did not need much help with his writing,' McCormack told me, 'but in later years, yes. He was not at the height of his powers all his life and I guess he had other sorts of distractions of many kinds later in his life. You could see sometimes that the focus was not as tightly drawn as it was in the first couple of books, where he was miraculous.' McCormack found himself increasingly having to suggest editorial changes. Now and then he even rewrote or added sentences that Alf would accept or reject as he chose. 'Occasionally in the later books James lost a total firmness of grip,' McCormack told me, 'certainly by the time he wrote *All Things Wise and Wonderful*, books five and six. By then I found myself going through the writing and saying "Look, how about this?" or "How about that?" He was always, always, *always* a pleasure to read, and better than anyone else trying the same sort of thing, but he was not as good as the very early James Herriot. Yes, he *did* take some editing but so did Dickens. It doesn't diminish the man's greatness.'

After publishing six books in seven years, Alf was not to write another book for four years. He was written out and exhausted and he wanted more time to be with the family and to indulge his lifelong love of reading – not fiction any more but biographies and history. In the article he wrote for the Christmas 1979 catalogue for Kroch's and Brentano's bookstore in Chicago he said that if he ever had to give up every activity except one he would choose to read. When the Literary Guild in America excitedly invited him to New York to be the star guest at its huge fiftieth anniversary dinner/dance at the Waldorf Hotel, and offered him two free return tickets on Concorde and a free weekend anywhere in America, he declined, explaining that he was on duty in the surgery that weekend and his partner was depending on him.

And yet it was now, just as he started to ease up and relax his punishing writing schedule, that his books were about to be given the biggest boost of all. In August 1977 the BBC began to film the television series that was to have its first broadcast in January 1978 and would make James Herriot a household name not just in Britain and America but all around the world. They called it, of course, *All Creatures Great and Small*.

CHAPTER TWELVE

Timothy, Tim and the TV Series

THE BBC TELEVISION SERIES of the Herriot stories was destined to make James Herriot internationally famous even in remote *kampongs* in South-East Asia and distant mud huts in the wilds of Africa. The two cinema films had not done especially well, perhaps because the Herriot stories were too gentle and episodic for a cinema audience that was growing increasingly accustomed to explicit scenes of violence and pornography, but the TV series was light, gentle family entertainment and it soon became compulsory viewing for millions. The programmes did not, however, make Alf as much money as they might have done. 'He made the big mistake of selling the film rights for the first forty-one programmes of *All Creatures Great and Small* – the ones that made the most money – to an American, David Susskind, who then made a fortune out of them,' said Eddie Straiton, who was hired as veterinary adviser for all the rehearsal and studio work on the first forty-one episodes and whose hands were often to appear on screen – along with those of the series' other veterinary adviser, Jack Watkinson – when it was necessary to show skilful veterinary work close up. But the series gave such a boost to the sales of the books that as the wealth cascaded in during the 1980s Alf became a multimillionaire. After the election in 1979 of Margaret Thatcher's Conservative government, which reduced income tax rates dramatically, he was able for the rest of his life to keep more than half of his vast earnings.

'We tried before the feature film to persuade Yorkshire Television to make a series,' John Rush told me, 'but they wouldn't and subsequently the BBC took it. We were never overexcited by the very first film – Simon Ward was not the best Herriot – and none of us thought the first two films were brilliant. They weren't the right vehicle for Alf's kind of work, which is very episodic. I always saw his books as having television serial potential, not feature film potential. Alf was almost a reluctant seller of the film and television rights. The feature films were not a huge success in my view, whereas the television series was, but none of them made Alf much money. He made his money from the books. David Susskind had a financial interest in the first series – he had acquired the right to produce the spin-off series – and Susskind had a co-production with the BBC on the first two TV series but then he just let the BBC get on with it. Afterwards the BBC secured the right to make subsequent series. But people do not make a fortune from the television rights in a work. Of course Alf got a decent up-front sum and repeat sums and overseas sales. Sure, they were substantial, but it was not the sort of money that he made out of his books.'

It was John Alderton, the star of the second feature film, who finally managed to persuade Alf to let the BBC make the television series. 'The BBC asked me to try and get the television rights,' Alderton told me, 'but Alf didn't want to sell them. I went up to Yorkshire with a BBC man to talk to him and we had a tremendously long and wonderful liquid evening in which Alf in his cups agreed that the BBC could do it. But eventually for some reason I couldn't do it after all – I can't remember why, I may have been into something else – but I know that Chris Timothy [who did eventually play the part] was sticking pins into a model of me saying "turn it down, John, turn it down". I know that he thought he was next in line for the part if I didn't do it, but I think Alf was a bit pissed off that I turned it down. I think he understood that I was going to do it and he was not too impressed with the fact that I backed out of it.'

When Alderton decided not to play the part again it was then offered to Richard Beckinsale, the charming young British actor who had been immensely popular in the British TV series *Porridge* and *Rising Damp*. It was not until Beckinsale declined as well that the part went instead to the unknown thirty-three-year-old Christopher Timothy. Robert Hardy played Siegfried, Peter Davison was Tristan and Carol Drinkwater was Helen, and the series was produced by Bill Sellars, who said that he first realised that the Herriot books were naturals for television when he picked up one of the paperbacks at a railway station bookstall. The books were adapted for the series by Ted Rhodes, who became a friend of Alf's and went on to edit two more series. Filming took place mainly amid the stunning scenery of Swaledale and Wensleydale, where 'Darrowby' was played by the picturesque little village of Askrigg, which even in 1996 still seemed to be caught in a nineteenth-century timewarp, with a bull-baiting ring set into the cobbles of the marketplace. Cringley House, opposite the market cross, became Skeldale House and the King's Arms was turned into the Drovers' Arms of the books. James and Helen's TV wedding took place in the village church at Wensley, while the famous introduction to every episode, when James and Siegfried are seen laughing as they drive over a little bridge at Langthwaite and through a ford, was filmed in Arkengarthdale.

It was in the little village of Reeth, home to the Skeldale House of the second Herriot film, that Alf first met Christopher Timothy and Robert Hardy in the first week of filming. Timothy and Hardy (whose first name, by strange coincidence, was Timothy, so that he was 'Tim' to his friends) were shooting one of the stories Alf had told in *It Shouldn't Happen to a Vet* – about the gipsy, Mr Myatt, and his sick pony – but rain had stopped filming for the time being and Hardy and Timothy were sheltering in a lane and going through their lines. Timothy, wearing a woman's plastic see-through rain hat, suddenly felt a hand on his shoulder and a Glaswegian voice said softly: 'I am your *alter ego*.' It was Alf, who said later that Timothy played the part exactly right throughout the series. Timothy had in fact prepared for the part before filming by staying in Leyburn with Jack Watkinson and by going out with him on his rounds to see every side of a vet's life. Alf said later that he was highly impressed by the way that Timothy had captured perfectly the essence of the nervous young city boy trying to be a vet in the wilds of Yorkshire. The two men were later to meet occasionally in Thirsk in later years. 'He poured the meanest glass of whisky,' said Timothy.

Alf also paid tribute to Robert Hardy as well as to Carol Drinkwater and Peter Davison, saying that they too had all got their characters absolutely right, a remark that probably infuriated Joan, who said more than once that Carol Drinkwater's portrayal of her made her look 'too much of a slut' and that she much preferred the way Lisa Harrow – 'more elegant and ladylike' – had played the part in the films.

Donald Sinclair, of course, disagreed violently with Alf, hating the way that Hardy portrayed Siegfried as a rude, selfish, impatient, bad-tempered curmudgeon. Luckily for Alf, Sinclair liked Hardy personally and they became such friends that in later years Hardy often came to stay with him in Yorkshire; otherwise he might have been tempted to issue another threat of a libel writ.

The actors were dissuaded once again from meeting their real-life *alter egos* until after they had established their characters and started filming. Robert Hardy told me that he took his portrayal of Siegfried entirely from the books. 'One or two people who knew Donald quite well said I was like him,' said Hardy, 'but I got a fearsome amount of flak from him and we quarrelled about it from time to time. His wife, Audrey, thought that I was ludicrously unpleasant, and he said "I don't mind what you do, it's Audrey who can't bear it." When I pointed out that he had now been played by several actors he said "Yes, and you're the worst of the lot." It was useless to try to persuade them that people abso- lutely loved the extraordinarily unpredictable, explosive

Siegfried, and I toned it down later.

'Some people found Donald unpleasant. He could be downright rude and he was to me once: he said "Come to lunch, some people would like to meet you", but halfway through lunch he opened up on me with all guns blazing. But otherwise I found him great fun and genuinely eccentric. He was absolutely sweet to me – I think we had horses in common – and I was fascinated by him. We had many happy hours together – I was observing him like mad – and the most revealing moment was when I took Peter Davison to meet him and suddenly there was a thundering of hooves and Donald and his horse came straight over the iron railings. "What the devil are you doing here?" he yelled. That was absolutely Donald. One of the most percipient phrases in Alf's books was when he described Siegfried taking him to a pub and wrote "Siegfried was at his most ducal." That was Donald.'

Alf's son Jimmy told John Woodcock of the *Daily Mail* in 1995, after both Alf and Sinclair had died, that he thought Sinclair was well portrayed by Hardy 'because he could be abrupt, rude even, as well as utterly charming, especially to the ladies. Hardy was aware of Donald's disapproval and tackled him about it one day. He asked him who he would have liked to have played him. Donald replied "Oh, Rex Harrison, someone with manners." '

Alf's old Glasgow Veterinary College friend Jimmy Steele also disagreed with Alf about the casting for the series. 'I didn't think the casting of Alf was good,' Steele told me. 'Christopher Timothy was a shackly [untidy] sort of guy and Alf was always tidy. And *physically* he wasn't like Alf, either. Alf was upstanding and had a finer figure than he had. A *presence*. But that chap had no presence.'

Carol Drinkwater, who was twenty-six when filming started, was terrified by her first encounter with Joan at a dinner organised by Bill Sellars during her first week of playing the part. 'Joan looked like a tartar to me at the time,' she told me at her home in the South of France in 1997. 'I'd hardly sat down at the table when Joan opened up her handbag and drew out a photograph of herself when she was twenty-eight and pushed it across the table – like she was going "Snap!" with a pack of cards – and said "*That*'s who you're playing. *That*'s who I am." It was like a challenge to me, like "You'd better live up to something." I thought "My God, this is terrifying." In fact I got to love and like her very much indeed but at that first meeting I felt really inadequate. There is the story of course that the character of Helen wasn't based on Joan at all.'

Really? On whom, then? Nan Elliot, perhaps?

'I don't know. Maybe Helen's a bit of several women. But maybe that's why Joan was so challenging – she knew Helen wasn't based on her. Alf was very much more quiet and charming. I very much felt that Joan was the power. He was absolutely adamant that he didn't want to get involved in the making of the series – he said he was busy enough doing his writing and his practice – and in the beginning he didn't seem all that pleased that it was being made. At first he was rather reticent about it, but as it became so popular and he became a real cult figure, a national hero, he couldn't help feel some sense of pride.

'Alf was very charismatic because he had a wonderful

sense of humour and he was a natural storyteller. He told us the same stories after dinner after several whiskies that were in the books – and that we'd *filmed* – and we still laughed. We went to their bungalow in Thirlby for dinner in 1978 and a lot of whisky was drunk and everyone was getting talkative, and on that occasion I felt that the balance in the relationship was different because although Joan was powerful in the sense of being challenging, when he actually got going and started telling his stories and talking he was very much the centre of the universe. Alf loved a drink or two. I found him rather loquacious. Yes, he was shy, but once settled in company where he felt secure he was witty and loquacious and flirtatious – but flirtatious only in the sense of being appreciative.

'Joan was very much the sterner of the two and the more responsible of the two. Alf liked to let go, to play. And he had an extraordinary twinkle in his eye. He liked women. I wouldn't say he was a womaniser, because that has a particular tone about it, but he appreciated good-looking women, maybe all women.'

Carol Drinkwater believed that Joan eventually approved of the way she played Helen: 'Several years later Joan told another woman "I'm very flattered and honoured that I've got somebody as lovely as Carol playing me" so I thought "Oh, I'm vindicated. It's all right."'

She was horrified to hear that Joan had described her performance as sluttish. '*Sluttish*? She didn't say that to me. Wow! I don't think that my rendering of Helen was at all sluttish. I'm rather hurt that she said that. I'm very proud of the programme and my part in it. It's classic television.'

Other writers produced the scripts for the series and Alf 'absolutely refused to have anything to do with the programmes', said Eddie Straiton. 'He never became close with any of the actors – he didn't choose them or anything – and he never came on set. He was lucky that I got involved with the first forty-one programmes because I was able to supply all the old-fashioned veterinary equipment.'

Most of the animals that appeared in the series – whose owners were each paid £25 by the BBC – genuinely needed treatment for the complaint that was being depicted on screen, and Straiton and his partner Alex Talbot often operated in earnest on the animal immediately after filming, either in the studio or outside in Straiton's mobile surgery van. 'I was a kind of veterinary stuntman doing the real doctoring,' Straiton told Mileva Ross of the *Sunday Mirror* in 1980. 'You may see a close-up of my hands on the screen, but clever camera work and editing make it look as though Christopher and Robert are really doing the surgery. That very professional surgical stitching you see them doing never actually touches the animal. They are sewing pieces of material skilfully prepared by the make-up girls to blend with the animal's natural colouring.' Straiton was surprised to discover that Timothy, Hardy and Davison were such professional actors that 'they could all pass for real vets. I've seen Christopher show real courage in situations that would scare off many professionals.' On one occasion Timothy boldly tamed a vicious wildcat by grabbing it firmly, and Hardy – who kept his own horses, a whippet and even a polecat – seemed to have a special rapport with animals. It was not all acting on the screen, by any means.

There was a brief crisis when Christopher Timothy broke his leg in a car crash just before Christmas, temporarily interrupting filming, but the first of the forty-five-minute television programmes – the first of a thirteen-part series directed by Christopher Baker and Terence Dudley – was still broadcast on schedule in Britain on the evening of Sunday 8 January 1978. It immediately became compulsive weekly viewing for half the country. For not only were the programmes about lots of cute animals (always a British weakness) but they also had an old-fashioned, leisurely charm, humour and gentle nostalgia – something essentially *English* – that was becoming increasingly rare on television. They made clean, cosy, wholesome family viewing and were so hugely popular that the BBC was to broadcast forty-one episodes in the next five years. It seemed the public could never have enough of them. The series was indeed so cosy that there was uproar in the British press when Christopher Timothy, a married man and father of six children, had an affair with Carol Drinkwater and moved in briefly with her. Even though she was not the cause of the break-up of his marriage, since he had already left his wife eight months previously, 'the publicity was terrible,' Carol Drinkwater told me. 'There was so much bad feeling towards me that I was nervous of going back on set at all.' She and Timothy had made the mistake of tarnishing the immaculate, idyllic Herriot image. 'Alf was upset about that,' John Rush told me. 'He disapproved of adultery.'

Even when the programmes had all been repeated the BBC issued expensive videos of some of the episodes and sold piles of them. Looking at them again in 1996, however, it was difficult to believe that they would be anything like as successful had they been launched on the world twenty years later, since some of the acting now seems gauche and stilted and the whole atmosphere is cloyingly sentimental. It is not difficult to see why Donald Sinclair objected to Robert Hardy's over-the-top portrayal of him, for Hardy's pink, chubby Siegfried was loud and patronising. Christopher Timothy's Herriot was decidedly gormless, making the young vet out to be a wet, overobliging prat. Carol Drinkwater – who left the part after three series 'because the BBC didn't want in any way to expand the role' and was replaced by Lynda Bellingham – was certainly sexy as Helen but she came over as a hefty girl, not like the real Joan at all. Many modern viewers might well consider some of the episodes to be embarrassingly awful: for example 'Sleeping Partners' (transmitted on 26 March 1978), in which James and Helen are on honeymoon and go tuberculin-testing and James is made to look absurd when he has to wear a ridiculous 'calving suit'. The acting in this episode was stilted and melodramatic and the extended 'joke' allowed to go on for far too long. Carol Drinkwater as the ripe, mumsy new bride was big, luscious and fruity, but Christopher Timothy was awkward and clumsy and Robert Hardy mannered and pompous. Yet nothing could stop the series becoming vastly popular and it is pointless to criticise it.

'The movies were flops in the USA,' said Tom McCormack, 'and the TV series was remarkably slow-paced for this country. They'd take an eight-page chapter and stretch it out over the three-quarters of an hour, so it never got on one of the major networks here. But it did get people going in to buy a book who hadn't bought a book in a year.'

Alf was by now so famous that everything he did made news and even things he did not do appeared in print. False stories were spread about him, as they are about anyone in the public eye. In October 1978, for instance, *The Observer* reported that he had been approached in a shop in Thirsk by a cigar-smoking American film director who asked if anyone could tell him where James Herriot lived. Certainly, said Alf: he knew the writer very well and would be happy to show the stranger the house, and he is said to have led the director and film crew up a hill to a large stone house where he pointed out a room in which he said he knew for a fact that the Herriot books had been written. As he left the film people to knock on the door of the empty house he declined the director's grateful offer of a £1 note, said *The Observer*.

It is a most unlikely story. Firstly, any American film director looking for James Herriot would have known by then exactly what Alf looked like. Secondly, keen though Alf may have been to protect his privacy and to keep secret where he really lived, he would never have been cruel enough to have played a trick like that on a group of people who were only doing their job. It is indicative of the accuracy of the piece that *The Observer* seemed for some reason to think that Thirsk was called Borrowby.

Fame became such a burden for Alf that Tom McCormack began to feel 'a slight pang' of guilt for having made him famous, though he consoled himself by remembering that when they had first met over lunch at the Connaught in 1972 he had warned Alf that fame was not necessarily all it was cracked up to be but Alf had laughed that he would "lap it up". 'He did lap it up for about two years,' McCormack told me, 'but then it became more and more oppressive and one of the results was that over the years he looked less and less happy. I wondered indeed if this success that I played a part in had eroded his life in some fashion. He wouldn't be the first man to have said "I've never been so happy as I was in the old days." You get to the point where every time the phone rings you're praying it's not for you.'

Alf became so reclusive by the end of the 1970s that 'he actually turned down the opportunity to be on the cover of *Time* magazine,' said McCormack incredulously. 'He just wasn't going to sit for the portrait! *Time* magazine! I told him about John Cheever, a wonderful writer, who only ever had a number 1 bestseller – even though it wasn't his best book – when he appeared on the cover of *Time* magazine. But James wasn't interested. He was number 1 already. He turned down national network television people from the United States even when they said "We'll send teams of people up there, he doesn't have to move." As he became more famous, journalists would turn up year after year and expect to be taken by him on his rounds and it became a pain in the ass. And he knew he didn't need it.'

In fact McCormack understood Alf's reaction very well and never tried to bully him into doing things he did not want to do, no matter how advantageous they would have been commercially. McCormack obviously suffered more than just 'a slight pang' of guilt because in June 1979 he wrote Alf a heartfelt letter begging him to relax. 'I know you're writing a new book,' wrote McCormack. 'I'm delighted, but the crucial thing in my mind is what it has been these past few years: I want you to enjoy what you're doing, I want you to do it at your own pace and for your own pleasure, not ours. I'm haunted by the thought of how much stress and pressure and unrelenting petition has crowded into your life like a scavenging horde of camp-followers, crushing out much of the joy that should be the real pay-off for what you've achieved. You've done, for all the people that live off you, all that can be asked; from here on you must do what you want to do and only when you want to do it.'

*

Apart from the making and broadcasting of the TV series, with which Alf was barely involved at all, these years of the late 1970s were fallow ones for him. He and Joan even managed to get away to Crete for a holiday in October 1978. Two months later he was given the OBE for services to literature and in February he, Joan, Seamus and Rosie travelled to London to collect the medal from Prince Charles, who told him that he much enjoyed watching the television series and asked him how he had managed to drag himself away from Thirsk during the lambing season. The Queen, too, was a Herriot fan: she once invited Alf to one of her Buckingham Palace dinners and told him that she loved his books and that they had made her laugh aloud. The honour delighted Alf, as did another later in the year when Edinburgh's appropriately named Heriot Watt University made him an Honorary Doctor of Literature. But after writing *Vet in a Spin* in 1976 he produced no more new books for four years and allowed himself to watch television once again, for the first time in years, without tapping away on the typewriter at the same time. This did not mean, of course, that there were no more new James Herriot books. Far from it. By now the Herriot industry was in full swing and his publishers were beginning to produce books that were cobbled together from the others. In 1978 Alan Brooke suggested to Alf that they should put together *James Herriot's Yorkshire*, a lavishly illustrated guide to the Dales and moors with striking landscape pictures by the young freelance photographer Derry Brabbs, who was to go on later to illustrate similar books by the English fell-walker A. Wainwright. Alf was unsure about the new project. 'Do you think it will sell any copies at all?' he asked doubtfully.

'He was terribly modest about it,' Brooke told me. 'He thought it was a very bad idea and wouldn't sell.' It was in fact a brilliant commercial idea and went on to sell more than a million copies in Britain alone. Victor Morrison remembered that it was at first suggested that the distinguished photographer Fay Godwin should be commissioned to work with Alf on the book but that Alf greeted the suggestion 'with horror. Fay was a very nice person but very serious,' said Morrison. 'The *Radio Times* had once sent her to photograph him and he thought the photos were rather sad and gloomy, so he said no to her and we came up with Derry, who was very good with Alf.'

In fact *James Herriot's Yorkshire* turned out to be a very odd production – a bitty scrapbook album in which Alf seemed to be more confused than ever as to what was fact and what was fiction. Even though the book was meant to be non-fiction he referred time and again to Siegfried, Tristan and Helen when in fact he was writing directly about their real-life *alter egos*, Donald, Brian and Joan. He also recycled stories that were blatantly untrue, like the hoary old one about how he had been in Scarborough with the RAF in 1943 when Jimmy was born and went absent without leave to see Joan and the baby in Thirsk. It was almost as though he no longer knew who he was and was facing an identity crisis. Was he Alf? Was he James? What had been true and what had not? Despite the beautiful photographs, Alf's contributions to the book were little more than captions and much of the material was recycled from the earlier books. He seemed merely to be going through the motions and could not really bring himself to work closely with Derry Brabbs. 'It wasn't done intimately,' Brabbs told me. 'He'd write a chapter and then I'd go off and illustrate it. Then we'd edit it on a slide projector, but that's all we did together.' Alf faced the book's publication, however, with his usual genial good humour. When he first saw the cover, which shows him standing on a snowy hillside and holding a walking stick in an unfortunate position, he remarked: 'Good God, it looks as though I'm holding my cock!'

Not long after the publication of *James Herriot's Yorkshire* the book publishing arm of *Reader's Digest* magazine approached Michael Joseph and persuaded the company to let them put together *The Best of James Herriot*, a beautifully illustrated compendium of his stories with additional photographs and articles about Yorkshire life and history. The book, which was eventually published in 1982, was edited by Jenny Dereham of Michael Joseph, who had succeeded Anthea Joseph as Alf's British editor. She went up to Yorkshire and stayed with Alf while he was choosing his favourite episodes to include in the book.

Thousands of other people started trekking up to Yorkshire too in those years. The television series brought a flood of Herriot fans to Thirsk, especially from America and Japan, and both Richmond and Hambleton District Councils started enticing visitors to the area by renaming it Herriot Country. It was estimated before long that tourism in the area had increased by 45 per cent and that Alf and the series had been responsible for the creation of three thousand new jobs in the Yorkshire Dales. Not everyone was happy about this invasion: some locals complained about the crowded streets, the TV vans, the new gift shops with their Herriot knick-knacks and souvenirs; and some muttered that it weren't right for t' telly to keep showing Yorkshire farming folk who seemed to be soft in t' head. The majority, though, seemed to be grateful for the extra business as the hordes of tourists crowded the streets of Thirsk and Askrigg and clattered across Thirsk's cobbled marketplace to stare at the surgery in Kirkgate, hoping for a glimpse of 'James', 'Siegfried' and 'Tristan', despite the fact that the real Tristan, Brian Sinclair, had left many years earlier after just six years in the practice. Coaches arrived in convoy to clutter the narrow streets. Cameras clicked at anything that moved. An average of fifty people – and sometimes more than a hundred – queued every day outside the surgery, holding books for Alf to sign. And if he happened to be there that day he always did sign them. 'It was incredible,' Seamus told Fergus Kelly of *Today* in 1992. 'One American just marched in with a camcorder and went through the whole house, straight into the surgery while my father was operating on an animal. But most of the Americans are lovely and very generous. We have collection boxes for animal charities in the waiting room and they often used to stick £50 notes in them.'

Despite the constant demands on his time and tolerance Alf always had a smile and a kind word for his fans. They went away with their eyes glowing. Who would believe it, back home in Kansas or Kentucky? They had met the real James Herriot. They had shaken his hand, the hand that wrote the books, the same little 'lady's hand' that had been inside all those cows and mares. And he had looked right into their eyes and had smiled at them. No wonder they went home and spread the word. No wonder Alf's reputation grew. What other bestselling author would be so approachable and go to so much trouble to make his readers happy? Very few indeed, if any at all. Alf was unique. Alf actually *liked* his readers. And they in turn loved him.

Occasionally, however, all the adulation was too much for him. 'He told me once,' said Alan Brooke, 'that he often used to be approached in his garden by people asking for James Herriot and if he didn't want to talk to them he would pretend to be the gardener, saying that James Herriot was out.'

Nor was he always quite as self-effacing and unassuming as he seemed. Now that he had become such a huge success he was beginning to realise his true value and he was no longer prepared to be underestimated or treated unfairly. He even began to exhibit a steeliness that until now had been well hidden. 'James changed a little bit over the years, very understandably,' Tom McCormack told me, 'and one of the ways in which he changed was because his life was well and truly screwed up by this intrusion that fame brought him. One time we were up there with him out on the patio having afternoon tea at about 4.30, a perfect June or July day, watching the ducks, and by God this car comes rolling up to the bottom of the drive and out get these people, with their cameras around their necks. James got up out of his seat and said "more damned Americans" and he rushed down the driveway to stop them and turned them away. He came back and said "Australians." But it gummed his life up. This was an angry man running down that driveway to shoo people away.'

There is, however, something baffling about Alf's apparent desire for privacy: if he really wanted to keep his fans from turning up at his front door, why did he include his full address under his entry in *Who's Who*? There it is, year after year, until he died: Mire Beck, Thirlby, Thirsk, Yorkshire, YO7 2DJ. He might just as well have placed an advertisement in every American newspaper.

On another visit to Thirsk, in 1980, McCormack was astonished to find that Alf had actually developed a dictatorial streak. 'I want the emphasis of whatever I say about him to be generally an appreciation not only for his *immense* talent but in those early years the appreciation of the man that he was,' said McCormack, 'but I think that in his later years he was so goddamn *crowded* by Americans, and his life was so obliterated, that something happened there. In his later years he became a bit autocratic. We were up there in 1980 and we all went out to dinner – all of the families, Jimmy and Gill and the kids and Rosie and the kid, Sandra and I and Daniel and Jessie – and during the course of the damn dinner James was at the head of the table. President Carter had declared that the US would not go to the Moscow Olympics because of the Afghan incursion and James was pronouncing that politics should never intrude on sport in any way. So I said to him "Look, James, suppose the Olympics was scheduled to be in Uganda and everyone would have to salute Idi Amin, who was one of those vicious madman killer leaders at the time, would you really wanna go and perform for Idi Amin right now, a man who eats people for breakfast? Imagine all of us going into that stadium in Uganda and tipping our flags to Idi Amin." And James said: "I declare this subject closed." *I – declare – this – subject – closed!* He was angry. He just stopped the discussion. He never would have done that years earlier. So I dropped it and we went on to other things.

'I tell you this because I want to help you get an accurate picture of a man who I thought was a very, very great writer. But it's important to me that people understand the multi-dimensionality of greatness, whoever the writer is. Even with James Joyce you've also got to realise what a pain in the ass he could be. In James Herriot's later years, as he was burdened with illness and worries that come with money – and he was so saddled with money considerations, tax considerations – and with people invading his life and everyone wanting a piece of him, he became more and more autocratic and his humour did not manifest itself as much.'

Dick Douglas-Boyd had a similar experience when he took Alf to Barnsley in June 1981 to address a literary dinner at which one of the other main speakers was the bestselling novelist Jeffrey Archer. 'I went to the organisers first and said I'd like to do some publicity for Alf,' Douglas-Boyd told me, 'but they said "Sorry, we're not allowing any posters or publicity material, this is a literary occasion." So I told Alf "no razzmatazz" but when we turned up there was a great big archway of Jeffrey Archer posters and Alf was furious. He said "What *is* this? You told me there would be no publicity for anyone." I said "That's what I was told." I went straight up to the manager and he said "I didn't do it, the publishers came in and they did it." I said "They can't do it" but they said "It's Jeffrey Archer and they just did it." That was the only one time when Alf and I had a flicker of disagreement.'

Douglas-Boyd's relationship with Joan Wight was much less smooth. 'Joan was rather different,' he said. 'She was aggressive when everyone was doing their utmost because they liked Alf, but she never gave praise, she'd never say "Isn't this nice?" Joan was *always* critical of *everything*: jackets, promotion.'

'She was definitely the boss in that marriage,' I was told by another Michael Joseph employee who asked not to be named. 'She was typical of many successful authors' wives, insisting that "he's not being treated properly". Alf was such a gentle person he allowed it to wash over him. He just wanted a quiet life.'

'She was the one who made sure that when they came up to London they stayed in the hotel just behind the Ritz, just off Dover Street, a small hotel, very expensive,' said Douglas-Boyd. 'She insisted. Joan was a very strong character. She was always there to make sure that he was treated as the top guest everywhere, and of his position when the photographs were taken.'

Because Alf himself was so modest and unassuming?

'Well, I don't know how *deeply* modest he was, actually,' said Douglas-Boyd. 'I'm sure he was aware of his own worth. Talking to him about writing indicated to me that he did reckon his writing quite highly. He was very confident that he was writing good English, expressing himself well, and had a good pace. He was quite conscious of that, even though he liked to disguise himself as a simple, jobbing hack. Because that was true too, I think, in a way. That's what made him such a good guy.'

*

Alf published only one brand-new book throughout the 1980s and Michael Joseph printed 289,000 copies of it. *The Lord God Made Them All*, his seventh volume, was published in 1981, four years after his previous book, *Vet in a Spin* – and then after that he was silent again for more than a decade.

The Lord God Made Them All, which was dedicated to his latest grandchild, Jimmy's daughter Zoe, showed serious signs that Alf's long rest had been bad for his writing. Tom McCormack found himself having to make numerous detailed suggestions for changes and improvements to the text, especially to give more bite to the pay-off lines at the end of each story. The first chapter is still hilarious: about the old rogue gate that keeps attacking young Herriot whenever he visits Mr Ripley's farm and about his attempts to castrate Mr Ripley's gigantic young bulls. So is the tale of Mr and Mrs Whithorn and their two spoiled, savage West Highland White dogs. There is also one genuinely moving story: the heartbreaking tale of Amber, the beautiful honey-coloured young bitch that develops a dread skin disease that spreads relentlessly and finally kills her despite everything that Herriot can do for her, including taking her home and cosseting her himself for weeks. And the book still offers evidence of Alf's sense of mischief: he called one of the Yorkshire farmers in it Robert Maxwell (after the crooked, litigious British newspaper tycoon) but avoided the threat of one of Maxwell's many libel writs by describing the character as being nice, dynamic, clever and highly principled. Not even Robert Maxwell could sue over that, however much he might have suspected that Alf had his tongue firmly wedged in his cheek.

But otherwise the book exhibits definite signs of strain and weariness. It reads as though Alf was really scraping the bottom of his memory. Too many of the stories are tired, dull and just peter out with no real denouement, too many are overweight with unnecessary padding and rather too many tell fond but dull little stories about Seamus and Rosie when they were small children. The book is also shapeless and confusingly disjointed, with constant irritating jerky flashbacks and flash-forwards. It starts in 1943 then chops and changes to 1951, 1961, 1947, 1945, 1961 again, 1947 again, 1963 and so on and on, ending finally in 1953. Throughout the book Alf kept interspersing not very interesting snippets from the amateurish diaries he had kept during his trips to Russia and Turkey in 1961 and 1963, an intrusive device that makes the reader restless. His style, too, had become careless and humdrum: a young veterinary student actually hangs his head in shame and Herriot himself not only shudders and slaps his brow when he makes a mistake but even hangs his head 'sheepishly' – though on second thoughts a vet would, I suppose. When the book eventually came out in Britain in paperback it seemed that even its publishers, Pan, had given up on it: it was so villainously proof-read that after a few pages I gave up counting the misprints.

The spark seemed to have gone out of Alf's writing. He was sixty-four now and beginning to wilt under the exhaustion of trying to be a bestselling writer and public speaker as well as a full-time vet. 'I've been on a treadmill,' he told me then. 'It's time to get off.' He vowed that that was it. He'd had enough. He had said what he wanted to say and would never write another book.

He still had the energy, however, to continue fibbing about his diaries. 'Diaries?' he said to William Greaves of the *Daily Mail*. 'I never kept a diary. You wouldn't have had any energy left at the end of a working day to keep anything.' This denial was particularly cheeky since the book he had just published, *The Lord God Made Them All*, was packed throughout with extracts from his 1961 and 1963 diaries.

Away from the adoring crowds of fans, the book launches, the signing sessions, the literary lunches and dinners, the public speaking, the honours – Liverpool University made him an Honorary Doctor of Veterinary Science in 1983 – Alf decided to cut back too on the amount of time he was going to devote to vetting in the 1980s. By now he had four grandchildren and he wanted to spend more time with them and the rest of his family. There were now five young vets working in the practice as well as Seamus, two of them women, so he was not needed at the surgery nearly as often as before even though Donald Sinclair was badly injured in an accident with a motorcyle in July 1981, breaking a leg and having to spend a month in hospital. There was also another good reason for Alf to start taking things more easily. 'Being a vet isn't as much fun as it was when I began,' he told Paul Vallely of the *Sunday Telegraph Magazine*. 'The old small farmers who lived at the ends of the Dales, cut off from modern society and its ways, were the real old characters. They still held to all the old superstitious cures. Science and modern methods have put an end to all that. Farms are bigger; the old men's sons are scientific chaps; antibiotics, steroids, and special hoists and crushes to immobilise the beasts while we examine them. No, it's not as much fun now.'

He certainly did not need to work for money, even though he told Vallely: 'People seem to think I'm a millionaire, but I'm not. I wrote six of the books under Mr Healey [the Labour Party Chancellor of the Exchequer] and paid 95 per cent tax on them. It has not made me enormously wealthy, but it has brought me financial security and I'm grateful for that.' It was another of his naughty little fibs, because he was in fact a multimillionaire. *The Lord God Made Them All* sold an astounding 585,000 copies in hardback in the USA alone, Bantam paid $3 million for the paperback rights and millions more copies were sold in the *Reader's Digest* edition. Despite having had to pay all that tax, when Alf died fourteen years later he was still to leave more than £5 million. It is however quite true to say that over the years he had been harried mercilessly by the Inland Revenue. 'His accountant had a terrible argument with the taxmen,' John Rush told me, 'because when the films and television series were going on Alf wanted to acquire a video recorder to see the material that was sent up but the taxmen would not allow it as a tax-deductible expense.'

He started to go into the surgery no more than two or three days a week and was able to spend much more time with the family and to walk even more in his beloved countryside. He also at last found a puppy to replace the much-mourned Hector and Dan: a Border terrier, Bodie, named after the character played by one of Joan's favourite actors, Lewis Collins, in the TV series *The Professionals*.

But Alf's life was not always as calm and idyllic as it seemed to be on the surface. 'What worries me,' he told the *Saturday Review* in 1986, 'is that people believe I have some secret of living – which of course I don't. Or that I am devoid of troubles or problems of any kind – which I am not.' The major problem that faced him at the end of 1980 was that his mother, who was by now eighty-nine, was suffering severely from cerebral arteriosclerosis and could no longer look after herself properly. 'She went wandering,' said her Anniesland Road neighbour Mrs Jean Schreiber. 'She used to wander out in the road in her dressing gown. I suppose now you'd say it was Alzheimer's.' Hannah was deeply confused and kept falling down but refused to be moved elsewhere. December and January were traumatic months for Alf as he kept having to drive to and from Glasgow on nightmarish winter roads to see her and to try to persuade her to go into an old people's home. The long journeys and the worry left him exhausted but eventually he was able to move her down to Yorkshire and into the Oval Nursing Home in his favourite town, elegant Harrogate, just twenty miles south of Thirsk. There he and Joan could visit her regularly whenever they made their half-day visits to the town and Alf was able to sell the house in Glasgow.

In 1981, too, Brian Sinclair became seriously ill. In July Alf himself had to be rushed into hospital in the middle of the night because of an agonising kidney stone and he was away from work for a month. Donald Sinclair was still on crutches after his accident and Rosie had to go into hospital for a cartilage operation. And then Alf's old friend Eddie Straiton fell out with him after Straiton found himself in trouble with the Royal College of Veterinary Surgeons – 'I hold the record of having been up before the disciplinary committee three times' – and Alf refused to appear at the hearing on his behalf.

On 30 September 1981, the day before his first wife Lorraine's funeral, Straiton – who claimed that because of his success some jealous people in the RCVS were 'always gunning' for him – was found guilty of 'disgraceful professional conduct' that was 'calculated to bring discredit on the profession and to undermine public confidence in it'. His offence had been to tell a fictitious joke on the *Jimmy Young Show* in January about how he had once had a race with some fellow vets to see who could spay a cat the quickest, and he was warned to behave himself in future. Two days later an editorial in the *Daily Mail* said of the disciplinary committee: 'What a silly and pompous way for grown-up professional men to behave. Are they simply jealous of the man who has done more than almost anyone else to popularise their way of life?' Straiton may have had the support of the national press, which reported the case at length, but he never fully forgave Alf for what he saw as a betrayal by one of his oldest friends, a man whose evidence at the hearing could have had the charge dismissed.

'Listen, I've got *nothing* but admiration for Alf,' Straiton told me, 'but he did let me down very badly. My son was killed when he was fourteen and my wife never got over it. She suffered serious depression, got brain cancer and fifteen years ago she died. While she was dying I got into trouble with the RCVS because I told a funny story on the Jimmy Young programme. I was due to appear before them on 29 September 1981 on this facetious charge but for three or four weeks beforehand I was sitting up every night with my wife. And the night before I had to go down in front of them my wife died.

'My solicitor had been very good: he'd got Robert Hardy, Peter Davison and Chris Timothy to go down and give me a character reference, and even the chief surgeon from Stafford, and he said to me "If you could get Alf

Wight to come down with you and say 'Now look, these stories that Eddie tells are just the same as my apocryphal stories', which they were, that would be a strong point in your favour." So I phoned Alf – and he said no. I said "Why, Alf? I don't understand. If the boot was on the other foot you must realise that I'd walk barefoot to London for you." He said "I'm not going." And the following week in the *Veterinary Record* I saw that he'd just been given an honorary Fellowship.' Alf was about to become an FRCVS – a fellow of the Royal College of Veterinary Surgeons. 'He was afraid he would lose the fellowship, or at least he did not want to upset the Establishment,' said Straiton. Alf's behaviour was in striking contrast to that of their old Glasgow Veterinary College friends Jimmy Steele and Aubrey Melville: Steele came down from Scotland to stay with Straiton for his wife's funeral and for several days afterwards and Melville attended Straiton's trial and defended him there by attacking the RCVS's Disciplinary Committee.

Yet according to Straiton, Alf was also capable of great kindness and generosity: 'When his great friend Denton Pette was desperate – he was on his uppers and had had a stroke – Alf secretly gave Eve Pette some money several times.'

On 7 December 1981, a few weeks after Eddie Straiton's disciplinary case, Alf's mother died in the Oval Nursing Home in Harrogate. She had suffered a coronary thrombosis as well as cerebral arteriosclerosis. Despite his sadness at her passing, Alf felt a sense of relief, for Hannah had just turned ninety and was no longer mentally capable. He confessed to Tom McCormack in a letter written in January that it was a pleasure to have been able to spend Christmas for a change in Yorkshire with Seamus, Rosie and the grandchildren. His mood in that letter was almost jocular and he told McCormack that he had been most amused that summer by a bed-and-breakfast advertisement in the local paper that had read: 'Excellent accommodation in Herriot country. No pets.'

When his father had died twenty-one years earlier Alf had described him on his death certificate as a shipbuilder's clerk (retired) but this time for some reason he described him on his mother's death certificate as a musician. It was Alf's final act of filial piety and loyalty to the memory of the parents who had struggled so hard and sacrificed so much to give him the best possible start in life.

CHAPTER THIRTEEN

The Mellow Years

THE TV SERIES *All Creatures Great and Small* had by the end of 1983 become such a British institution – with an estimated thirteen million regular viewers – that the BBC broadcast at Christmas a special full-length film as the final, farewell episode. But although the forty-one programmes that had been put out since January 1978 had covered every aspect of the Herriot books, television refused to loosen its grip on such a popular money-spinner. 'We exhausted the books very quickly, about halfway through the series,' John Rush told me, 'and then we came to an arrangement with the BBC where they would come up with storylines which Alf had a right to approve or disapprove. Alf was reluctant – he had to be persuaded each time, he thought there'd been enough – but the BBC were on a winner and all concerned thought it wasn't such a bad idea, so it went on. Alf would see the storylines, approve or disapprove, and then the BBC would commission the writers to write the scripts based on the storylines.' Other writers – Roger Davenport, Alfred Shaughnessy, Anthony Steven – were commissioned to concoct further adventures for Herriot & Co 'based on the books by James Herriot' which showed the vet in later life as an older man with children. In that way the series was kept alive until 1990 and Alf did not need to raise even his little finger for the money to keep pouring in.

He had done enough already. To date his books had sold about forty million copies and the TV series was being repeated on cable television in the USA. In 1984 *Moses the Kitten*, the first of his children's books to be cobbled together from stories he had already used in the adult books, was published and for the next seven years a new one came out every year in time for Christmas – from *Only One Woof* in 1985 to *Smudge, the Little Lost Lamb* in 1991, ending in 1992 with yet another compendium, *The James Herriot Storybook*, which was published in America as *James Herriot's Treasury for Children*. Yet another omnibus volume of selections from his work, *James Herriot's Dog Stories*, was packaged by Michael Joseph and published in 1986, to be followed in 1994 by *James Herriot's Cat Stories*. The books had acquired a momentum of their own. James Herriot had become an industry and had long ago outgrown Alf himself.

Alf had by now signed so many books and autographs that he contracted osteoarthritis and developed 'trigger finger', where his little finger was bent back permanently against his palm, and although he had an operation on it he could still hardly clench his right hand and Joan had to take over the chore of signing cheques. But still the Herriot fans – mainly Americans – descended in their thousands on Thirsk, expecting autographs. Throughout the summer of 1982 he had had a daily average of fifty admirers, with a high of sixty-three on one day, so instead of writing books in front of the television every evening he would slowly and painfully autograph bookplates that he then handed out to the fans. All he asked for in exchange was a small donation towards a local animal shelter that he was supporting. In 1984 the American summer invasion of Thirsk was bigger than ever. In a letter to Dick Douglas-Boyd in October Alf reported that there had been queues of as many as 150 fans outside the surgery every day and that although they were all nice people – and had all bought piles of his books – he confessed that it did become wearing by the end of the summer. Even so he tried not to forget how much he owed to his American fans. 'I'm all too pleased to see American visitors down at the surgery and to sign the books because they bought Baby new shoes,' he told *People* magazine in 1985.

Despite the wealth that was now cascading into his bank account his daily routine was as simple as it had always been. He and Bodie would go for a long walk every morning before returning to Mire Beck for lunch with Joan. 'I don't eat much meat,' he told *People* 'with a nod to his patients'. 'I prefer vegetables.' In the afternoons he would go walking again with Bodie, Rosie and her own dog, a yellow labrador called Polly, before settling down to read a biography or history (rarely fiction) or to listen to music or watch television. Whenever possible he tried to spend time with his four grandchildren. Even when he and Joan went on holiday it was all as low-key as ever. As usual they took their holiday that October at their simple little cottage in the hills of North Yorkshire, in the Cover Valley near Coverham. He still loved it there because, he told Douglas-Boyd, there was not another person to be seen. His craving for remoteness and solitude was as strong as ever.

His memory for dates, too, was as firmly unreliable as it had always been. In 1985 he was asked to write an article for the Hillhead High School centenary magazine in which he claimed that he had joined the old school in Cecil Street in 1927. In fact he had not joined until September 1928 and one wonders how he could possibly have forgotten. Nobody forgets the date of his first day at school and certainly not someone as sharp and intelligent as Alf. Or did he perhaps choose the incorrect date deliberately? So many millions of his readers were by now convinced that he had become a vet in Thirsk in 1937 that if he now admitted that he had not even started at Hillhead until the end of 1928 some of them might have begun to ask how on earth he had managed to go right through five years of high school and at least five years of veterinary college in just eight years.

Now that he was nearly seventy the shadows were beginning to lengthen across the twilight years of his life. In 1982 Anthea Joseph died of cancer and in 1983 Miss Marjorie Warner – the real woman from Sowerby on whom he had based the character of Tricki Woo's rich, doting mistress Mrs Pumphrey – died in Saltburn, Cleveland, aged eighty-six. Alf went to her funeral in Sowerby and later discovered that she was not in the end all that rich after all: she left just £90,270 to be shared among various charities, including two animal charities, and because she had always enjoyed a daily 10p flutter on the horses she also left £100 to the Injured Jockeys Fund. Miss Warner had been one of the very few real people depicted in the Herriot books to recognise herself and, like Brian Sinclair but unlike his brother Donald, she was only too delighted to have become part of the Herriot legend.

Alf was also depressed when Joan began to suffer from bronchitis, which was bad enough in March 1986 to make them cancel their acceptance of an invitation to one of the few London literary gatherings that they really enjoyed, Hatchard's bookshop's annual Authors of the Year party. He was cheered up a little when Dick Douglas-Boyd sent him a cutting of an amusing article that had appeared in *The Cricketer*. The article, 'Shakespeare on Cricket', by the Edinburgh classics professor E. Kerr Borthwick, was a clever and minutely researched spoof piece in which the author suggested tongue-in-cheek that Shakespeare must have been a great cricket fan himself four hundred years earlier. He gave dozens of examples to make it look as though the Bard had mentioned the game often in his plays, such as: 'I see you standing like greyhounds in the slips' (*Henry V*); 'Let me be umpire' and 'Give him a box' (*Henry VI Part I*). To add piquancy to the jest it is of course just possible that Shakespeare *did* know something about cricket since the game was being played in Guildford in Surrey at least as early as 1550, fourteen years before he was born. Alf wrote back to thank Douglas-Boyd for the article, saying that he thought it was brilliant and confessing that he had particularly appreciated it because he was feeling a bit depressed about Joan's condition.

After years of nagging by Rosie, who had long been telling her parents that they were 'stick-in-the-muds' because they never went anywhere different, Alf and Joan actually went on a cruise around Italy in 1987 – the first time in ten years that they had been on holiday anywhere except for the Yorkshire Dales or Scotland, where Alf's favourite regular holiday places were still Skye and Ardnamurchan. 'I love Scotland and we go back regularly,' he told me the following year, 'but I love North Yorkshire too.'

He was not always all that well himself in those years of the 1980s. Despite his virtual retirement he was still signing books and autographs, even though the pressures on him had caused such stress that it had brought on several angina attacks and he had had to have several electro-cardiogram tests. 'Alf's too kind and nice,' Joan told me. 'I try to protect him but he'll help anyone.' In February 1988 he also had to have a minor operation to remove stones in his bladder and kidneys and already he was suffering the early symptoms of the prostate cancer that was to kill him seven years later: he was finding it difficult and painful to urinate. Brian Sinclair, now seventy-two, was also in Leeds General Hospital after a serious operation; Donald Sinclair was seventy-six by now and obviously could not go on for ever; Sinclair's wife Audrey, now seventy-nine, was going blind; even Joan was almost seventy. Time was catching up with them all.

Even so after seven years of comparative idleness as a writer Alf broke his vow never to write another book. In 1987 the BBC approached him again, told him that there was a desperate shortage of decent family viewing on television and begged him to let them have some skeleton plots on which other scriptwriters could build a new TV

The wedding scene from the first film, *All Creatures Great and Small*,
in which Simon Ward played James Herriot and Lisa Harrow was James's
wife Helen . . . *(Ronald Grant Archive)*

. . . and Alf and Joan Wight watching the shooting of the scene, which
was in fact inaccurate since in reality, during the dark wartime days of 1941,
they did not have a white wedding at all but only a simple ceremony.
(Greenwood of Leeds)

From left to right: Donald Sinclair, Alf Wight and Brian Sinclair, with their *All Creatures Great and Small* movie *alter egos* standing behind them: Anthony Hopkins (Siegfried Farnon), Simon Ward (James Herriot) and Brian Stirner (Tristan Farnon). *(Daily Mail)*

Ward, Hopkins and extras on the set of that first film. *(Ronald Grant Archive)*

Alf and Joan with their screen counterparts John Alderton and Lisa Harrow, who starred in the 1976 film version of *It Shouldn't Happen to a Vet*. (EMI)

Alderton and Harrow pore over a copy of *The Veterinary Journal*. (Ronald Grant Archive)

After a hard day's work Alf often tapped away at the typewriter in the evenings – but usually in front of the television set. 'Alf had a drawer absolutely full of his stories,' said Dick Douglas-Boyd. The black labrador was his beloved pet Dan. *(The Press Agency (Yorkshire) Ltd)*

Left and opposite: The immensely successful BBC television series *All Creatures Great and Small* quickly established young actor Christopher Timothy in the role of James Herriot. Alf said later that Timothy played the part exactly right. *(BBC)*

Above: The 'real' James Herriot with a newborn calf. 'Delivering calves is the toughest job.' *(Ian Cook / Us Magazine-NYT)*

Left: The TV Herriot (Christopher Timothy) discusses tactics with new boss Siegfried Farnon (Robert Hardy) in the first ever episode of *All Creatures Great and Small*, which was transmitted on Sunday 8 January 1978. *(BBC/Ronald Grant Archive)*

Shaggy dog stories?
Tristan (played by Peter
Davison) attempts to treat
Mrs Farmer's (Madeline
Smith) dog in the episode
entitled 'Pride of Possession';
while James (Christopher
Timothy) cuddles Mrs
Pumphrey's pampered
Pekinese Tricki Woo.
(BBC/Ronald Grant Archive)

Alf Wight OBE: with daughter Rosie at Buckingham Palace in 1979 after collecting his medal. *(Express Newspapers)*

Alf's son Jimmy (pictured with his father in 1988) has followed very closely in his footsteps. Alf was immensely proud of both his children.

series. How could he resist such a plea? He started writing gently again, taking his time, but now using a word processor. 'It's fun and a challenge and it makes me feel I'm modern,' he told me when I went to see him in Thirsk and we lunched together at the Golden Fleece Hotel, 'and I'm enjoying writing again.' The great thing was that he could write at leisure. The pressure was off. He was still fit and spry but he was seventy-one and white-haired now and no one was going to hurry him. And afterwards he could also expand his skeleton plots into a new batch of stories that he could collect for another book. Why should he rush? He was going to enjoy himself and enjoy himself he did, doodling away on his computer – no longer in front of the television but in his sunny study overlooking the bluebell wood and the ducks on the stream at the back of the bungalow. He was to work on and off on the book for five more years until he was ready to let it go. It was published in 1992 under the title *Every Living Thing* and was the final Herriot chronicle.

'I'm the most part-time writer ever,' he told me over lunch in his soft voice with its gentle Scottish accent. 'I spend just the occasional hour at it. I couldn't work office hours. I'm still writing about the fifties: that's the place with the rosy glow. The end of the fifties was a grand time for me, with the children growing up. Writing's been fun and fulfilling but my deepest satisfactions in life have been from vetting, especially in the old days when we were going full blast. That was a marvellous thing. My son and the others still feel the same, I'm sure. Being a vet was very much part of your life, the very smell of the place, the smell of aromatic powder, baking soda, Epsom salts, filled the whole house, the smell of our trade. It was a marvellous life: I spent my life in an open car and got through seven Triumph Heralds, seven Morris Minors and a Ford Zephyr. I had the best of it, I think. It was a wonderfully healthy life. It was terribly rough and you were always getting hurt and it was filthy: you couldn't even get soap and towels on the farms, just mucky sacking full of cow dung. Now there are crushers to hold the animals so that a bullock might as well be a kitten, and everything has changed, though there are still one or two of the funny old men of the late thirties and forties still alive: men who still use old Yorkshire words like *lile* instead of *little* and *ya* instead of *one*. But otherwise things are completely different. We got kicked and knocked about – but I'd do it all over again.'

He told me that people kept blaming him for inspiring such a huge upsurge in young people's interest in animals and the countryside that the veterinary profession had become oversubscribed. Nowadays hopeful entrants needed to be very clever, with at least three excellent passes in the A-level exams. 'That's good up to a point,' he said, 'and I get hundreds of letters from little kids: whole classes send me drawings about my books. But academics don't always make the best vets. Anyway, I'm blameless. When I went into the profession nobody wanted to be a vet and they'd take anybody: they took me!'

After lunch we wandered across the marketplace and down Kirkgate to the famous surgery to see Alf's jaunty, bearded, forty-five-year-old son Jimmy, who was living in the next village with Gillian and their children and was running the Thirsk practice with three other young vets. The surgery now had become as modern and computerised as Alf's own writing but on the day I visited it in 1988 both Alf and old Donald Sinclair were there to lend the youngsters a hand. 'I still love vetting,' Alf told me, 'but now I avoid the hairy things and I don't do any operating any more. The pressure is off. I do only two days a week and just the easy jobs.' Sinclair – aged seventy-seven, thin, emaciated and sharp-featured – was rushing out to deal with a difficult lambing and had by now become resigned to being known around the world as the original Siegfried. 'He's used to it,' Alf told me. 'Sometimes he even introduces himself as Siegfried to the tourists.'

One of the vets in the surgery that day was a pale young man with exhausted, red-rimmed eyes, who had just spent thirty-six non-stop hours calving. For a moment it felt as if time had suffered a sudden half-century slippage and that he could have been the young Alf Wight starting out on his own career in this very room nearly fifty years before.

Alf slipped on a crisp white coat to treat a couple of sick dogs – a ten-month-old Labrador with diarrhoea, a five-year-old sheepdog with a temperature of 105 degrees. The sheepdog was accompanied by its gnarled old owner, whom Alf introduced to me as Old Tot. Old Tot was not nearly as daft as he looked. 'His son went to Oxford,' said Alf after the old man had gone, 'and got a double first and coxed the Blue boat!' Alf took the animals' temperatures, gave them antibiotics, chatted to their owners and behaved generally just as any genial, ordinary vet would do. Out in the streets later he nodded at passers-by and nobody who did not know could possibly have imagined that he was a multimillionaire and famous all over the world. I asked him whether some of his fans, especially foreign admirers, might perhaps have offered him a fortune to fly to America or Japan to treat their animals so that they could tell their friends that James Herriot was their vet. 'If anyone came to consult me as James Herriot I wouldn't see them,' he said, correct and steadfast as ever. 'That would be wrong. It would be taking advantage of someone else's client.'

We went out into the back garden, where in the first book James fell asleep in the grass beneath an acacia tree and woke up to see Siegfried for the first time. In those days the garden had been immaculate but now it looked neglected, with grass and weeds growing over the asparagus and strawberry beds. The coachyard where once glossy horses had been stabled now housed just three owls, a golden pheasant and a tumbledown look.

Afterwards Alf drove me home in his four-wheel-drive Audi Quattro to have tea with Joan at their cosy but startlingly small two-bedroom bungalow in Thirlby. He shrugged. 'Why would I need a mansion or a Rolls?' he said. He could have been anyone's favourite uncle and yet his fame was as massive as ever. Recently he had been mobbed by a crowd of 250 people and he had had to set aside special times when he would agree to meet his fans: at 2.45 p.m. every Wednesday and Friday, after his small-animal surgery, he would hold his human surgery for admirers. 'The locals get a giggle out of it when they see the queues outside,' he grinned. 'The Americans

always know when I'll be there and they always want to
have their photographs taken with me. They're a very nice
crowd – country lovers and animal lovers – and one of
them said to me how wonderful it must be for me to be
giving so much joy through my books. I don't pay as
much credit to that as I should. I get a lot of letters from
people with depression, or anxiety, or who have passed
through a bad period, who say that they have turned to
my books and the books have pulled them through. That
gives me a kick. It does. Oh, my! But some letters are
heart-rending, about broken marriages and other trag-
edies, and there's me in the books in awkward situations
and laughing my way out: maybe that helps. One very
prestigious American psychiatrist who came to see me
once uses my books as therapy when he is fed up. I think
I should use one myself!'

American vets were continually trying to persuade him
to fly to the USA – he always refused – and they often
came to visit him in Thirsk and to offer him awards and
medals. The previous day even the deputy leader of the
Labour Party, Roy Hattersley, had come up to Thirsk to
interview Alf for some newspaper or magazine and to
lunch with him as I had done at the Golden Fleece Hotel.
Hattersley was apparently such an important journalist,
Alf chuckled, that he had even brought with him a girl
assistant to take notes of the interview. It was a somewhat
bizarre encounter considering Alf's staunchly right-wing,
Conservative, Thatcherite politics. 'He does like his food,
Hattersley, doesn't he?' Alf grinned mischievously. 'I
noticed he got stuck into the wine too!'

Already a Herriot's Café and a Herriot's Wine Bar

had opened in the town – 'Neither of them asked my permission,' said Alf, though to be fair neither had he asked permission of Jim Herriot the footballer before he had decided to use *his* name. Another Thirsk shop was doing a brisk trade in prints of the surgery and the local council was trying to cash in on his celebrity by putting up notices on the approach roads reading THIRSK – JAMES HERRIOT'S TOWN. He had agreed. 'I'm not a great lover of the limelight and I do get embarrassed by all the attention,' he said, 'but I'm glad to do anything to help the town. It has a superb centre and the country round about is very pretty. It's an ideal tourist centre for the Pennines and the moors.' He was also trying to raise money for a local dog sanctuary, but some people were never satisfied and despite all his efforts there were still people in Thirsk who were critical of him. 'Some locals say I haven't done enough for Thirsk,' he told me. 'One has even suggested that I should write a book and give all the royalties to the town! But I've done my bit by meeting all the tourists personally. Very few writers do. And I don't want the town cheapened in any way. It would be awful if Thirsk became tatty like Stratford.'

He was still trying to pretend that his books were 90 per cent fact: 'I only changed a few small things to avoid offending somebody,' he said. 'I'm not inventive at all. I couldn't be like Dick Francis and think out plots. I just picked over my memories.' He was also a fan of his own TV series. 'They're filming the sixth series now and I always watch the programmes,' he said. 'I like to see what they've done with my little bit of writing. Thirteen million people watch the TV series, the only one with more viewers than *EastEnders, Neighbours* and *Coronation Street*. I think that's terrific for a gentle little series that's non-sexy and non-violent. I'm really tickled pink.'

As for all the money he had made, he said: 'It's a very liberating thing, the security of money. But you must remember that I wrote all the books when Mr Healey was Chancellor of the Exchequer and he took it all away: I had to pay 83 per cent in income tax and 98 per cent on income from investments. My accountant said to me: "For every book you write for yourself you have to write five more for the taxman." So I've bought nothing much, just the new Audi and a caravan. Luxuries as such don't appeal to me.' His claim that he had lost most of his earnings in tax was an exaggeration: although he had indeed paid huge amounts of tax in the 1970s, Mrs Thatcher's Tory Government of 1979 had lowered income tax dramatically, and Alf continued to earn vast amounts of money throughout the 1980s. Considering his enormous wealth, he seemed absurdly pleased that by 1988 the value of his bungalow in Thirlby had increased in eight years from £28,000 to about £100,000. Once a Scot, always a Scot.

He told me that his greatest pleasure came still from walking, gardening, going to Harrogate – and eating Chinese food, which he adored. 'I never enjoyed fishing, shooting, hunting or riding,' he said, 'and I don't know anything about birds or wild flowers. I'm a townie, raised in Glasgow. But I love the open spaces, the feeling of being close to the wild.' He was inordinately proud of the ducks on his part of the stream, especially the rare white one he had recently saved from a marauding mink that he had managed to trap.

He told me that he had always seen himself as a vet as 'the grey man in between two flamboyant characters', Siegfried and Tristan. We talked about how he had hated other famous animal books such as Richard Adams's *Watership Down*; about how he preferred nowadays to watch cricket on television rather than to read; about the great England cricketers Geoffrey Boycott and Ian Botham. Then Alf drove me several miles to the nearest railway station. He had spent almost an entire day with me, despite all the calls on his precious time, and never once did I feel that it was time to go. Afterwards he wrote me another delightful, flattering letter to thank me for the subsequent article I wrote that week for the *Sunday Express*. He was always the perfect gentleman.

Apart from the worry over his health, he seemed utterly content. 'If you get married and have kids, that's the main thing, isn't it?' he told Liz Nickson of the *Sunday Express Magazine* in September 1988. 'And I've lived in this beautiful district, having the great pleasure of being associated with animals. Oh, aye, it's been a marvellous life.'

In 1989 he finally decided to retire for good. 'The actual moment came one day when I was stitching up a cow's teat and my glasses were sliding down my nose,' he later told Jonathan Margolis of the *Mail on Sunday*. 'Suddenly I thought, "Wight, you're too old for this." '

The swift passing of the years was brought home even more fully when Brian Sinclair, 'Tristan', died that year. 'He was an amazing bloke,' said Alf, 'with an almost overdeveloped sense of humour.' Perhaps Alf was increasingly conscious of his own growing prostate problem but whatever the reason, on 14 August he drove to his solicitor's office in Darlington and signed a new will.

Rosie persuaded her parents to go abroad yet again that year, this time to Interlaken in Switzerland in August, and it was the year too when Alf finally met the footballer Jim Herriot. The ex-goalkeeper, now a bricklayer living in Larkhall, Strathclyde, was not a pet-lover and had never read a Herriot book – 'I think I've read only two books in my life,' he told Dick Barton of the *Sun* a few years later – but he had long been a regular viewer of the TV series. Yet for twenty years he had had no idea that the author of the books had hijacked his name after seeing him on television. It was not until 1989 that his niece told him about it after reading an article in the *Reader's Digest* and he decided to make a special journey down to Thirsk to see his famous namesake. Alf received him warmly. Herriot gave him one of the eight precious Scotland football jerseys he had earned as an international player, Alf gave him a signed copy of one of his books, and they ended up having a gentle game of football 'headers' in the garden. 'He was very excited about meeting me,' the real Herriot told Ben McConville of the *Sunday Express* with surprise in 1995, 'which I found puzzling because he was the big star and I am just another ex-footballer.' They talked about football and the TV series and from then on, every year, they sent each other Christmas cards. Alf's would always be addressed 'To the real James Herriot'. Herriot came to consider it a great honour that Alf had stolen his name and he glowed a little in reflected glory.

'People say to me "You've got the same name as that vet",' he told McConville gleefully. 'You should see their faces when I tell them the vet was named after me.'

A year or two later there was a nice twist to the story: this time the real James Herriot was sitting at home watching a televised football match in which one of the teams was Sunderland and there on the screen, in the crowd, he suddenly spotted Sunderland's staunchest and most famous fan. 'There's Alf!' he yelled to his wife. 'There's Alf!'

History had turned full circle.

CHAPTER FOURTEEN

The Rich Man in His Castle

IN APRIL 1990, as literary editor of the *Sunday Express*, I asked Alf to be a judge for the *Sunday Express* Book of the Year Award, but the task of reading about twenty new novels was beyond him and he declined in the nicest possible way. He was still being deluged with so many invitations, he said – even more than during his writing prime in the seventies – that now he was saying no to everything. He and Joan tried increasingly to escape the fans by taking refuge in their secret hideaway cottage and in his letter to me he said that he was constantly bewildered by his increasing popularity. Fame was becoming a serious burden. He was by now seventy-three and his signature was shaky. He was getting old.

There certainly seemed to be no end to his success, which blossomed greater and greater every year. No wonder Tom McCormack had sent him a Christmas present of eight Waterford crystal glasses and six bottles of Dom Perignon champagne at the end of 1989. By now Alf's books had sold about fifty million copies around the world and by the end of 1990, when the last of all the episodes of *All Creatures Great and Small* was finally broadcast as a ninety-minute special on Christmas Eve, it was still attracting a British audience of about eleven million viewers even though there had now been eighty-seven episodes and two Christmas specials. In the USA each episode was watched by an estimated thirty-seven million people and the six series had been sold to forty-two countries all over the world. In Germany they had all been screened no fewer than four times. 'James Herriot' had become such an icon that when it became known in 1989 that the Government was thinking of closing Glasgow University's Veterinary School thousands of Alf's fans signed a petition which eventually kept it open: it did not seem to matter to them that the school was not actually the same college at which Alf had studied.

'We had an enormous number of people who wanted to turn *All Creatures* into a stage play,' John Rush told me. 'Alf was reluctant. We couldn't conceive how they could do it. One company did write a treatment but it didn't work. We were also constantly approached for Alf to endorse commercial products but he made it clear that he would never do so – Spillers Dog Food, whatever – because he felt it impinged upon his professional life as a veterinarian. We could certainly have made huge sums from James Herriot endorsements.'

Even though Donald Sinclair also finally retired in 1990 the fans still hung around the surgery in Thirsk hoping for a glimpse of their heroes. In the village of Askrigg the house that the series had adopted as the vets' surgery, Skeldale House, had been renamed just that and although it was now an old people's home Herriot fans were still queueing up to be photographed outside it, some with their dogs, as though the animals were about to go into the building to be treated by the famous vets. 'Some of them wander into the kitchens looking for the surgery,' the home's secretary, Ann Hawkins, told Peter Davenport of the *Daily Telegraph*. A visitor to the Yorkshire Dales could go there on a Herriot tour with a Herriot guide, or rent a car from a Herriot car-hire firm, go walking along The Herriot Trail, have lunch in a Herriot restaurant, buy photographs of the stars of the Herriot TV series as well as Herriot writing paper, Herriot calendars and Herriot guidebooks in a Herriot gift shop, take tea in a Herriot tea shop (and buy some Herriot marmalade there as well) and have a drink and dine in 'The Herriot Pub', which was what the King's Arms in Askrigg – the pub that had been used in the series as The Drovers' Arms – was now calling itself on a brass plate above the door. One American couple, said the pub's landlady, had been so excited to see that the table at which they had eaten when they had been staying at the pub had later appeared in the TV series that they returned all the way to Askrigg to photograph it.

The series had made 'Herriot Country' so popular, attracting millions more tourists there every year, that voices of dissent began to be raised even though the hordes of visitors provided a great boost to the local economy at a time of serious recession and unemployment. Richard Harvey, the park officer of the Dales National Park, put Askrigg and several other Herriot sites on his list of a dozen parts of the Dales that had been seriously harmed by increased tourism. 'In some ways the series has cheapened the area,' he said. 'The Dales had their own majesty before this programme for people who made the effort to see them. When all the interest began we thought it was no bad thing. Only later did we realise it was a mixed blessing.' The chairman of Askrigg parish council, John Abraham, agreed and announced that he was delighted that the series was ending at last since it meant that the village would no longer be blighted by all the TV cameras, actors and crews, let alone the trippers, cars and coaches. 'There has been too much publicity for a place this size,' he said.

*

There were many moments of great family happiness for the Wights during these years. They made sure that they kept up with Brian Sinclair's widow Sheila and still met her every week for tea in Harrogate. Alf and Joan celebrated their golden wedding anniversary on 5 November 1991 and in October of the following year their seventeen-year-old granddaughter Emma, Rosie's daughter, was made head girl of her school in York. In 1992, as well, Alf became the first winner of the British Veterinary Association's new Chiron Award for 'exceptional service to the veterinary profession' and his old veterinary college friend Jimmy Steele – who was by now 78, long retired from the Ministry of Agriculture and living in Ayr in Scotland – travelled down to Thirsk with his wife Bette and stayed overnight with Alf and Joan. 'He wasn't a heavy drinker,' Steele told me, 'but he was certainly on the whisky that night! It was some night! They treated us royally. After his success as a writer he hadn't changed one iota. Even physically Alf hadn't changed or aged much.'

'He had a gentle face,' said Bette Steele.

'Aye,' said her husband, 'he was an open book, Alf.'

When Alf discovered that the Steeles had six grand-children he signed no fewer than eighteen of his books for them – a gesture of immense generosity – but the Steeles were slightly disconcerted over the matter of the breakfast banana.

'I have half a banana every day for breakfast,' chuckled Jimmy Steele. 'I don't know why. I always do.'

'Joan was quite astounded when he asked for half a banana,' said Bette Steele, 'and the next morning when he came down there was the other half of the banana all tied up in plastic, sitting on the table! They didn't change their lifestyle. They were very simple.'

One special honour delighted Alf more than any other: in March 1992 he was voted life president of Sunderland Football Club, the club he had supported for seventy-two years ever since his father had started drumming the names of the Sunderland team of 1920 into him when he was three years old. It was a wonderful tribute and came with perfect timing: 1992 was Sunderland's centenary year as a Football League club and a month later, in April, the club beat Norwich 1–0 in the semi-final of the FA Cup. Alf announced that he could now die happy. On Saturday 9 May he enjoyed one of the proudest days of his life when he and Joan travelled down to London to the great national soccer cauldron of Wembley and not only watched Sunderland play Liverpool in the FA Cup Final – the greatest of all great English football occasions – but watched it from the coveted VIP seats. It was Sunderland's greatest moment – and maybe Alf's too – since the team had beaten Leeds United in the 1973 final. 'You can't rationalise the pleasure you get from watching your team win but it gives you a tremendous kick,' he told Edward Marriott of the *Sunday Telegraph* the week before the match.

This time, sadly, Sunderland were beaten but Alf's heart was bursting with emotion as he watched the red-and-white flags unfurled and waved aloft like medieval banners in English football's greatest temple. I suspect there were tears in his eyes, then. If only his father could have been there to see him standing there with all the bigwigs. How proud old Jim Wight would have been of his only son. And when Alf was president of Sunderland Football Club in those last three years of his life he must surely have popped around the corner once or twice to Brandling Street on his way out of Roker Park for a final glimpse of the tiny house where he was born. If he did then surely the ghosts of generations of shipyard Wights must have raised their cloth caps and nodded with approval.

*

When Alf's final book, *Every Living Thing*, was eventually published in October 1992, a full eleven years after his previous one, it turned out to be his longest book – and happily a great deal better than *The Lord God Made Them All*. Alf was back on form and it was a fitting finale to his work as a writer, telling as it did of life in Thirsk during the 1950s. The book – the title of which comes from the Book of Ecclesiastes – was dedicated to the dogs, Polly and Bodie, and exhibits all his old skills of warmth, control and timing. Several of the tales are beautifully paced, others are genuinely moving and many of the anecdotes are as good as anything he had ever written: the story of the emaciated sweetshop cat, for instance; the one about Mrs Pumphrey, Tricki Woo, the Milk Committee and the Lovat tweed Savile Row suit; the one about the cat that kept mysteriously passing out. There is also the wonderfully lively character of the young veterinary assistant Calum Buchanan, who turns up with a badger sitting on his shoulder and who is based on Brian Nettleton, the young vet who had worked with Alf and Sinclair for two years back in the 1950s. And now and then there are some perfect touches – like the remark of the harassed, overworked hill farmer, Ted Newcombe, who says that one of his greatest luxuries is to wake up in the middle of the night and know that he can roll over and fall asleep again.

Every Living Thing also offers yet more evidence that Alf had always kept a regular diary, despite his constant denials that he had done so: in Chapter 19 he explains that he is able to reproduce verbatim the dialogue of the chattering tailor, Mr Bendelow, because he wrote it all down at the time. The book shows, too, how far Alf was prepared to go to twist the facts of his real life to create his fiction: in Chapter 42 he describes his and Joan's move from Rowardennan in Sowerby to Mire Beck in Thirlby but claims that it occurred in the 1950s when in fact they did not move until 1977.

The book also contains a classic example of how Alf would take even a simple pub joke or anecdote and turn it into a story that millions believed was absolutely true. One tale that was going the rounds when I was working in Fleet Street in the 1960s told of a boastful Northerner, Joe Arkwright, whose friends are so fed up with his

stories about how he knows dozens of famous people –
among them Winston Churchill, Princess Margaret,
Brigitte Bardot and all four of the Beatles – that they keep
betting him that they can prove he is lying, only to find
that when they force him to meet these luminaries they
greet him with delight like an old friend. Eventually – so
the story went – when Joe Arkwright mentions his old
chum the Pope his infuriated friends bet him a final £100
that he cannot possibly know him and they all go off
together to Rome to prove the bet one way or another.
In St Peter's Square Arkwright suggests to his cynical
friends that since His Holiness has not been very well
lately he will go into the Vatican alone to see him, but to
prove that they are old friends he and the Pontiff will
come out on to the balcony arm in arm and wave at them
in the square below. His friends, being considerate men,
agree, and ten minutes later they see Joe Arkwright and
the Pope emerging together on to the balcony high above
the square, arm in arm, grinning and waving excitedly at
them. As they stare up at the unlikely couple in amazement, still unable to grasp that Joe Arkwright and the
Pope really are old friends, a Zulu warrior in a loincloth
lopes into the square and up to them. 'Say, *bwana*,' says the
Zulu, 'who am de little old guy in de white dress up dere
wid old Joe Arkwright?'

In *Every Living Thing* Alf told a strikingly similar story,
only this time Joe Arkwright is called Arnold Braithwaite
and the famous people he knows are not Churchill,
Princess Margaret, Bardot and the Beatles but Lew Hoad,
Tom Finney, General Allenby, Stanley Matthews, the
entire England and Australian cricket teams, a horde of

international hockey players and a rich assortment of Indian rajahs. Alf had taken the Arkwright story, toned it down to make it credible, given it a specially Yorkshire flavour and passed it off as fact – like any other writer of fiction.

Tom McCormack did not agree that *Every Living Thing* was one of Alf's better books. He was particularly unhappy about it, feeling that it needed some serious editing, but by now Alf had become so successful that he was stubborn about his writing and no longer prepared to make all the changes that McCormack wanted. 'James did not need editing early on,' McCormack told me. 'He was a very, very great writer. There came a stage when he did need editing – and he took it – but finally there came a stage when he was not taking editing, to the detriment of the book. His judgement about his own writing became concretised but his readiness to take editorial suggestions diminished. He took some: I reversed the last two chapters in *Every Living Thing* because they seemed wrong and he accepted it. But in Chapter 8 he used the word "but" thirty-seven times in eight pages, so I went through it and circled them all and said "I just call this to your attention but I'm happy to fix it and change it for you." He said "It hasn't bothered anyone else", to which I said "Look, it's a bloody flaw." But he wouldn't have it changed. "I insist," he said. And that was disappointing. What the hell is an editor for? Playwrights and actors need directors and if you are a writer you *pray* for a good editor. They're so few and far between.'

McCormack was in fact being a little pernickety: the thirty-seven occurrences of 'but' in Chapter 8 of *Every*

Living Thing are spread over twelve pages, not eight, and they do not jar at all on a casual reading even though two pages have seven of them each.

Alf in turn was unhappy with the painting on the jacket of the American edition, which showed for the first time his own likeness rather than that of a hunky young male model. He was particularly upset by the whiteness of his hair in the illustration, but his protests were in vain. McCormack could be equally stubborn. He refused to budge. 'I must go with my judgement, not London's, about what is right and effective for the American audience,' McCormack wrote to Alf's New York agent, Claire Smith. 'I certainly don't want to distress James, but . . . I am sure enough about the rightness of my decision, and I must report to you that I have released the final art to the printer.'

Despite the disagreements behind the scenes the *New York Times* gave the book a rave review. It went straight to No 1 in the bestseller list two weeks before publication, sold an astonishing 650,000 hardback copies in America in just six weeks and stayed in the *New York Times* bestseller list for eight months. Alf's books by now had been translated into more than twenty languages and were bestsellers in every one of them.

Once again a cavalcade of journalists made the pilgrimage to Thirsk. By now he had said everything he could possibly want to say about his life, vetting and writing yet still the journalists flocked to interview and photograph and film him. He must by now have been thoroughly fed up with it all but he bore it with immense tolerance and patience. Jonathan Margolis of the *Mail on Sunday* got

there first and like most journalists could not resist taking
Alf to lunch in the Golden Fleece Hotel's dining room,
which had been renamed Herriots Restaurant (without
any apostrophe). 'Being a country vet was like a long
holiday with pay,' Alf told Margolis, admitting that like
most vets he had always been sentimental about animals
'and that's a hell of a good thing, believe me'. He also
claimed he had been bitten only twice in more than fifty
years as a vet because he had always been careful to talk to
the animals before he approached them. 'I don't know
how much they can discern from your words,' he said,
'but a dog that might bite someone else won't bite me.'

By now Alf had given up going to the surgery altogether,
he told Tom McCormack, because he did not always feel
very well. The practice was now being run by Seamus and
three younger vets: Andrew Barrett, Peter Wright and Tim
Yates. A notice on the front door told the queues of fans
that 'Mr Herriot has now retired and is no longer receiving
visitors' and they had to settle instead for pre-signed
bookplates handed out to them by the receptionists.

Stephen Pile of the *Daily Telegraph*, who described Alf
as 'pink, dapper and slightly frail', also took him to lunch
at the Golden Fleece and asked him what he felt sitting in
a restaurant named after him. 'Nothing,' said Alf, typically.
Pile asked him how on earth his books could be so
popular in such an astonishing variety of countries, from
Israel and Japan to Russia and Serbia – even in Spain,
'where they don't even like animals'. This time Alf had no
doubt about his answer. 'The permissiveness of the horrible sixties changed people,' he said. 'My books reassert the
old values. I have read a couple of these sexy, modern

books and laughed out loud. I wouldn't want to write this sort of thing.' Pile agreed and ended the article with a perceptive summing-up: 'In Herriot's books people get married and, uniquely, stay married. The family is all important. People work hard and spend money only when they have it (credit cards are not mentioned). They breathe God's own fresh air and they do not go to a therapist three times a week to discover that everything is their parents' fault. Above all, his characters are incredibly and miraculously nice to each other. There are rude people in these pages, but they are swept aside by the rising tide of good nature. It is possible that the entire world reads Mr Herriot's books and, finding there is no rape, no murder, no hate, no anger, no child abuse, no whining, moaning or bitching, or wife-beating, heaves a huge sigh of relief.'

Of all the interviews with Alf that year, however, the most extraordinary and revealing was one he gave to Lynda Lee-Potter of the *Daily Mail*. Miss Lee-Potter had long been renowned as an amazingly engaging, persuasive and incisive interviewer who could charm even the vultures out of the trees and Alf found himself talking to her more openly than he had ever spoken on the record, for publication, to anyone else. He sang like the proverbial canary, even about his deepest, secret feelings for his family.

'Rosie's daughter is the apple of my eye, head girl at her school in York,' he said. 'She's just slightly taller than me now, a very glamorous girl and brilliant at art. She has a sunny nature like her mother, throws her arms round my neck as soon as she sees me. She phoned me this morning, in fact. She's a super girl, I love her to bits. I said to my wife "I'm so crazy about Emma, I give her a kiss and cuddle her every time I see her. You don't think Rosie believes I love Emma better than I ever loved her, do you?" It really worried me. Because much as I love Emma I can't love her as much as I love Rosie. It might sound daft but I couldn't bear it if Rosie thought that. So I think my wife passed the message on.'

He was also immensely proud of his son and not merely because Jimmy was now running the surgery. 'Jimmy's a natural-born entertainer,' Alf told Miss Lee-Potter. 'He could make a cat laugh. Every time there's a party you see a group in the corner surrounding Jimmy and everyone is rolling with laughter.'

As for his fifty-one years married to Joan, he confirmed that she was the stronger partner: 'She's the blaze of the family. She's a practical person. I'm very airy-fairy really. She's tall, dark hair, a lovely face.' But he did confess that sometimes he wished she would be a little more demonstrative towards him with her affection. 'She's the number one love of my life,' he said. 'She's not as emotional as me, we've never called each other darling or dearest or anything like that. I have asked her if she loves me and she says yes. She doesn't elaborate on the fact and I suppose I would like it if she did. My gosh, we're getting into deep water here! I'll be in trouble if you write that.'

*

It had been a triumphant year for Alf but also a tragic one, for it was in 1992 that he was diagnosed as having cancer of the prostate and given no more than three to five years to live. Time was running out. Even Bodie and Polly were growing old. Although he continued to take them out for walks – and every Tuesday he and his old childhood chum Alex Taylor would walk together with their dogs – throughout 1993 and 1994 he became increasingly frail. He had to endure painful treatment for his disease and the medication he was taking affected him in unpleasant ways. 'One night towards the end of his life,' said one old friend sadly, 'he drank too much, keeled over, and had to be helped to the car.'

Tom and Sandra McCormack lunched with him in Thirsk for the last time in the summer of 1993 and were appalled by how ill he looked. 'He was quite hobbled and by then his hands were so gnarled that he had a tough time just signing the bill,' McCormack recalled sadly. 'That encounter was sombre as hell because this was a man who was getting no satisfaction from anything. A lot of bad stuff comes with fame and fortune. I knew when I first met him at lunch in that June of '72 that his life was going to be changed and invaded in a way that would disrupt it. I thought then that he was going to be screwed up.'

Happily Alf had by now made it up with Eddie Straiton and had written to congratulate him when Straiton's young second wife, Penny, gave birth to their son Edward in April 1990. 'I got a lovely letter from Alf saying the birth announcement in the *Veterinary Record* had made his day,' said Straiton. They kept in touch now and then by post and telephone until Alf's death. 'On the last occasion he wrote to say his condition was terminal. I had known for some time about his prostate cancer and I told him I'd been praying for him every night.'

Alf still made valiant efforts to hide his illness from his

fans. Ever the professional, he agreed to help Christopher Timothy make a video film entitled *James Herriot's Yorkshire*. One afternoon, as the pair emerged from the surgery in Kirkgate, they were confronted by an American tourist who was almost delirious with joy at finding both of them together, the famous vet himself *and* his television *alter ego*. Alf suddenly seemed much younger and perkier, Timothy reported later, and acted up for his delighted fan, but as soon as they were alone again he reverted to being old and ill. He also allowed Simon Ward to interview him for Ward's video documentary about modern vetting, *Creature Comforts*, which shows him looking very tired and frail. 'I never made any money until I wrote the books,' he told Ward. 'A very obscure vet was Alf Wight, a run-of-the-mill vet.' He smiled. 'Real Herriots from all over the world have written to me to say "You're the image of old Uncle Marmaduke" and I have to say "I'm sorry, I'm only half a Herriot." '

During those last few months it was particularly agonising for Rosie, who was still living in the bungalow next door, to watch her father slowly dying. As a doctor she knew very well exactly what he was having to endure, even though he wasn't one to complain and you would never have guessed at his agony except for the occasional suppressed wince or frown. Jimmy's wife Gillian, who was also a doctor, must have known too precisely what her father-in-law was suffering. By the summer of 1994, when Alf was seventy-seven, he had become so weak that when a flock of black-faced sheep strayed into the garden at Mire Beck and he tried to stop them eating the flowers they turned on him, sent him sprawling and trampled him. He was taken to hospital with a broken leg. It shouldn't happen to a vet, of course.

Alf's last few months were haunted by such pain and illness that had he been an animal he would have been put out of his misery long before the end. By August 1994 he felt so fragile that his last letter to St Martin's Press – not to Tom McCormack but to a young associate editor there, Cal Morgan – had to be written for him in a girlish hand by Emma, who was now nineteen and studying Fine Arts at Newcastle University. Yet in November he accepted with pride an invitation from Glasgow University to open a new £330,000 James Herriot Library in the veterinary school there in February: a library with computer links, video facilities, a conference room and space for 120 students to study. He was so pleased about receiving an honour from his home city that he who had never sought publicity even telephoned local Yorkshire newspapers to tell them about the honour – and when it became obvious that he was far too weak to go to Glasgow for the ceremony he promised that Jimmy, who had himself been a student there in the 1960s, would open the library in his place. With typical generosity Alf also still found time to send me his 1960s short story 'La Vie en Rose' and then to write me an affectionate letter just seven weeks before he died to thank me for accepting it and to wish my short-story magazine every success. The letter was dated 6 January 1995 and his signature was very shaky.

Even so the family managed to get him up to Sunderland the next day to watch his last football match and in the first week of February Rosie drove him into Thirsk to have an eye test and a dental check. 'He was always looking ahead,' she told Brian Duffy of the *Sunday Express* after her father died. During his last days, she said, he was still taking delight in the sight of a pink rose and still laughing at *Hancock* and *Rising Damp* on television. He would certainly have enjoyed a bleak chuckle had he seen the issue of *Hello!* magazine that was published on 11 February. It contained a photograph of him under the ludicrous headline 'Inside Story' with a caption that appeared to know so little about him that it managed to make five mistakes in four short paragraphs – among them the claim that he had been born in Glasgow and that his veterinary partner was 'Siegfried Sassoon'!

Four days before Alf's death, on a darkening Sunday evening, he went for the last of all his walks, just down the garden path to the front gate and back, with Joan and Rosie at his side and faithful fourteen-year-old Bodie, now grey-haired himself, walking stiffly at his heels. 'On that final walk he was thinking positive,' Rosie told Brian Duffy the day after Alf died. ' "I have to keep moving", he would say. As the pain spread to his bones it got agonising.' Duffy spoke to Joan as well that day. 'Alf loved our little house,' she told him. 'He would look up at Sutton Bank and say: "I wouldn't swap it for Buckingham Palace." ' An Englishman's home is his castle, the English jurist Sir Edward Coke wrote in 1628, 'and each man's home is his safest refuge' – and that was exactly what Mire Beck had been for Alf. When he was there he had been as protected from the shallow hurly-burly of the world as if his little bungalow had had a drawbridge and a moat.

Alf had always said that he would like to die a good

vet's death, working hard in a cattle stall till the very end, just as his old friend Frank Bingham had done, but it was not to be. At the end he was far too ill to be anywhere near a cattle byre. He died in bed at home on the Thursday, 23 February 1995, with Joan and Rosie at his side.

The next day Jimmy drove up to Glasgow to keep his father's promise and open the James Herriot Library. 'Alf was incredibly pleased at the honour,' said the university's vice-principal, Professor Sir James Armour, himself a vet. 'He had been quite positive that, no matter what happened, Jim had to come and open the library.' Jimmy agreed. 'He got more enjoyment out of this honour than all the others put together,' he said. 'I think it's because he always regarded himself as a Glaswegian. He had a great affection for Glasgow.'

On the same day the Three Tuns Hotel in Thirsk received a fax from a fan in California, Sharon McLin, which read: 'It was on American TV news last night that James Herriot had passed away. We were so sorry to hear that. Like millions of Americans we were fans. So sorry.'

*

The funeral, on 1 March, was private and secret, restricted to family and only the very closest friends. It was held not in Thirsk, where the fans would have turned up by the thousand, but in the tiny village church of Felixkirk, near Thirlby, where even the most fanatical reader could not have found them, and of course they sang hymn number 573 from the Church of England's *Hymns Ancient and Modern*:

> *All things bright and beautiful,*
> *All creatures great and small,*
> *All things wise and wonderful,*
> *The Lord God made them all.*

Afterwards he was cremated and his ashes were scattered on the Yorkshire moors that he had loved so much for more than fifty years.

*

The obituaries were long and universally affectionate as was proper for a man who had been so widely and deeply loved. Many authors are admired or respected but few are actually loved by their readers. Alf was one of the rarities. He 'almost single-handedly transformed the image of the vet from a muddy figure in a distant field or an inoculator of urban cats and dogs to a romantic and sympathetic hero', said the *Daily Telegraph* the day after he died. 'The appeal lay in the fact that the animals always stayed animals, without any anthropomorphism, while the humans were richly comic or pathetic.' There was only one sentence in that obituary that might have upset Alf, after all those years he had spent trying to persuade everyone that his books were 90 per cent autobiographical: the *Telegraph* described them as fiction.

So did *The Times*, which called him 'one of the most successful popular novelists of the century'. The paper noted that in Alf's books 'the trade of vet seemed to go far beyond the mere business of healing animals; it became a unifying force in the far-flung farmsteads of Yorkshire's hills and dales'. *The Times* also pointed out that the books had enticed an entirely different sort of young person into the British veterinary profession: before then most vets came from a farming or rural background and there were very few of them; but afterwards many were townies like Alf himself and the profession became so popular that there were many more applicants than places available and the entry requirements had to be raised even higher than for those students who wanted to doctor humans. The paper recalled the one tribute that Alf had always put above any other: when one old Yorkshire farmer was told that his vet was also the famous writer James Herriot he paused, thought, and then said, 'Well, he's not a bad veten'ry, either.'

Alf would also particularly have appreciated two tributes by fellow professionals that appeared in the *Veterinary Record*. The main obituary, on 4 March, was written by John Crooks, who had been Alf and Donald Sinclair's assistant in 1951 and who had risen so high in the profession as to have become president of the British Veterinary Association. 'I knew I was in a busy, happy practice, but could never have believed that it would achieve such international fame,' wrote Crooks. Alf, he said, 'had small, sensitive hands and was especially skilled in obstetrical work. Although not long in the arm it was amazing with what facility he dealt with difficult calvings in the large shorthorn cows common in the 1950s. One farmer said to me "Aye, 'e got us a grand live calf – but 'e near 'ad to climb in to get it out." He handled animals with gentleness and firmness. He loved his work . . . Those of us who had the privilege of working with him, and those who had the privilege of having their animals cared for by him, will remember him for what he most aspired to be – a highly competent and caring veterinary surgeon.'

Eddie Straiton was in Jamaica, recuperating after a painful corneal graft eye operation, when Alf died, so his own obituary of Alf did not appear in the *Veterinary Record* until a month later, on 8 April. In it he said that he considered Alf to have been 'one of the world's outstanding authors' and that 'his books shall be read, reread and enjoyed by many generations to come. Personally, I class his work with that of Mark Twain, Dickens and Cronin.' And he concluded: 'As someone who knew Alf Wight probably better than any other veterinary surgeon I can say, without fear of contradiction, that he was not only a first-class veterinary surgeon and a brilliant writer but a perfect father and gentleman who bore his phenomenal success with modesty and dignity.'

In New York Tom McCormack was so saddened by Alf's death that he did not know what to say and it took him seven weeks to write a letter of condolence. He started it time and again, gave it up time and again, but in April finally managed it. 'I've been in books for thirty-six years,' he wrote to Joan, 'and there's reason to believe I've published more authors than any other living person in my industry. Of this multitude, no other author has ever approached the feelings that Alf stirred in me. I was proud of him, I admired him as a man . . .'

Alf would also have loved especially his son's tribute when he spoke at length to Noreen Taylor of the *Daily Mail* about his father ten months after he died. 'I've lost my best friend,' said Jimmy. 'We were so close. Told each other everything. I went to him with my problems, went to him for advice, and if I'd heard a joke, I'd think "Oh, wait till I tell Dad." People are always going on about me being Herriot's son and how it must have been a pain living in his shadow. I can honestly say that I never felt as though I was.'

But perhaps the tribute that Alf would have relished most of all came in the end not in words but in deeds – from his beloved football team at Sunderland. A year after he died the club achieved a dream that they and Alf had long shared: in May 1996 they won promotion at last into the giddiest heights of English League football, the Premier Division. His joyous spirit would have been at Roker Park that afternoon when Sunderland's delighted fans knew at last that the lads had done it and the terraces were awash with the red and white scarves and banners and trembled with the cheers and chanting and songs. You could hear the happy roars that afternoon all over Sunderland and especially maybe in the little terraced house two hundred yards away where little Alfie Wight had been born eighty years before.

*

Donald Sinclair was devastated by Alf's death. Whatever their differences and disagreements might have been, their lives had been irretrievably intertwined for fifty-five years and would be for ever because of the books. James and Siegfried would endure in literature long after their originals had been forgotten. In old age the two men had still lived no more than a mile from each other, both in Thirlby – Sinclair at Southwoods Hall – and they still met regularly and shared a million memories. 'I never heard Dad and Donald have a cross word,' Jimmy Wight told John Woodcock of the *Daily Mail* later that year, 'though they were certainly very different people. Father was the solid citizen type who kept things going at a down-to-earth level. Donald was explosive, chaotic, full of dreams and ideas, a true eccentric and blessed with a wonderful sense of humour. He was also a man of humility and would forever regale you with his failures, but not speak of his triumphs.' When Alf died, said Jimmy, Sinclair telephoned him and said brusquely 'I'm fed up about your Dad' before slamming the telephone receiver down again. 'It was his way of expressing grief,' said Jimmy, 'and it had taken all his courage to say it.'

But distraught though Sinclair was over Alf's death, worse was to come. In March his wife Audrey, now eighty-six and almost completely blind, fell, broke a hip and never fully recovered. At the beginning of June she died at home – according to her family in her husband's arms. Sinclair was inconsolable. They had been married for fifty-two years and claimed to have spent barely one night apart in all that time. The tragic, eighty-four-year-old Sinclair – who was himself unsteady on his feet and in pain because of an agonising hip – was racked now by grief, loneliness and despair and three weeks later, on 23 June, unable to bear it any longer, he committed suicide at home by taking an overdose of barbiturates. He left a loving note for his children Alan Sinclair and Janet Grey and instructions not to be revived. Quite rightly they honoured his wish. He lived on in a coma for five more days but died on 28 June. At the inquest that was held a month later the Acting Coroner, Jeremy Cave, recorded an open verdict although it is obvious that Sinclair had committed suicide. His friends said he had died of a broken heart.

It was a terrible way for the happy, homely Herriot saga to end. The stories in *All Creatures Great and Small* had almost always had cosy endings, but not this one. But then how in real life could there ever have been any good way to finish? Perhaps the only way to see poor Siegfried's end is not as a tragedy but as a tribute to his wife, as a last salute to the woman he had adored for so long, the woman he could not imagine living without.

*

Alf's funeral had been small and private but the memorial service of thanksgiving for his life was deliberately huge and magnificent. It was held on 20 October in the soaring splendour of York Minster and a vast throng of nearly two thousand people turned up to celebrate and give thanks for his life, from farmers whose cattle he had doctored to readers who had loved his books to the great and good – and bad – of the literary world. Among them were Tom McCormack, the Dean of Glasgow University and the presidents of the Royal College of Veterinary Surgeons, the British Veterinary Association and the Yorkshire Veterinary Society. Alf's beloved granddaughter Emma read the lesson, Christopher Timothy read an extract from *Vet in Harness* – the story of James and the tight-fisted Yorkshire farmer with the sick cow – and Robert Hardy read a piece by one of Alf's favourite

authors, P.G. Wodehouse, from *The World of Jeeves*. One
absentee was Carol Drinkwater. 'I wasn't invited nor even
informed that it was taking place,' she told me sadly.
'When Alf died I didn't find out until a week later. I was
a bit hurt that nobody had told me because in a way I felt
that I was a part of his life and his world. I wrote to Joan
and said I was so upset and what a wonderful man he was,
etc, and I send you all my love, but she never answered.
Maybe she was upset because I left *All Creatures Great and
Small* after the third series. Or maybe Joan was upset by
all that terrible publicity when Chris and I had an affair.'

The service was conducted by the Dean of York, the
very Reverend Raymond Furnell, Seamus gave an
address, Alex Taylor delivered a tribute and the Minster
rang with the glorious sounds of the organ, the trumpet
fanfares, the full choir. And of course they sang hymn
number 573:

> *All things bright and beautiful,*
> *All creatures great and small,*
> *All things wise and wonderful,*
> *The Lord God made them all.*

Again and again their voices bellowed out across the vast
old stones and up to the lofty rafters of the ancient
cathedral:

> *Each little flower that opens,*
> *Each little bird that sings,*
> *He made their glowing colours,*
> *He made their tiny wings.*

And the hymn goes on:

> *The rich man in his castle,*
> *The poor man at his gate,*
> *God made them, high or lowly,*
> *And ordered their estate.*

Had Alf really believed it? That all his struggles and successes had been ordained and sanctioned by God? That God at first had made him poor and lowly, setting him in the slums of Sunderland and Glasgow and then lifting him up on high to great wealth and a little castle of his own? Perhaps. Alf had never seemed to be a particularly religious man but he had seen the glories of God in the beauties of the Yorkshire Dales and the taciturn smiles of the Yorkshire farmers and the laughter of his children and grandchildren and in the beasts of the field, and I think he may well have believed it. 'I could never be an atheist,' he had told me in 1988. 'After all, I don't believe in television. How can it possibly work? Pictures through the air? But it does.'

Television again: television flickering throughout his long, happy life, from the ghost of John Logie Baird in the shadowy, rundown streets of Yoker to the famous, vibrant television voices of Christopher Timothy and Robert Hardy echoing the magic of beautiful English words in the magnificent splendour of York Minster.

It was fitting, and time to go.

Postscript

When Alf died he left more than five million pounds: £5,425,873 gross, £5,379,969 net. Since all but £150,000 of it was left in trust for Joan – Jimmy and Rosie each inherited £75,000 immediately – there would have been no inheritance tax to pay on it. It was a vast fortune for any writer to leave, especially when you consider that he had given huge amounts away already not only to his children and grandchildren but also to the taxman. His old friends Bette and Jimmy Steele were stunned to learn how big his legacy was and if even half of his earnings had indeed been taxed by the Labour Government at 83 per cent, as he always claimed, then to leave more than £5 million after he had already given millions to his family meant that he may well have earned at least £40 million during his lifetime, most of it from his writing – a figure that was easily possible since his books had sold an estimated fifty million copies world-wide by the time he died. But it should never be forgotten that his huge success so nearly did not happen. He understood that and it made him philosophical. Many years earlier he had laid down his own key for living the good life when he said with surprising hard-headedness: 'It isn't simplicity or anything like that. To be cynical, the key is *necessity*. I worked like hell for peanuts before I wrote any books only because I damn well had to. The spur was necessity – and that was a damn good thing.'

Under the terms of his will, which he had signed five and a half years previously, on 14 August 1989, he appointed Joan, Jimmy and Rosie as his executors and trustees and asked that his literary agent Jacqueline Glasser (*née* Korn) and her colleague Anthony Crouch, both of David Higham Associates in London, should be retained as literary agents and valuers of his works. If Joan had died before him he would have left £100,000 in trust for each of the four grandchildren, who would not have been able to touch the money until they were thirty, and £5,000 to the Wights' housekeeper, Flora Ianson. As it was, he had provided handsomely for his widow, children and grand-children. None of them would ever be nearly as poor as he had been.

There was one unhappy paragraph – a paragraph with the unlucky number of 13 – right at the end of the will. 'In the event of my Grand-daughter EMMA PAGE benefit-ting under the provisions of this my Will,' Alf declared, '*I DIRECT* my Trustees to exercise their influence upon her to advise and deter my said Grand-daughter Emma Page from allowing her Father CHRISTOPHER JOHN PAGE (the former Husband of my Daughter the said Rosemary Beatrice Page) to obtain from my said Grand-daughter any money whatsoever out of her inheritance under this my Will.'

Tom McCormack, who estimated that Alf's sales in America had totalled thirty-seven million copies and that worldwide sales must have been well over fifty million, was surprised that Alf had left nothing whatever to any charity: 'Did he give nothing to the veterinary school? That sort of thing? That's surprising.' But McCormack was immensely grateful to Alf for all he had done for him, his career and St Martin's Press, which sold in the end seven million Herriot books. 'He did more for me personally and my family than any writer I've ever published,' McCormack told me. 'He changed my life because when I took over at St Martin's as chief executive in 1970 the company was going to die but the Herriot books gave us clout in terms of money and in terms of convincing people that we could do it. By proving we could do it we began to get other submissions. Because of James's success, the number of big titles we did expanded massively in the seventies. When I got there in 1969 the trade department published forty-two titles in that whole year: now it does 650 and the whole company does 1,600 titles. The trampoline was *All Creatures Great and Small*. So the company owed him a very great deal. So did many other people, like veterinary students: because of him the number of veterinary schools in New York alone rose from twenty to twenty-seven over a few years. And there are many other writers, especially from Britain, who were published in the States by us only because James Herriot was a success. He was the beginning.'

As for poor, suicidal 'Siegfried', Donald Sinclair also died a millionaire, leaving an estate worth £1,133,390 net, though this would have been worth no more than £560,000 after the payment of inheritance tax – still a sturdy sum but only a fraction of Alf's legacy. Defying his reputation for meanness, Sinclair left £1,000 each to four of his employees and £500 to a fifth. In a codicil signed just a month before he killed himself, he left his car as well as £1,000 to his chauffeuse, Margaret Birch. The rest went to his two children.

*

In August 1996 I returned to Thirsk to try to detect the last lingering traces of the town's most famous son. In the Golden Fleece Hotel two American couples and a young Japanese were eating in Herriots Restaurant and admitted that they were in Thirsk because of the television series. They had come to worship at the shrine of Herriotdom. 'Worship' is the very word: throughout my stay at the hotel the guests in the Herriot Restaurant communicated in whispers, as though they were in church. Perhaps they felt they were. Less reverent was the hotel's information sheet, which managed with impressive nonchalance to make two mistakes in one short word by referring to the restaurant as Heriot's. The food on offer in the restaurant was not exactly hearty Herriot fare but tended to be more of the pretentious *Paupillettes of Plaice Stuffed With Prawns* variety. I ventured to wrestle with the plaice and was irresistibly reminded of dry cardboard. The wine took half an hour to arrive. I decided to round off the meal with some strawberries and when they arrived I sprinkled pepper on them (a delicious way to eat them) and a tiny greenfly staggered out of the fruit and across the plate. It appeared to be sneezing. All creatures great and small, for sure.

To be fair, 'The Herriot Breakfast' in Herriots Restaurant the next day was a great deal better: a full English fry-up with black pudding and a wonderful sausage that Alf himself would have relished.

Outside, across the cobbled market square, were two shops named after the fictitious town of Darrowby – one, a café, had been blessed with the excruciatingly twee name Darrowby Fayre – and another shop was selling boxes of Darrowby ('*The Town Of The Vet*') fudge, toffee and caramel. The town bookshop had on display every Herriot book as well as videos of the television series and Christopher Timothy's ninety-minute video *James Herriot's Yorkshire*, a tribute – part biography, part travelogue – that was warm and affectionate but despite the shots of wonderful scenery oddly stilted and contrived. It also managed to make the inaccurate claim that Alf had been a student at Glasgow University. Nor was it just the tourists who were still reading the Herriot books. The librarian in the public lending library told me that the books were still heavily borrowed 'not just by tourists but also by the locals: the older people like to read them over and over again'. The town's little museum, in Thomas Lord's old house opposite Alf's surgery, had a small James Herriot Room with scraps of Alf's manuscripts and old veterinary implements on display and the museum shop was selling Herriot plates, jerseys, postcards, car stickers and carrier bags. Even inside the beautiful parish church, St Mary's, where Alf and Joan were married in 1941, they were selling tea towels depicting the famous surgery.

The one truly awful example of Herriotisation was at a pub on the edge of the market square that had for two hundred years been called the Red Bear but had just been refurbished at a cost of £150,000 and renamed the

Darrowby Inne – complete with spurious extra 'e' – by its owners, the giant Vaux brewery. Thirsk residents and councillors had raised a stink when the twee new name had been revealed in May – 'We do not want to see the town becoming a sort of Disneyland,' the mayor, Miss Janet Marshall, told Jo Knowsley of the *Sunday Telegraph* – with the result that the brewery changed the word 'Inne' to 'Inn' on the signs outside the pub but for some reason failed to do so inside, on the mirrors behind the bar and on the menus. The result was irretrievably naff: the sort of modern pub that was heavy with olde-worlde mahogany and brass fittings, old country prints and photographs, with a facetious sign over the bar warning ROWDY OR UNRULY CHILDREN WILL BE SOLD AS SLAVES. The illustration on the sign swinging in the breeze outside the Darrowby Inne depicted a typically Olde Englishe scene: a vet and a farmer gazing at a calf; but inside the food on offer included Chicken Tandoori, Mushroom Korma and Beef Madras.

The biggest and saddest change, though, was that the famous, elegant Georgian surgery at 23 Kirkgate had been closed for good. I peered through the windows into the rooms where James and Siegfried and Tristan and Helen will be for ever young and saw only emptiness and dust. In February 1996 Donald Sinclair's children had sold the building for £225,000 to Hambleton District Council, which was in the process of turning it into a Herriot museum and visitor centre where it was hoped that some of the practice's old veterinary equipment from the 1930s and 1940s – microscopes, stethoscopes, even an old Gladstone bag – would eventually be laid out on display in rooms furnished with some of Alf's personal effects and kept as much as possible as they had been when Alf and Donald Sinclair had started working together in 1940. The new museum was scheduled to open by the autumn of 1997 and Jimmy Wight and the four other vets who were still working in the practice had moved to an ugly modern red-brick building on a bleak industrial estate some way out of town on the busy A19 main road to York. 'I'm sure my father would have approved,' Jimmy Wight told Andrew Morgan of the *Sunday Telegraph*, unconvincingly, in March. 'He often said we were out-growing the place and realised we must move with the times. He would not be too sentimental.' In fact Alf was incredibly sentimental – certainly with animals, as he admitted himself, and in his books as well. Jimmy was also surprisingly dismissive of the flood of tourists who had helped to make his family richer than they could ever have dreamed. 'I love the Americans,' he said, 'but it's not fair on the others having tourists constantly coming in here. They were becoming a nuisance.' This anti-tourist remark is especially strange given that Jimmy Wight and his fellow vets had also exploited the Herriot mystique just as much themselves, calling their new surgery 'Skel-dale Veterinary Centre' – after Alf's *fictional* surgery, Skeldale House.

It is, of course, quite hopeless to expect that Thirsk might be anything like the quiet, idyllic Darrowby of the books. It probably never was. In 1996 lorries thundered constantly through the market square, pounding down the A19 from Darlington and Middlesbrough to York, the same A19 where drivers were welcomed by signs saying

JAMES HERRIOT'S TOWN. The signs seemed to have been successful in attracting visitors: the pavements were bustling and cars, buses, coaches and vans rattled through the town relentlessly or sat belching in traffic jams from dawn to long after dusk. Whatever it had been like in the 1940s there was nothing much magical or nostalgic about Thirsk in 1996. Nor was it any longer especially olde-worlde English, what with its two pizza palaces, two Chinese restaurants and Indian restaurant.

Thirty-five miles away the village of Askrigg, where the television series was filmed, had survived the onslaughts of publicity much better. It had always been much more picturesque than Thirsk, with cobbled streets and every building made of solid stone, without even one modern eyesore anywhere, without any outdoor hoardings or advertisements, and in 1996 it was still quiet and idyllic, nestling like some miraculous relic of the 1930s beneath the pretty hills with their network of dry-stone walls and their bleating sheep. Many of the houses were lush with charming hanging baskets tumbling with colourful flowers. The elegant King's Arms (the Drovers' Arms of the TV series) was still calling itself 'A Herriot Hotel' and displaying framed photographs of stills from the TV series but it seemed to be the only place in the village to capitalise on its Herriot connections – even the little village store had no Herriot postcards or T-shirts – and the stylish Georgian hotel's wonderfully spacious bars and central courtyard still smelt of history. Above all there was still a silence in the streets that spoke of centuries. Dogs do not bark in an English village like Askrigg: they would never be that impolite.

The tiny settlement of Thirlby was timeless, too. Joan Wight was still living in Mire Beck, next door to Rosie, down a secretive, dead-end country road – so secret that the hamlet did not have even one shop and Mire Beck had no name on the gate. But Askrigg and Thirlby were exceptional: apart from them the world of the Herriot books seemed quite extinct by 1996. 'Sadly, the magical world of James Herriot doesn't exist any more,' Jimmy Wight admitted to Noreen Taylor of the *Daily Mail* in 1995. 'A lot of the wonder, the adventure, has gone out of the veterinary world that Dad knew when he started in the business. There are no longer small farms with animals that constantly need a vet's service. Farms everywhere have grown into huge conglomerates. These days farmers are far more educated and self-reliant than they used to be. Most of them now give their own injections, and are able to tackle calving and lambing themselves, unless there are complications. So, while my dad travelled the countryside, wading through muddy fields chasing cows, I spend most of my time in a surgery treating cats, dogs and gerbils.'

It does not sound quite the same and I suspect that some of the fun had gone out of vetting for Jimmy, too. Despite the fact that Alf had always said that Jimmy was a much better vet than he had been, in August 1996 Jimmy told me that he was giving up the veterinary practice to become a writer like his father – but, unlike Alf, a full-time writer. His first book, he said, would be a biography of his father – a brave endeavour for any son to undertake. The book is due to be published in 1999.

I spoke to a dozen residents of Thirsk to ask them

about Alf and every single one said what a lovely man he was, a man without one enemy. Several said he had been very good for the town. 'The town depends on tourism,' said Mrs Freda Roberts, an elected councillor who sat on both the town and district councils, 'and tourism here has increased tremendously thanks to Alf. We even had a Taiwanese vet here the other day who'd come because of Alf. He's done an enormous amount for this town. And he was a nice man, a *superb* man, with no side to him at all: he was just our vet, our working vet. I don't think he had any enemies at all. He was a lovely man and that's the only description that anyone will give you.' Pam Dunning, the town clerk, agreed. 'We're very proud of him,' she said, 'and he's done no harm to the town. He was a lovely gentleman, a super chap, a very genuine chap. We miss him a great deal.'

Perhaps the last word should be left to one of his oldest friends. 'I'm sure he had no enemies,' Jimmy Steele told me in 1996, 'because he would never do any dirty tricks. Alf was so loved by so many people.'

No man could ever want a better epitaph.

Index

100 Years of Glasgow's Amazing Cinemas (Peter) 35, 99–100

Abraham, John 322

Adamson, Audrey *see* Sinclair, Audrey

Alderson, Helen (fictional character) *see* Wight, Joan

Alderton, John 264–8, 274–5

Alexander, Cecil Frances 217, 263, 268–9

All Creatures Great and Small (Herriot, omnibus edition) 3, 199, 213–26, 230–36, 264, 347

All Creatures Great and Small, film 231–6

All Creatures Great and Small, TV series 4, 134, 136, 271, 273–84; casting 275; setting 275–6; viewer appeal 282; shortcomings 283–4; shown in USA 283–4; worldwide distribution 319–20; storylines for AW's approval 303; viewing figures 303, 319–20; proposed stage play 320

All Things Bright and Beautiful (Herriot, omnibus edition) 241–2, 245, 263–4

All Things Herriot: James Herriot and his Peaceable Kingdom (Sternlicht) 6–7

All Things Wise and Wonderful (Herriot, omnibus edition) 268–70

Ames, Alfred 220–21

Anatomy of the Domestic Animals, The (Sissons) 96

Anderson, Gerry 86

Anderson, Mary 48

Animals Are My life (Straiton) 20–22, 169

Anthony Hopkins: In Darkness and Light (Callan) 234

Archer, Jeffrey 293

Ardnamurchan peninsula, Scotland 159–60

Argo, William 220–21

Arkengarthdale 276

Arkwright, Joe, fictional story of adapted by AW 325–7

Armour, Prof Sir James 116–17, 336

Askrigg 119, 275–6, 289, 320–22, 352–3

At the Sign of the Mermaid 189

Avenue Theatre and Opera House, Sunderland 11

Baird, John Logie 25, 39

Baker, Christopher 282

Baldwin, James 192

Bantam (publishers) 224–5, 245, 298

Barbirolli, Sir John 69

Barclay, 'Big Bill' 63

Barnet, Lord 188

Barrett, Andrew 329

Barton, Dick 317

Baxter, Stanley 53

BBC (British Broadcasting Corporation) 271, 273–5, 281–3, 303, 308

Beaumont, Frank 52, 61, 69

Beckinsale, Richard 275

Begg, Hugh 87

Bell, Hannah *see* Wight, Hannah

Bell, Jane (maternal grandmother of AW) 10

Bell, Robert (maternal grandfather of AW) 10

Bellingham, Lynda 283

Bennett, Granville (fictional character) *see* Pette, Denton

Berry, Douglas 69

Berry, 'Wee Ned' 63

Best of James Herriot, The (Herriot) 183, 289

Bingham, Frank 124, 150, 336

Birch, Margaret 348

Blakely, Colin 264–5

Bodie (dog) 105, 298, 305, 324, 331–2, 335

Bolitho, William 19

Bolt, David 212, 214

Borthwick, E. Kerr 307

Both Sides of the Burn (Yoker secondary school) 27

Brabbs, Derry 287–8

Bragg, Melvyn 193

Braithwaite, Arnold (fictional character) 326–7

Brand, Gavin 26

Britannia Music Hall, Glasgow 35

British Veterinary Association 254, 258, 322, 342

Broadbent, Sam (fictional character) 206

Brooke, Alan 252, 257, 287, 290

Brooks, C.R.M. (Charlie) 63

Brown, W.H. 72

Bruce, Brenda 231

Buchanan, Calum (fictional character) *see* Nettleton, Brian

Busby, Thomas 113

Callan, Michael Feeney 234

Cameron, Ian 103–4

Campbell, Alastair 61

Campbell, Donald 102

Campbell, Dorothy 81–3, 86–7, 100

Campbell, Douglas 65, 162

Campbell, Heulwen 65, 117, 121, 161–2, 254

Cancer of Empire (Bolitho) 19–20

Carnegie Trust 84

Carruthers, Eliza 26

Carruthers, William 26

Cave, Jeremy 342

Cessford, Jim 70

Cessford, Maisie 62, 70

Channel Islands 243–4, 246–7

Chapman, Judge (York) 261

Charing Cross Electric Theatre, Glasgow 35

Charles, Prince of Wales 286

Cheever, John 285

cinemas: musicians 10–13, 15–16, 34–7, 55, 99; Sunderland 11–12; Glasgow 34–7, 45; introduction of sound 55, 99

Clark, Fergus 58

Clark, Nell 58, 71

Coleman, Jack 86

Collins, Billy 187

Collins publishers 186–7

Common Colics of the Horse (Reeks) 96

Connolly, Billy 37

Consumer Promotions Corporation 261

Cord Power Parts Ltd 261

Cord Power Parts (North) Ltd 261

Cotter, Jimmy 58

Crawford, William 23–4, 41–5

Creature Comforts (video documentary) 333

Cricketer, The 307

Cringley House 119, 276

Crooks, John 157–8, 178, 338–9

Crouch, Anthony 346

Cunningham, Ken 78

Daily Mail 17, 46, 121, 134, 154, 156, 171, 182, 196, 231, 238–9, 256, 278, 296, 300, 330, 339, 341, 353

Daily Mirror 224

Daily Telegraph 17, 115, 177, 181, 224, 236, 239, 243, 252, 254, 321, 329, 337

Dan (dog) 230, 246, 255, 258, 263, 269

Danbury, Horace 126

Danbury, Joan *see* Wight, Joan

Danbury, Laura 161

Darrowby (fictional village) *see* Thirsk

Darrowby Inne, Thirsk 350

Davenport, Peter 321

Davenport, Roger 303

David Higham Associates 188, 212, 346

Davison, Peter 278; as 'Tristan Farnon' 275, 277, 281; gives Eddie Straiton character reference 300

Dawson, A.J. 75

Day, Peter 190–91, 194, 199–200

Dereham, Jenny 189–90, 289

Disenchanted, The (Schulberg) 182

Dolce Vita (restaurant) 186, 193

Don (dog) 55, 58, 67

Donovan, Harry 104

Douglas, Robert 140

Douglas-Boyd, Dick 116, 237, 250, 252, 305, 307; on publishing AW's books 178, 200–202, 207, 210–11, 224; with AW at Imperial Hotel 255–6; on AW's autocratic streak 293; relationship with Joan Wight 293–4

Douglas-Boyd, June 255

Drinkwater, Carol: as 'Helen Herriot' 3–4, 127, 275, 277, 279–80, 283; meets Joan

Wight 279; affair with
Christopher Timothy 282;
not invited to AW's memorial
service 343
Dublin 91–2
Dudley, Terence 282
Duffy, Brian 209, 335
Duncan, Alex 190
Dunning, Pam 354

Edward VII, King 16
Elizabeth II, Queen 148, 286
Elliot, Nan 94, 126, 129–30, 279
Emslie, Professor 96
Era, The 15–16, 34
Evening Standard 210
Every Living Thing (Herriot)
157–8, 309, 324–8
Everybody's Dog Book (Dawson) 75

Faichney, John 73
Falk, Quentin 234–5
Farmers Weekly 210
Farming Press 186
Farnon, Siegfried (fictional
character) *see* Sinclair, Donald
Farnon, Tristan (fictional character)
see Sinclair, Brian
Felixkirk 336
Field, The 224
Filshie, James 61–3, 68
Fisher, Joe 52
Forty Hours Strike (John Brown's
shipyard) 31
Four o'Clock (J.A.W. and D.M.M.)
73–4
Francis, Dick 201
Furnell, Rev Raymond 343

Gardner, John 98
Gibb, Johnny 73
Gibbs, Patrick 236
Glasgow: social conditions (poor)
19–27, 36; 750 Yoker Road
23–4, 26, 48; shipbuilding
27–31, 57; cinemas 34–7, 45;
746 Yoker Road (later 2172
Dumbarton Road) 48–50;
724 Anniesland Road 98,
106, 110; 694 Anniesland
Road 110; air raids 130–31
Glasgow Encyclopaedia, The (Fisher)
52
Glasgow Herald 61
Glasgow High School 53
Glasgow Rangers FC 47
Glasgow University 105, 320
Glasgow Veterinary College 6–7,
67, 106; shambolic operation
79–88; pass rates 80, 83–6,
90; fees 84; attendance 85–6;
gambling 86, 88; drop out
rate 103; taken over by
Glasgow University 105
Glasser, Jacqueline (*née* Korn) 189,
214, 346
Godwin, Fay 287
Golden Fleece Hotel, Thirsk 313,
329, 348–9
Golden Pan awards 264
Gordon, Richard 190
Gorman, Edward 84
Grand Hotel, Scarborough 136–9,
141, 160, 171
Greaves, William 296
Green family (cinema owners)
35–7
Greene, Graham 243

Grey, Janet (*née* Sinclair) 120–21, 239, 341

Grey, Rupert 121, 238, 240

Hall, Mrs (fictional character) 185

Hardisty, Tony 17, 32, 227

Hardy, Robert: as 'Siegfried Farnon' 4, 119, 238, 275–8, 281–3; meets AW 276; friendship with Donald Sinclair 277–8; gives Eddie Straiton character reference 300; reads extract at AW's memorial service 342–4

Harold Ober (literary agency) 213

Harrogate 172

Harrow, Lisa 231, 233–4, 264, 277

Harvey, Alex 183, 230, 247

Harvey, Richard 321

Hatchard's (bookshop) 307

Hattersley, Roy 313

Hawkins, Ann 321

Heaton Park, Manchester 143–4

Hector (dog) 230, 246, 254–5, 258, 263, 269

Hello! 335

Hepburn, John 83

Herd, Douglas 75

Heriot Watt University 287

Herriot Country 6

Herriot, Helen (fictional character) *see* Wight, Joan

Herriot industry 287, 289–90, 304, 313–14, 320–22, 348–52

Herriot, James *see* Wight, James Alfred

Herriot, Jim (Scotland footballer) 4, 183, 314, 317–18

Herriot museum, Thirsk 350–51

Hill, Susan 253

Hillhead Album, A (Morton) 51

Hillhead High School, 1885–1961 (Campbell) 61

Hillhead High School: academic standards 52–4, 71; costs 54–7; sporting excellence 58–9; discipline 61–2; move to Oakfield Avenue 71–2; science jinx 72–3

Hind, Gillian (daughter-in-law of AW, *married name* Wight) 245, 262, 333

Hopkins, Anthony 231–2, 234–7

How to Be a Writer 181

Humphreys, Graham 202

Hutchinson, Tom 236, 265

Hutchison, Eddie 101, 136

Hutton, Sir Len 252

Ianson, Flora 346

If Only They Could Talk (Herriot) 1, 4, 117, 176, 183–97, 201–2, 207, 212–14, 216, 230

Imperial Hotel, Torquay 255–6

Iris Clausen 179

Irvine, George 83

It Shouldn't Happen to a Vet (Herriot) 2, 193, 202–11, 213, 230, 276; film 264–6

Ivy Dene School, Thirsk 156, 162

Jackson, Gordon 53

James Herriot Library (Glasgow University) 105

James Herriot Storybook, The (Herriot) 304

James Herriot's Cat Stories (Herriot) 304

James Herriot's Dog Stories (Herriot) 86, 105, 304

James Herriot's Treasury for Children (Herriot) 304

James Herriot's Yorkshire (Herriot) 115, 117, 140, 166, 287–8

James Herriot's Yorkshire (video film) 333, 349

Japan 230–31

Jarron, James 84

Jenkinson, Rod 245

Jimmy Young (Young) 170

John Brown's shipyard, Glasgow 27–8, 31, 33, 110

Jones, Freddie 231

Jones, Isabell 23

Jones, Rowland 75

Joseph, Anthea 189–92, 194, 201–2, 204, 210, 221, 248, 255, 269, 306

Junor, Sir John 23, 26, 29, 47–8, 209–10

Katz, Jennifer 191

Kelly, Fergus 290

Kennedy, Margaret 52

Kinematograph Weekly, The 13

King's Theatre, Sunderland 11

Klaipeda, Lithuania 179

Knowsley, Jo 350

Korn, Jacqueline (*married name* Glasser) 189, 214, 346

Kroch's and Brentano's bookstore, Chicago 95, 270

La Vie en Rose (Herriot) 5, 174–6

Laker, Jim 160

Langtry, Lillie 16–17

Lee-Potter, Lynda 17, 46, 134, 154, 171, 330–31

LeRoy, Jean 188–9

Let Sleeping Vets Lie (Herriot) 193, 215–16, 221, 223–4, 230, 241–2, 249, 263

Let's Talk of Dogs (Jones) 75

Lewis, Peter 256, 268

Library Journal, The 221

Listening For a Midnight Tram (Junor) 23, 47

Literary Guild (America) 270

Liverpool University 297

Locke, Harry 70

Lord God Made Them All, The (Herriot) 294–8

Lord, Thomas 112, 133

Lord's (cricket ground) 112, 133

Luke, Fred 63–4

McAloon (Glasgow Veterinary College student) 85

McArthur, Tom 25

McCallum, Allan 64

McColl, Ian 57–8, 60–63, 70, 73

McColl, Neil 70–71

McConville, Ben 317–18

McCormack, Daniel 218, 254

McCormack, Sandra 211, 213, 218, 253–4, 332

McCormack, Tom 229–30, 240, 244–6, 251, 256, 283–4, 301–2, 319, 329, 346; publishes AW in USA 188, 199, 211–27; on AW's writing 222–3, 226–7; relationship with AW 225; tones down Siegfried

character 241–2; on Joan
Wight's attitude to AW's
writing 244–5; keeps AW
from Wimbledon tennis final
253–4; editing of AW's later
books 270, 295, 327–8; guilt
for AW's burden of fame
284–6; on AW's autocratic
streak 291–3; last lunch with
AW 332; effect of AW's death
339; at AW's memorial
service 342; debt to AW 347
MacDonald, Ramsay 65
Mackay, Diana 252
McKinlay, Alan 28–31, 34, 57
Maclean, Alistair 59, 243
Maclean, Banytine 84
Maclean's 7, 269
McLin, Sharon 336
McMorran, Maurice 104
Macrae, Malcolm 72
McSween, Eddie 70
Mail on Sunday 316, 328
Making Ships Making Men
   (McKinlay) 28, 57
Malcolm, William 41
Margolis, Jonathan 316, 328–9
Marked Money 11–12
Marriott, Edward 171, 324
Marshall, Janet 350
Martin, Jim 57
Maxwell, Robert 295
Mayle, Peter 201
Meccano Magazine 67
Melville, Aubrey 89–90, 93, 301
Michael Joseph Ltd 2, 116, 178,
   188–92, 199–203, 207, 210,
   214, 218, 230, 252, 264,
   268–9, 289, 293–4, 304

Mire Beck, Thirlby 245–6, 291,
   325, 335
Mohd, Qasuria Ashiq 83
Moorehead, Caroline 115, 119,
   177, 181, 252, 254
Morgan, Andrew 351
Morgan, Cal 334
Morrison, John 186, 193–4
Morrison, John ('Johnnie') 88, 92
Morrison, Kathleen 92–3
Morrison, Victor 178, 201, 244,
   250, 253, 287
Morton, Henry Brougham 51
Moses the Kitten (Herriot) 304
Mowbray, Robert de 112
Murder, Murder, Polis! (Sinclair)
   43–4
Murdoch, Copey 58

Nettleton, Brian 158, 325
New York Times 219–20, 328
Newcombe, Ted (fictional
   character) 325
Newhouse, Gobber (fictional
   character) 206
Nickson, Liz 316

Observer, The 224, 284
Only One Woof (Herriot) 304
Oval Nursing Home, Harrogate
   299, 301

Page, Christopher John 227–8,
   261–2, 346
Page, Emma (granddaughter of
   AW) 258, 262, 322, 330–31,
   334, 342, 346
Page, Rosemary Beatrice *see*
   Wight, Rosemary Beatrice

Pan Books 210–11, 249, 264, 269, 296

Panopticon, Glasgow 35

Partick Thistle FC 47–8

Paton, James 83

People 305

People's Palace, Sunderland 11

Peter, Bruce 35, 37, 99

Pette, Denton 172, 237, 250, 301

Pette, Eve 172, 301

Picturedromes, Glasgow 35–7

Pile, Stephen 17, 243, 329–30

Plater, Alan 264

Playing to Pictures 13

Ploughman of the Moon (Service) 53–4

Poland 179–80

Polly (dog) 305, 324, 331–2

Pumphrey, Mrs (fictional character) *see* Warner, Marjorie

Queen, John 83–4

Queen Mary 33

Raconteur 5

Radio Times 287

Rae, Gordon 172

Rae, Jean 172

Rae, William 63, 72

Ratcliffe, Arthur 12

RCVS (Royal College of Veterinary Surgeons) 299–301, 342

Reader's Digest 183, 222, 230–31, 264, 268, 288–9, 298, 317

Records of 80 Years' Progress (Glasgow Veterinary College history) 82

Reeks, Caulton 96

Reeth, Swaledale 264, 276

Rhodes, Ted 275

Risk, Jimmy 71

Ritchie, Douglas 163

Ritchie, May 163

Roberts, Freda 354

Roger, Mary 75

Roker Variety Theatre, Sunderland 11–12

Ross, Ewan (fictional character) *see* Bingham, Frank

Ross, Mileva 281

'Rowardennan' 159, 245

Royal Air Force *see* Wight, James Alfred (RAF)

Royal College of Veterinary Surgeons (RCVS) 299–301, 342

Rush, John 235–7, 274, 282, 298, 303, 320

St David (horse) 122, 148

St Martin's Press 188, 199, 207, 211–12, 216–17, 334, 347.

San Francisco Chronicle 220

Saturday Review 223, 241, 298

Scarborough 135–41, 160, 171

Schreiber, Graeme 109

Schreiber, Jean 109–11, 171, 251, 299

Schulberg, Budd 182

Secret Life of John Logie Baird, The (McArthur and Waddell) 25

Sell Them a Story (LeRoy) 189

Sellars, Bill 275, 279

Service, Robert 53–4

Shakespeare on Cricket (Borthwick) 307

Shaughnessy, Alfred 303

shipbuilding: slump 14, 32–4, 57; Sunderland 14, 33–4; Glasgow 27–31, 57

Shuei-sha 231

Simmons, V. 200

Sinclair, Alan (son of Donald) 148, 238–9, 341

Sinclair, Audrey (*née* Adamson, wife of Donald) 115, 122, 240; background 147–8; marriage 147; son (Alan) born 148; character 239; objects to Robert Hardy's portrayal of 'Siegfried Farnon' character 277; blindness 308; death 341

Sinclair, Brian (brother of Donald) 114, 123, 147, 157, 193, 236, 243, 289; 'Tristan Farnon' character 114, 185, 195, 206, 238, 288; receives percentage of AW's film/television income 237–8; illness 299; operation 308; death 316

Sinclair, Donald 5, 193, 308; interviews AW for Thirsk job 111, 114, 117–20; buys Thirsk practice 114; first wife's death 114–15; character 120–22, 129–30, 153, 157, 239–40, 278, 341, 347–8; exploits AW 120–22, 153, 157; marries Audrey Adamson 122, 147; presents Queen with horse 122, 148; attempts to join RAF 129; dismisses Eddie Straiton 129; AW's best man 136; godfather to

Seamus 143; angered by royal gifts 148; becomes Queen's adviser on horses 148; becomes Thirsk Racecourse resident vet 148; pigeon fancier 148–9; son (Alan) born 148; relationship with AW 235–43, 267–8; friendship with Robert Hardy 277–8; accident with motorcycle 297; at work in Kirkgate surgery 311; retires 320; devastated by AW's death 340–41; devastated by second wife's death 341–2; suicide 341–2; value of estate 347

'Siegfried Farnon' character 5, 7, 117, 119, 184–5, 194–5, 206, 288, 311; objects to choice of name 115, 239; objects to screen portrayals 234–8, 264–5, 277–8; unhappiness with portrayal in books 236–9, 241–2; receives percentage of AW's film/television income 237–8; threatens legal action over AW's portrayal 237–9

Sinclair, Janet (daughter of Donald, *married name* Grey) 120–21, 239, 341

Sinclair, Maureen 43

Sinclair, Sheila 322

Singleton, George 34–5

Skeldale House (fictional location) *see* Thirsk, 23 Kirkgate

Smith, B., & Son (Thirsk) 113

Smith, Claire 213–14, 328

Smithsonian Magazine, The 243

Smudge, the Little Lost Lamb
(Herriot) 304
Sowerby 159
Steele, Bette 322–3, 345
Steele, Jimmy 81, 86–9, 94, 116,
120–22, 127, 151–2, 157,
261, 301, 322–3, 345, 354;
objects to casting of *ACGAS*
(TV series) 278–9
Sternlicht, Sanford 6–7
Stettin, Poland 179–80
Steven, Anthony 303
Stevenson, Margaret 83
Stewart, David 83
Stirner, Brian 231
Straiton, Eddie 24, 38, 54, 91,
109, 116, 121, 136, 152, 157,
169–70, 193–4, 197, 199,
204, 237, 244, 262, 332;
Animals Are My Life
(autobiography) 20–22, 169;
childhood 20–22; at Glasgow
Veterinary College 80–81,
84–5, 87–94, 102–4; AW's
obituary 89–90, 124–5, 339;
seeks work 108; on AW's
salary 120; at Thirsk practice
122–5, 129; relationship with
Joan Wight 126–7, 173; air
raid destroys house 130;
planned partnership with AW
153; and AW's nervous
breakdown 165–70;
brucellosis 166; encourages
AW to start writing 167–9;
pays for AW's Majorca trip
168, 170; runs Thirsk practice
in AW's absence 168, 170;
trains Seamus in practice 173;

aids AW's literary
breakthrough 186–8, 193;
veterinary books published
186; veterinary adviser on
ACGAS (TV series) 273,
281; appears before RCVS
disciplinary committee
299–301; AW's refusal to
appear on behalf of 299–301;
character references 300; son's
death 300; son (Edward) born
332; eye operation 339
Straiton, Lorraine 299–301
Straiton, Penny 332
Summers, Harold 99, 110, 111
Sun 183, 230, 247, 317
Sunday Express 1–3, 17, 32,
208–10, 224, 227, 316–17,
335
Sunday Express Magazine 316
Sunday Mirror 281
Sunday Sun 240
Sunday Telegraph 171, 236, 265,
324, 350–51
Sunday Telegraph Magazine 49, 177,
181, 187, 248, 297
Sunday Times 224
Sunday Times Magazine 244
Sunderland: 111 Brandling Street
9–10, 13, 18; cinemas 11–12;
shipbuilding 14, 33–4
Sunderland Empire 11
Sunderland FC 9, 31–2, 47, 102,
162, 178, 227, 260–61, 318,
323–4, 334, 340
Sunnyside Maternity Home,
Thirsk 139, 154
Susskind, David 231, 233–6, 264,
273–4

Switzerland 159, 174–6, 317

Talbot, Alex 281
Taylor, Alex ('Sandy') 42, 90, 101, 136, 143, 160, 162, 259, 332, 343
Taylor, Lynne 160, 162, 259
Taylor, Noreen 156, 182, 196, 339, 353
Teach Yourself to Write 181–2
Telegraph Magazine 190
'The Count' (Glasgow Veterinary College student) 86
Theatre Royal, Sunderland 11, 18
Thirlby 245, 353
Thirsk 3–5, 112–14, 353–4; 23 Kirkgate (veterinary surgery) 119, 184–5, 264, 310–11, 320, 350; as 'Darrowby' 184, 275; Herriot industry 289–90, 313–14, 348–52; Golden Fleece Hotel 313, 329, 348–9; Darrowby Inne 350; planned Herriot museum 350–51; Skeldale Veterinary Centre 351
Till, Eric 264
Time 219, 285
Times, The 158, 337–8
Timothy, Christopher 3, 275–9, 333, 349; as 'James Herriot' 275–6, 278–9, 281, 283; meets AW 276; affair with Carol Drinkwater 282; breaks leg 282; gives Eddie Straiton character reference 300; reads extract at AW's memorial service 342, 344
Today 290

Too Good to Waste (Falk) 234
Torquay 255–6
Turnbull, Alex 26
Turnbull, Jane 26

United States of America 187–8, 199–201, 207, 211–26, 230, 251

Vallely, Paul 49, 177, 181, 187, 248, 297
Vernon-Hunt, Ralph 210–11
Vet in Harness (Herriot) 112, 133, 230, 249–50, 252, 263–4, 342
Vet in a Spin (Herriot) 216, 268
Veterinary Record 81, 89, 108, 120, 124, 200, 332, 338–9
Veterinary Surgery as a Career (article) 67
Vets Might Fly (Herriot) 133, 138, 264, 268
Villiers, Marjorie 187
Villiers Theatre, Sunderland 11

Waddell, Peter 25
Ward, Simon 231–5, 264–5, 274, 333
Warner, Marjorie 238–9, 306–7
Watkinson, Jack 273, 276
Watson, Elizabeth 49
Wear Music Hall, Sunderland 11
Weipers, Sir William 102–3
Wensley 276
West Scrafton 159
Whatham, Claude 231
White, John 98
Whitehouse, A.W. ('Old Doc') 7, 67, 79–80, 82, 85, 97, 101
Whiteley, Richard 262–3

Whitemore, Hugh 233

Who's Who 291

Wight, Gillian (*née* Hind,
    daughter-in-law of AW) 245,
    262, 333

Wight, Hannah ('Nan', *née* Bell,
    mother of AW) 10, 26, 98,
    110, 153, 162; musical career
    10–11, 37, 48–9, 58, 100,
    111; dominant personality 14,
    38, 109; and family move to
    Glasgow 14, 16–18;
    appearance 109; work as
    seamstress 111; husband's
    death 170–71; delight at AW's
    success 250–51; cerebral
    arteriosclerosis 298–9; death
    301–2

Wight, James Alexander ('Jimmy'
    or 'Seamus', son of AW) 3,
    6–7, 121, 160–61, 182, 196,
    228, 239–40, 290, 329, 341,
    343, 345–6; birth 139–43;
    childhood 154–6; relationship
    with father 154–6; trained by
    Eddie Straiton 173; joins
    Thirsk practice 181; musical
    talent 181; marriage 245;
    Nicholas (son) born 262;
    endorses Robert Hardy's
    portrayal of 'Siegfried Farnon'
    character 278; runs Thirsk
    practice 310–11, 351; opens
    James Herriot Library
    (Glasgow University) 336;
    tribute to father 339–40;
    anti-tourist remark 351; gives
    up veterinary practice to
    become writer 353

Wight, James Alfred ('Alf'): birth
    9; and Sunderland FC 9,
    31–2, 47, 102, 162, 178, 227,
    260–61, 318, 323–4, 334,
    340; family links with
    entertainment 10; love of
    football 31–2, 46–8, 178–9,
    255, 317–18; character 38,
    60, 70–71, 88–91, 93–4,
    251–3, 262–3, 266–8,
    279–80, 290–94, 299–301;
    relationship with father 46;
    relationship with mother 46,
    109, 162, 171; love of music
    49, 69, 89–90, 162–3, 258–9;
    diaries 65, 116, 151–2, 178,
    180, 184, 223, 248, 296–7,
    325; and opposite sex 68–9,
    92–5, 126, 129–30, 280; anal
    fistula 75, 123, 140, 143–4;
    love of reading 96, 218, 270,
    343; family move to 724
    Anniesland Road 98;
    develops love of countryside
    101–2; family move to 694
    Anniesland Road 110;
    affection for Glasgow 112;
    entranced by Yorkshire Dales
    118–19; financial problems
    121–2, 136, 149, 156–7, 172,
    182; meets Joan Danbury
    126–7; dominated by Joan
    127–8, 262, 279–80, 293–4,
    331; courts Joan 128–9;
    marriage 129, 134–6; Seamus
    (son) born 139–42; married
    life 149–52; Rosie (daughter)
    born 154; family holidays
    156, 159–60; sends children

to fee-paying school 156; builds 'Rowardennan' 159; trips to Switzerland 159, 175–6, 317; love of cricket 160; and mother-in-law 161; contracts brucellosis 165–70; nervous breakdown 165–70; depression 166–7; Majorca trip 168, 170; father's death 170–71; wedding anniversaries 180, 182, 240, 322; dissuades Rosie from studying veterinary medicine 181; watches Sunderland Cup Final victory 227; impact of success 229–30; watches *ACGAS* filming 231–4; relationship with Donald Sinclair 235–43, 267–8; payments to Sinclair brothers 237–9; considers tax exile 243–4; taxation 243–4, 274, 297–8, 315; visits Channel Islands 243–4, 246–7; Jamaica trip 244; builds Mire Beck 245–6; failure to grasp extent of wealth 245–6; self-portrayal 252–3; irritated by public attention 254; fears self corrupted by success 256–7; daily routine 258–60, 305; Emma (granddaughter) born 258; love of dogs 260; builds house for Rosie 262; Nicholas (grandson) born 262; and Rosie's divorce 262; death of dogs 263; sells *ACGAS* film rights 273–4; mixed emotions over

ACGAS TV series 274–5, 279, 281; endorses *ACGAS* TV performances 276–7; disapproves of Timothy/Drinkwater affair 282; burden of fame 284–6, 290–91, 293, 319; film director story 284; turns down *Time* magazine cover offer 285; at Buckingham Palace dinner 286; receives OBE 286; possible identity crisis 288; ambivalence regarding privacy 291; increasing strain of lifestyle 296; mother's illness 298–9; kidney stone 299; moves mother into nursing home 299; refusal to appear on Eddie Straiton's behalf at RCVS hearing 299–301; mother's death 301–2; osteoarthritis 304; Cover Valley cottage holidays 305–6; health problems 308; Italian cruise 308; politics 313; meets Jim Herriot 317–18; will 317, 346–7; refusal to endorse commercial products 320; made life president of Sunderland FC 323; watches Sunderland FC in 1992 FA Cup Final 323–4; feelings for Emma 330–31; for Joan 331; for Rosie 331; for Seamus 331; prostate cancer diagnosed 331; congratulates Eddie Straiton on birth of son (Edward) 332; trampled

by sheep 333–4; invited to
open James Herriot Library,
Glasgow University 334;
watches last football match
334; death 336; funeral 240,
336–7; memorial service
342–4; obituaries 89–90, 231,
337–9; value of estate 345;
exclusion of Christopher
Page from will 346; leaves
nothing to charity 347
childhood: family move to
Glasgow 13–18; football fan
31–2, 46–8; mother's
influence 38; primary school
38–9, 41–5; father's influence
46, 49; reading 46, 55, 65–6;
family move to 746 Yoker
Road 48; love of music 49;
passion for animals 55, 58, 67;
decision to be a journalist 65
Hillhead High School: wealth
gap with other children
59–60; academic performance
62, 64–6, 68, 75, 77; belted
by James Filshie 62; subjects
studied 62–3, 69; ambition to
specialise in dogs 67–8; seeks
advice on academic
requirements for veterinary
career 67; first date 68–9;
wins athletics medal 68; wins
English prize 68;
contemporaries' memories of
69–70; meets John Barbirolli
69; illness 75
Glasgow Veterinary College:
football 48, 90–92; failed
exams 84, 97, 103, 118;
subjects studied 84, 96;
laboratory accident 85; social
life 88–94; Dublin footballing
weekend 91–3; football
match against The Dick
(Edinburgh) 93; abandons
dream of specialising in dogs
95; attacked by coalman's
horse 95; learns about horses
95–6; learns to ride 96;
record sheet 96–7, 101;
laziness 97–8, 100; academic
results 101–2; improved
academic performance 101;
hands-on experience 102–3;
final exams 103–4; models
self on William Weipers 103
veterinary career: decision to
become a vet 66–7; poor job
prospects 107–9; interview
for Thirsk job 111, 114,
117–20; exploited by Donald
Sinclair 120–22, 153, 157;
salary 120–21, 153, 157; buys
Thirsk partnership 121; runs
practice in Donald Sinclair's
absence 122–6; appointed
MAF Local Veterinary
Inspector 124; initially
daunted 125; develops
small-animal side of business
150; dedication to job 152–3;
planned partnership with
Eddie Straiton 153; takes
children on rounds 154–5,
158; Istanbul trip 178, 180;
USSR trip 178–80; joined by
Seamus 181; elected Yorkshire
Veterinary Society president

227; wins US award for services to veterinary world 251; elected honorary member of British Veterinary Association 254, 258; swinging cat story 268; cuts back on veterinary work 297–8; made Honorary Doctor of Veterinary Science (Liverpool University) 297; on veterinary practice past and present 309–10; at work in Kirkgate surgery 311–12; overseas offers 312–13; retires 316; wins British Veterinary Association Chiron Award 322

RAF: fictionalisation 6, 133–4, 138–42; volunteers 130–31; training 135, 137, 140–44; missing year 138–41; phantom pregnancy 138; vertigo 142; discharged 144–5

fictionalisation of life: circumstances of RAF service 6, 133–4, 138–42; father's occupation 17–18, 49, 56, 136, 302; time taken to qualify as vet 84, 118; gambling at Glasgow Veterinary College 88; Herriot books 115–18, 161, 223, 248–9, 288, 314, 337; when started writing 116; circumstances of interview with Donald Sinclair 117–20; courtship of Joan 128–9; honeymoon 136; events surrounding birth of first

child 138–41; claim not to keep diary 151–2, 184, 248, 296–7, 325; goaded into writing 167, 177; date of father's death 171; finding first literary agent 188–9; first two books' lack of British success 199–200, 207; dates 257–8, 306; earnings from writing 297–8, 315; date became vet 306; date entered Hillhead High School 306; date of move to Mire Beck 325; Arnold Braithwaite story 326–7

writing: rejections 1, 176–7, 187–8; choice of pseudonym 4, 7, 182–3; 'James Herriot' character 7, 184–5, 194–5, 204–6, 217–18, 222–3, 232, 265–6, 288; 'Siegfried Farnon' character name 115, 239; working environment 161, 182, 248; starts writing as therapy 168–9; years of 'practising' 173, 176–8, 180–82; considers writing football book 179; studies other writers 181–2; agents 188–9, 213–14, 346; discovered by Anthea Joseph 189–92, 201; failure to recognise Jean LeRoy's contribution 189; earnings 192, 196, 245–6, 269, 273–4, 297–8, 315, 345; dedications 193, 236–7, 269, 294, 324; failure to recognise John Morrison's contribution

193–4; US publication 199–201, 207, 211–27; print-runs 200–202, 207, 219–20, 224, 230, 294; reviews 200, 207–10, 219–21, 224, 270, 328; productivity 203–4; sales 207, 212, 225, 230, 263–4, 268, 298, 304, 319, 328, 346–7; royalties 215, 224–5; alternative titles 216–17; appeal of Herriot books 217, 222–3, 249, 266, 329–30, 337; publishers' attitudes 218; US publicity tours 221–2, 225–6; fans 226, 229, 231, 250, 289–90, 304–5, 312–13, 320, 333, 336; desire to write straight novel 230, 269; popularity in Japan 230–31; translations 230–31, 328; asks McCormack to tone down Siegfried character 241–2; Len Hutton fan letter 252; failure to write about early years 257–8; self-confidence 257; receives Golden Pan awards 264; decline in powers 269–70, 295–6; made Honorary Doctor of Literature (Heriot Watt University) 287; assessment of own work 294; effect on veterinary profession 310, 338, 347

writings: *If Only They Could Talk* 1, 4, 117, 176, 183–97, 201–2, 207, 212–14, 216, 230; *It Shouldn't Happen to a Vet* 2, 193, 202–11, 213, 230, 264–6, 276; *All Creatures Great and Small* (for TV series see main heading) 3, 199, 213–26, 230–36, 264, 347; *La Vie en Rose* (short story) 5, 174–6; *Four o'Clock* (possible) 73–4; *Words* (possible) 76–7; *James Herriot's Dog Stories* 86, 105, 304; story of Dublin footballing weekend 92–3; Kroch's and Brentano's bookstore catalogue article 95, 270; *Vet in Harness* 112, 133, 230, 249–50, 252, 263–4, 342; *James Herriot's Yorkshire* 115, 117, 140, 166, 287–8; short stories 116, 173–7; *Vets Might Fly* 133, 138, 264, 268; *Every Living Thing* 157–8, 309, 324–8; early writings 181; *The Best of James Herriot* 183, 289; *Let Sleeping Vets Lie* 193, 215–16, 221, 223–4, 230, 241–2, 249, 263; *Vet in a Spin* 216, 268; *All Things Bright and Beautiful* 241–2, 245, 263–4; *All Things Wise and Wonderful* 268–70; *The Lord God Made Them All* 294–8; *James Herriot's Cat Stories* 304; *James Herriot's Treasury for Children* 304; *Moses the Kitten* 304; *Only One Woof* 304; *Smudge, the Little Lost Lamb* 304; *The James Herriot Storybook* 304

Wight, James Henry ('Jim', father of AW) 9–10, 98; musical

career 10–12, 14–18, 34–7,
48–9, 55–6, 99–100, 110–11;
and family move to Glasgow
13–18; possible reasons for
leaving Sunderland 14–17;
shipyard work 27–8, 30–34,
54; football fan 31–2, 46;
unemployment 32–4, 48, 54,
56–7; character 38, 109, 162;
encourages son's reading 46;
struggles to send son to
Hillhead 54–7; tries to
dissuade son from veterinary
career 77; struggles to keep
son at Glasgow Veterinary
College 84, 98; improvement
in family finances 98–100;
death 110, 170–71

Wight, James (paternal grandfather
of AW) 10, 99

Wight, Joan (*née* Danbury, wife of
AW) 4, 6, 117, 130, 162–3,
189, 193, 216, 218, 233, 266,
345–6, 353; 'Helen Herriot'
character 117, 126–7, 206–7,
277, 279–80, 288; meets AW
126–7; relationship with
Eddie Straiton 126, 173;
character 127–8, 221–2, 245,
262–3, 279–80, 293–4, 331;
courted by AW 128–9;
marriage 129, 134–6; first
pregnancy 138–9; Seamus
(son) born 139–42; married
life 149–52; helps AW in
practice 152; Rosie
(daughter) born 154; trips to
Switzerland 159, 176, 317;
money worries 172; wedding

anniversaries 180, 182, 240,
322; attitude towards AW's
writing 244–5; refuses to live
abroad 244; Emma
(granddaughter) born 258;
Nicholas (grandson) born
262; relationship with
son-in-law 262; and Rosie's
divorce 262; meets Carol
Drinkwater 279; relationship
with Dick Douglas-Boyd
293–4; bronchitis 307; Italian
cruise 308; at AW's death
336; no reply to Carol
Drinkwater's letter of
condolence 343

Wight, Nicholas (grandson of AW)
262

Wight, Rosemary Beatrice
('Rosie', daughter of AW,
married name Page) 3, 7,
160–62, 209, 217, 240, 305,
307–8, 317, 345–6, 353;
birth 154; childhood 154–6;
nearly trampled by cow
154–5; relationship with
father 154–6; dissuaded from
studying veterinary medicine
181; musical talent 181;
studies human medicine 181;
marriage 227–8; Emma
(daughter) born 258; divorce
261–2; romantic relationship
with Richard Whiteley
262–3; cartilage operation
299; and father's illness
333–5; at father's death 336

Wight, Zoe (granddaughter of
AW) 294

Wilson, Hetty 63

Winkfield airfield, Berkshire
    141–3

Winn, Godfrey 200

Wodehouse, P.G. 343

Woodcock, John 238, 278, 341

Words (J.A.W.) 76–7

World of Jeeves, The (Wodehouse)
    343

Wright, Peter 329

Yarrow shipyard, Glasgow 27

Yates, Tim 329

Year in Provence, A (Mayle) 201

Yoker Athletic FC 46

Yoker Fernlea FC 47

Yoker, Glasgow 18, 23–7, 45–6,
    49

Yoker Primary School 38–9, 41–5

York Minster 342–4

Yorkshire, Herriot industry
    289–90, 313–14, 320–22,
    348–52

Yorkshire Veterinary Society 227,
    342

Young, Canon John 136

Young, Jimmy 170, 300

Young, Lailan 244, 246–7, 251

Ziegler, Philip 187